The Chinese Adoption Handbook

The Chinese Adoption Handbook

How to Adopt from China and Korea

John H. Maclean,
author of *The Russian Adoption Handbook*

iUniverse Star
New York Lincoln Shanghai

The Chinese Adoption Handbook
How to Adopt from China and Korea

iUniverse Star
an iUniverse, Inc. imprint

For information address:
iUniverse, Inc.
2021 Pine Lake Road, Suite 100
Lincoln, NE 68512
www.iuniverse.com

John Maclean and his wife Brigitte have adopted twice from Russia. He is an attorney and can be reached at wassaw2@email.com.

ISBN: 0-595-29784-6

Printed in the United States of America

For my two wonderful Leaps of Faith

Alexander and Catherine

Contents

Introduction

This handbook is written to assist those who have decided to adopt from China or Korea. Some of the discussion is relevant to adopting internationally in general, however the focus is on Asia. Americans are now adopting annually over 5,000 children from China and 1,700 from Korea. The purpose in writing this handbook is simply to provide a roadmap and give you more control over the process. You will not find the answers to all of your questions in this book, but it will cover most of them. As to the remainder, between your agency and the Internet, you should be able to find the rest. Opinions expressed in this book all come with the caveat that they apply *generally* to situations. Exceptions will always exist.

The best way to use this book is to read all the chapters, even those pertaining to a country in which you are not interested. Chapters on packing, traveling, and medical conditions apply universally. Also, some references to Chinese children apply equally to Korean adoptees.

Finally, adopting is an art, not a science. Whether your experience is a happy one depends in some part on your expectations, comfort level, and demeanor. Further, your adoption is full of important choices that are *yours*, and yours alone. No one has the right to second-guess you. This includes your choice of agency or your choice of whether to adopt this particular child. The decisions and consequences are yours alone. You will find that there is no such thing as a stress-free adoption. The Chinese have a saying that progress is two steps forward and one step back. You should expect that in adopting there might be a few bumps in the road, but there is nothing that you cannot handle with a good attitude. You might not like the food. It might be colder than you thought. The Chinese might ask you a question you didn't anticipate. The INS—now known as the Bureau of Citizenship and Immigration Services (BCIS)—or foreign country want yet another piece of paper. In comparison to having and loving your child, it's all small stuff.

Now for the usual disclaimer: All opinions expressed in this book are those of the author. The information contained within these pages is intended to educate and not to serve as legal or medical advice on a particular problem. Discussions and links relating to web sites, medical conditions and tax aspects of adoption are not intended to be endorsements or professional advice whether in this book or on the aforementioned web sites. The companies and products referred to in this book maintain their trademarks and copyrights, and no infringement is intended. They are simply mentioned for information only.

Thanksgiving Prayer

Gracious and generous God,

We come before you today
with grateful hearts.

In the beauty and bounty of creation
we see the work of your hand;
in the loving faces around us
we know your own love for us.

May this meal nourish us and strengthen us,
so others may know your plenty
in our kindness,
and see your care and concern
in our witness.

Let us live true lives of gratitude,
as we pray in thanks to you, our God
who lives forever and ever. Amen.

CHAPTER I

Overview Of International Adoption

International adoption began as a response to the growing number of orphans (Displaced Persons) in Europe after World War II. The next wave began in the mid-1950s, during the Korean War. Currently, there are more than 100,000 Korean adoptees in the United States. The third wave of children came predominantly from Latin and Central America. These adoptions began to grow in 1973, peaking at 2,500 children in 1991. The fourth wave of adopted children occurred with the fall of the Iron Curtain. Russia and Romania became the primary sending countries. At the same time, China began to allow intercountry adoption of infants. The top ten countries over the past ten years are within Asia, Latin America, and Eastern Europe. Below are some of the adoption statistics since 1995.

IMMIGRANT VISAS ISSUED
TO ORPHANS COMING TO THE U.S.

TOP COUNTRIES OF ORIGIN

	FY 1995	FY 1996	FY 1997
1	2,130.......CHINA	3,333.......CHINA	3,816......RUSSIA
2	1,896.......RUSSIA	2,454.......RUSSIA	3,597......CHINA
3	1,666.......KOREA	1,516.......KOREA	1,654.....S. KOREA
4	449........GUATEMALA	427........GUATEMALA	788.......GUATEMALA
5	371.........INDIA	555.........ROMANIA	621........ROMANIA
6	351........PARAGUAY	380.........INDIA	425........VIETNAM
7	350........COLOMBIA	354.........VIETNAM	352.........INDIA
8	318.........VIETNAM	258........PARAGUAY	233.......COLOMBIA
9	298........PHILIPPINES	255........COLOMBIA	163.......PHILIPPINES
10	275.........ROMANIA	229........PHILIPPINES	152........MEXICO

	FY 1998	FY 1999	FY 2000
1	4,491......RUSSIA	4,348.......RUSSIA	5,053........CHINA
2	4,206......CHINA	4,101.......CHINA	4,269........RUSSIA
3	1,829....S. KOREA	2,008......S. KOREA	1,794......S. KOREA
4	911.......GUATEMALA	1,002......GUATEMALA	1,518......GUATEMALA
5	603........VIETNAM	895.........ROMANIA	1,122.......ROMANIA
6	478.......INDIA	712.........VIETNAM	724..........VIETNAM
7	406........ROMANIA	500.........INDIA	659..........UKRAINE
8	351........COLOMBIA	323.........UKRAINE	503..........INDIA
9	249........CAMBODIA	248.........CAMBODIA	402.........CAMBODIA
10	200.......PHILIPPINES	231.........COLOMBIA	399.........KAZAKHSTAN

	FY 2001	FY 2002
1	4,681........CHINA (mainland born)	5,053........CHINA (mainland born)
2	4,279.........RUSSIA	4,939........RUSSIA
3	1,870.........S. KOREA	2,219........GUATEMALA
4	1,609.......GUATEMALA	1,779........S. KOREA
5	1,246.........UKRAINE	1,106........UKRAINE
6	782...........ROMANIA	819..........KAZAKHSTAN
7	737...........VIETNAM	766..........VIETNAM
8	672...........KAZAKHSTAN	466..........INDIA
9	543...........INDIA	334..........COLOMBIA
10	407...........CAMBODIA	260...........BULGARIA
11	297...........BULGARIA	254...........CAMBODIA
12	266...........COLOMBIA	221...........PHILIPPINES
13	219...........PHILIPPINES	187...........HAITI
14	192...........HAITI	169...........BELARUS
15	158...........ETHIOPIA	168...........ROMANIA
16	129...........BELARUS	105...........ETHIOPIA
17	86...........POLAND	101...........POLAND
18	74...........THAILAND	67.............THAILAND
19	73...........MEXICO	65.............PERU
20	51...........JAMAICA and LIBERIA (both 51)	61.............MEXICO

In FY 2001 out of 4,629 (this is slightly less than the total figure) adoptions from China, 166 children were male and 4,463 female. 2,173 children were under the age of 1, 2,348 from 1-4 years of age, 84 from 5-9, 23 over 9 years of age and 1 unknown (what?). In the same fiscal year, out of 1,863 Korean adoptions (again slightly lower figure) there were 1,029 male children and 834 female. There were 1,736 children under 1, 114 from 1-4, 7 from 5-9, 5 over 9 years of age and 1 unknown. A country's numbers that are missing or very low from one year to the next usually reflect a change in the sending country's laws or the imposition of a moratorium.

Two kinds of visas are issued by the Department of State for children who have been or will be adopted, and thus qualify for an "immediate relative" (IR) visa. One is the visa for the "orphan" (as defined by the Immigration and Nationality Act) who is to be adopted abroad by a U.S. citizen, the "IR-3." There were 13,803 IR-3 Visas issued in FY 2001. The other is for the "orphan" who is to be adopted in the U.S. by a citizen, the "IR-4." There were 5,334 IR-4 Visas issued in FY 2001. The main distinction is that an IR-3 is given when a single parent or both married parents have seen the child prior to adopting abroad. An IR-4 is given when only one married parent has seen the child or the child is escorted to the U.S. before anyone has met the child. The IR-4 Visa means that in the eyes of the State Department the adoption is "not final" for purposes of immigration even though it may be "final" under the laws of the foreign country. Instead, the child is considered in guardianship status or if one parent has seen the child then it is a "proxy" or "simple" adoption. Both parents do not have to attend court, but they both have to have seen the child before or at the court hearing before an IR-3 can be issued. The importance is that children with an IR-3 Visa obtain automatic citizenship once they reach the United States. A child with an IR-4 Visa must await re-adoption or adoption if in guardianship status, or must be in a state like Michigan that recognizes foreign adoption decrees regardless of the visa type. You can read more on this distinction at: *http://travel.state.gov/state105804.html.*

CHAPTER II

China Today

The People's Republic of China is the most populous country in the world with over 1.3 billion people divided among 23 provinces, 5 autonomous regions and 3 autonomous municipalities. China has one of the highest population densities in the world. The 1990 census reported 118 people per square kilometer. This population, however, is unevenly distributed. In the densely populated east coast there are 360 people per square kilometer. China is a multi-ethnic nation of 56 nationalities, which make up 8 percent of the population. The majority ethnic group is the Han.

Starting in 1978, China's leadership moved the economy from Soviet-style central planning to more of a market-based economy—all within Communist Party political control. In place of collectivization in agriculture, national leadership has stressed "household responsibility," allowing households to produce and sell, which has boosted farm production tremendously.

China has been capturing the lion's share of foreign direct investment in Asia. The peaceful handover of power at the 16th Party Congress highlighted China's political stability. It may be authoritarian, but it is stable. China is now a member of the WTO, which should encourage the development of some economic transparency.

History of Chinese Adoptions

In 1979, the Chinese Government began to address the problem of an increasing population by advocating a one-child policy which encouraged all couples to have one child, allowed certain couples (i.e., those having only one daughter) to have a second child with appropriate birth spacing, and strictly forbade third and higher-order childbearing. In early 1983, a PRC State Council Bulletin announced a new nationwide policy. The provisions of this policy (which is still in effect) are as follows:

1) Women with one child are required to have an IUD inserted.

2) Couples with two or more children are required to have one partner sterilized.

3) Women pregnant without official permission are required to have an abortion.

During the 1980s China went through periods of lenient implementation of the one-child policy, but began the 1990s with a return to a policy of strict enforcement using coercive means. Also in the 1980s China instituted restrictive marriage laws. Men under 22 years of age and women under 20 were forbidden to marry. In general, enforcement has varied depending on the mood of the central government. Sometimes central and provincial regulations are "flexible" and exceptions exist to child limitations and penalties prescribed by family planning guidelines. Violators might only pay nominal fines. During other times there are draconian measures such as forced abortion or property confiscation. The government also offers incentives as well such as privileges in housing, medical care, and education.

The one-child policy has been more successful in urban than in rural areas. This success can be attributed to stricter governmental control and more stringent enforcement. IUDs and tubal ligations constitute the majority of contraceptive methods used in China.

In Dr. Kay Johnson's recent study of Chinese birth families she found that birth order and the presence or absence of a brother were "crucial in determining which girls were abandoned." 82 percent of Chinese adoptees have sisters and 88 percent were from rural areas. Most birth parents in the study were married. The birth mothers do feel the loss greatly, but time seemed to heal the sharpest pain.

Dr. Johnson found that abandonment is not the first option for these birthmothers. They come to that decision slowly. She learned that families often go to great lengths by 'hiding' their daughters or paying fines before turning to abandonment. It is seldom the first or even second oldest girl who is abandoned. She also found that birthparents "abandoned their daughter[s] not because they were poor or [because] the child would have a better life. The Chinese were afraid of their future[s] without the support of a son." They have great pressures placed on them. See the articles at: *http://www.rainbowkids.com/303foundfacts.htm* and *http://www.popcouncil.org/mediacenter/newsreleases/pdr24_3_china.html.*

There has been a lot of criticism of China's policy as the policy encourages abandonment, which does not do anything about the population problem. However, in understanding China's dilemma you have to appreciate that the U.S. population is expected to double to 500 million by 2035. The pressure on our resources to clothe, house, and feed everyone will also demand solutions.

Adoption Today

As an outgrowth of the one-child policy there was an increase in the abandonment of, primarily, female infants. One solution was to allow international adoption. The Chinese established a central authority for international adoptions, the Chinese Center for Adoption Affairs (CCAA). The CCAA's web site has a lot of very good information on the requirements at *http://www.china-ccaa.org/english-index.htm.*

The CCAA matches individual children with prospective adoptive parent(s) whose completed applications have been submitted and approved by the CCAA. Once a child is identified, the CCAA will send a letter of introduction about the child, photographs, and a health record of the child through the U.S. adoption agency to the prospective adoptive parent(s). The CCAA's address is No. 7 Baiguang Road, Zhongmin Building, Xuanwu District, Beijing, Postcode: 100053, People's Republic of China; Tel & Fax Nos: Administration Department: Tel: (8610) 6357 5768; Fax: (8610) 6357 5769; Liaison & Service Department: Tel: (8610) 6357 5785; Fax: (8610) 6357 5786.

After accepting the referred child, you then receive a formal notice from the CCAA to proceed to China called a "Notice of Coming to China for Adoption." You need this approval before leaving for China. Parents then travel to the city in China where the Civil Affairs Bureau with jurisdiction over the appropriate Children's Welfare Institute is located. Thereafter, a series of interviews with the adoptive parent(s) will occur, a contract will be signed with the Children's Welfare Institute, and the contract will be registered with the provincial Civil Affairs Bureau. You then pay requisite Chinese fees and obtain a Chinese passport and exit permit for the child.

You do not have to travel to Beijing, but can go directly to the local city where your child is located. Children's Welfare Institutes are administered by the Ministry of Civil Affairs through provincial Civil Affairs Bureaus and are government-operated homes for orphaned or abandoned children. Children can only be placed in the welfare institutes if their parents have died or abandoned them.

If a married couple travels to China to adopt, the child will receive an IR-3 Visa. If only one adopting parent comes to China, then the traveling spouse must bring a power of attorney from the non-traveling spouse that has been notarized and properly authenticated by the Chinese Embassy or one of the Chinese Consulate Generals in the United States. The child will then receive an IR-4 Visa and must be re-adopted in the United States. In FY 2000, 4,520 IR-3 visas and 533 IR-4 visas were issued to adopted children by the U.S. Consulate in China. In the past 10 years, U.S. parents have adopted over 20,000 Chinese children.

After the Chinese paperwork is through you then must complete the U.S. side by obtaining a medical clearance form, filing an I-600 form and having the I-604 investigation. The BCIS Petition to Classify an Orphan as an Immediate Relative (I-600) may be filed at BCIS Beijing, BCIS Guangzhou, or any of the U.S. Consulate generals in Chengdu, Shanghai, or Shenyang for forwarding to the consulate in Guangzhou, formerly Canton. Since all immigrant visas in China are issued at the consulate in Guangzhou, petitions filed at other posts will be sent to Guangzhou for processing. Thus, your child will receive her U.S. visa faster if the petition is filed with the U.S. Consulate General in Guangzhou.

The whole process, beginning from when you file your I-600A to when you bring your child home should take between 15 to 20 months. Most children are between 6 to 20 months in age. Parents normally request a specific age range that they would prefer and the CCAA tries to match it, although following your age range is not a priority with the CCAA. Obviously, which child you adopt depends entirely on the available children at the CCAA when it's your dossier's turn for matching. The children wait a long time to be matched. If there are small infants needing placement when your time comes up, then there is a good chance for that type of match. But if there are not many infants then the babies are usually placed with the youngest families and the other families will be matched with a toddler. This is why the odds are high that a family under 35 will be able to adopt an infant, but one over 45 will not. Another factor in the selection is how you are grouped by your agency. When your "group of dossiers" reaches the CCAA, they search among the children up for placement for a group of similar size from one children's home. Then, among that group of children, they try to satisfy the particular requests of the parents. Most people ask for the youngest child possible. Therefore, in most groups, the youngest couples will get the youngest children in that group and the older ones will tend to get the older ones. So, learning the ages of the others in your dossier group might help you predict the age of the child with which you will be matched. There is also an indication that in order to adopt a baby under one year the youngest parent must be 45 or under. The CCAA also claims it tries to match a child with parents that look most like them. It is a little difficult envisioning how that actually works since we all look alike. Finally, a family might request a particular province or children's home. This is given only slight consideration by the CCAA.

While most available children are girls, there are some adoptions of boys. Unlike the case in other countries, you may have to wait longer for a boy. The majority of the children come from 15 provinces, with the largest numbers from Hunan, Jiangsu, Jiangxi, GuangDong, GuangXi, and Hubei. A parent's list or directory of families who have adopted from various provinces and welfare institutions can be found at *http://wwwchinaconnectiononline.com* under *dirslist.htm*.

China's Children's Homes

In the last several years China has implemented a foster care system with some success. The children that come from the foster care system appear to be in better health, have better nutrition and be able to bond more quickly than children from a children's home. One of the first questions to ask of any agency is if their children come from foster care or from a children's home and then verify the answer by speaking with families that have just returned. It is not that adopting from a children's home is a huge problem, but rather you just have to realize and prepare for the fact that the child will be underweight, developmentally delayed more than a foster care child and possibly have a slightly longer period before bonding is complete. All it means is that you have a little more work ahead of you.

There are still some children that come from children's homes or orphanages. The conditions range from good to terrible. In the bad ones, babies spend long periods lying in a crib, cold and wet. They are cared for on a schedule determined by the availability of staff. Cries can go unheeded for hours. Even if their physical needs are met, they do not engage with another human being or gain comfort from having their upsets soothed by loving hands. They lack physical contact. In a bad children's home a baby might even be restrained in a crib and know nothing of playing with toys. Several years ago China was criticized over their treatment of children in the orphanages. China's response was to limit access to orphanages by foreigners and to limit adoptions of children with noticeable, although correctable, medical conditions. Here are two web sites with descriptions of children's homes: *http://www.orphandoctor.com/wwo/research/laurarobertson.html* and *http://my.execpc.com/~microop/orphan.html.*

Chinese orphanages are rarely heated and the children are bundled in many layers of clothes for warmth. This practice prevents a baby from moving freely and gross motor delays are common. Many babies overcome these delays quickly within the first weeks and months of arriving home. Other babies benefit from early intervention or infant stimulation programs designed to address developmental delays. Children in a Chinese orphanage usually receive little stimulation. There are few toys. There may be four to six children in each large, table-sized bed. Many children have rashes. Different orphanages "specialize" in certain problems. Scabies and lice might be present in one, while in another ear infections and impetigo might be more common. You can sometimes see impetiginized areas on the back of the scalp. Respiratory problems are not uncommon.

Chinese children's hospitals are very antiquated by our standards, and a decision to treat with antibiotics is reviewed each day. Thus, children receive only three days of medication for problems routinely treated in our country for ten days. The children show significant improvement with "Western medications" not obtainable in China, including Elimite, Nix, hydrocortisone cream, and antibiotics, which is why you should take some with you. The good news is that because these are infants, physical development can catch up quickly. Emotional development might take a little longer to resolve with initial problems ranging from sleep issues to initial attachment problems.

CHAPTER III

Research

To complete a Chinese or Korean adoption, parents must fulfill the requirements of their state, the BCIS, and China or Korea. This may appear to be an endless paper chase and quite overwhelming at first. However, if you break down the process to its component parts, then it becomes just another manageable checklist. The checklist can be divided into three parts: Home Study, BCIS, and Foreign Country requirements. If possible, you will find your stress reduced if you work on the home study and BCIS contemporaneously before choosing an adoption agency. The reason is that an agency may refer a child to you, and you will then have the significant added stress of deciding whether to accept the referral while you are undergoing the paper chase. Choosing an agency should be the last step you take, not the first.

Do not just jump in to the adoption process. Understand the process and some of the issues. Thanks to the Internet, there are hundreds of web sites devoted to foreign adoptions. Just type in "Chinese adoption" or "Korean adoption" on your search engine and you will be inundated with sites.

The BCIS regulations governing international adoption can be found at 8 CFR 204.3, which can be found at web site: *http://www.access.gpo.gov /nara/cfr/waisidx_99/8cfr204_99.html*. The U.S. Department of State has good overviews of the adoption process for each country. These overviews or flyers are on the State Department's web site and provide a good starting point. They cannot be relied upon too much as they are usually out of date or don't reflect the practical realities. You should read BCIS publication M-249, *The*

Immigration of Adopted and Prospective Adoptive Children, at *http:// www.immigration.gov/graphics/lawsregs/handbook/adopt_book.pdf* as well as the Department of State publication, *International Adoptions.* Another good outline of the process can be found at *http://www.foia.state.gov/masterdocs /09fam/0942021N.pdf.*

Remember too that each state will have its own rules. Some, like Georgia, are relatively painless and are handled within the home study process. Others, like Arizona, require several fingerprint checks and a court resolution. Here is a web site listing the states' laws: *http://www.calib.com/naic/laws/index.cfm.*

One of the very best research sites is Families with Children from China (F.C.C.) at *http://catalog.com/fwcfc/welcome.html.* For Korea it is *http:// www.adoptkorea.com/.* Other Korean sites are *http://www.kaanet.com* and *http://www.koreanfocus.org.*

Here are some other informative sites:
http://www.chinaconnectiononline.com
http://www.immigration.gov/graphics/services/advproc.htm
http://www.jcics.org
http://www.pshrink.com/chinadopt
http://www.rainbowkids.com
http://www.calib.com/naic

There are many families who have posted their adoption stories posted on the Internet. If you read these, you will soon get a flavor for the journey. Two such stories are at *http://catalog.com/fwcfc/adoptchina2.htm* and *http://members. tripod. com/gtkelle/adoption.html.* A large catalog of stories is at *http://www.tussah.com/ lara/chinasto.htm#Personal%20China%20Adoption%20Stories*

A great resource is the Adopt-Parent-China list on Yahoo at *http://groups.yahoo.com/group/a-parents-china.*The U.S. Embassy in Beijing has a good web site outlining the process at *http://www.usembassy-china. org.cn/english/us-citizen/adoption.html* and at *http://www.usembassy-china. org.cn/english/us-citizen/adopt_acs.html.* The later site gives a good overview, but is only current to 1998, so its information is 4 years out of date. A list of various Chinese children's homes can be found at http://www.lotustours. net/orphanages.htm.

If you need BCIS forms or information, you can retrieve them at *http://www.immigration.gov/graphics/index.htm*. The BCIS will now accept downloaded I-600A and I-600 forms on white paper.

If you want to compare countries, the January-February 2002 issue of Adoption Medical News contains a survey by medical professionals relating to the health of the children adopted from different countries. You can obtain back issues at 814-364-2449 for $10.00. You can also go to *http://www.adoptionnews.org/pub3.html* for more information on obtaining back issues.

Finally, and you may have already done this, do not fall in love with a picture of a child posted on the web. That child may not be available for adoption or it might not be 6 months later until you are ready to travel. Someone else might adopt that child. It just adds to your stress in addition to all of the paperwork. Of course, it is a great motivator, and many people have adopted children that they first saw posted on the web. Just be careful. Protect your heart.

Also, remember that everything about the adoption is your responsibility. You have to educate yourself. You have to ask questions and get involved. You have to make decisions. If you really just want to pay money to an agency and have them deliver a child to you without much involvement on your part, then you need to look deeper within yourself. Adoption is just a prequel to parenting. You have to be *involved* when you adopt or parent.

Adoptive Children and Families

Since the popularity of international adoption is a fairly recent phenomenon, it is too soon for any long-term studies to have been completed. Most of the recently published books and studies are based on the early Romanian adoptions where the children's institutional lives were horrendous. However, you cannot simply say that all children's homes are alike no matter where they are located. Certain issues *may* have a commonality, yet each child's story is by its very nature an individual event with its own peculiar history. Know that history and you will know that child. So much is dependent on such factors as whether your child was abused or neglected, in a good children's home or a bad one, in foster care or raised by a family member, her age, the presence of loving caregivers or not, and length of stay in the home, that it is hard to compare your child with a study.

If you read a study, check its relevance by first checking for the country of origin of the study group, then for the ages of the children, and finally for whether it is a self-selective group. For example, a specialist who treats attachment issues may say that all internationally adopted children have an attachment issue because that is the only population of children that he sees.

One recent study by Dr. Laurie Miller of the Floating Hospital was published in *Pediatrics* in June 2000. You can find it at *http://www.pediatrics.org /content/vol105/issue6/index.shtml#ELECTRONIC_ARTICLE* by scrolling down to the article. This study surveyed 452 adopted children from China. They were adopted between 1991 and 1998. The findings were similar to those found in other international adoption populations. 39% of the children were delayed by 2 standard deviations for height, 18% for weight, and 24% for head circumference. The duration of orphanage life was inversely proportional to the linear height lag, with a loss of 1 month of height age for every 2.86 months in the orphanage. Of the children, 75% had significant developmental delay in at least 1 domain: gross motor in 55%, fine motor in 49%, cognitive in 32%, language in 43%, and social-emotional in 28%. Elevated lead levels were found in 14%, anemia in 35%, abnormal thyroid function tests in 10%, hepatitis B surface antigen in 6%, hepatitis B surface antibody in 22%, intestinal parasites (usually *Giardia*) in 9%, and positive skin test results for tuberculosis in 3.5%, none seriously ill. One child each had hepatitis C exposure and congenital syphilis. No child had HIV. Unsuspected significant medical diagnoses, including hearing loss, strabismus, hip dysplasia, orthopedic problems, and congenital anomalies were found in 18% (81/452) of the children.

One finding is that the percent of high lead levels in adopted Chinese children is greater than in other international adoption populations and you should insist that your pediatrician test for lead when you bring your child home. It is an easily correctable condition, if known. This survey also shows that you must also insist that your pediatrician conduct the entire list of recommended tests for adoptive children in order to catch unsuspected problems. As might be expected, scores for height, weight, and head circumference were lower in children with developmental delays as compared with developmentally normal children. Dr. Miller made an interesting finding that delays in language and activities of daily living skills tended to increase with duration of orphanage confinement, whereas delays in other domains did not show this pattern.

Dr. Dana Johnson at the University of Minnesota's International Adoption Clinic has also conducted a study of 154 Chinese adoptees, 98% of which were female. Children arrived at a mean age of 10.4 months and had been in orphanages for an average of 9.2 months. Of five tests for infectious diseases, 3.5% of Chinese adoptees were found to be positive for hepatitis B; 3.7% tested positive for intestinal parasites; 1.4% tested positive for tuberculosis; 0.8% were found to have syphilis; and none had the HIV virus. In contrast to the study described above, 90% had normal lead levels. In a much smaller sample (19) Dr Johnson found that the area of development with the most abnormality was strength, with 63% of children lagging in development. That was followed by gross motor skills, 58%; fine motor skills, 42%; language, 26%; social skills, 16%; and tone, 5%. Delays usually improved rapidly after arrival, researchers found. Stature was affected with children falling behind one month of linear growth for each 3.4 months in the orphanage. Rickets was not obvious in any child, but biochemical markers indicating early rickets was more likely to be found as children grew older. Hepatitis C seems to cluster in infants from Yangzhou. This may indicate that there is a commonality such as a common clinic using unsterilized needles. This study can be found at *http://catalog.com/fwcfc/healthdanajohnson.html*.

Other studies of adopted children in general have demonstrated that under normal circumstances, while early experience may confer a temporary advantage, ultimately IQ is strongly determined by genetic factors. In essence, a good environment can help, but only if the genetic groundwork is first present. Environment cannot create intelligence, but it can damage it. Michael Rutter concluded in another study that "...[e]nvironmental effects on IQ are relatively modest within the normal range of environments, but the effects in markedly disadvantageous circumstances are very substantial." My analogy is that you have no control over the genetic potential of the seed you buy at a greenhouse, but whether it flourishes to its potential depends on the soil you give it.

A summary of some other Chinese-oriented studies can be found at *http://www.arches.uga.edu/%7erojewski/WelcomePage.html*. Also, there are other studies listed in Dr. Boris Gindis' articles in the *Communique* (a professional journal for school psychologists) at: *http://bgcenter.com/communique-article.htm*. You can also read some in the *Pediatric Annals* issue on international adoption in Volume 29, Number 4, April 2000. Back issues can be ordered at 856-848-1000.

In order to remedy this paucity of research, in 2001 the NIH funded a Minnesota study under the auspices of Dr. Dana Johnson of the University of Minnesota's International Adoption Clinic. The project has provided a wonderful snapshot of adoptive parents and their children. The web site for the International Adoption Project is at *http://education.umn.edu/icd/IAP/.* Findings from the survey are also on this web site. In February of 2001, surveys were sent to the Minnesota parents of 3,751 children adopted internationally between 1990-1998. Parents sent back 2,299 surveys, a response rate of 61%. The 2,299 children live in 1,857 families. About 50% of the families filled out surveys for more than one child. As of 2001, the moms were approximately 45 years of age (plus or minus 5 years and dads were 46, give or take 6 years). Most parents were between 35 and 40 years old when they adopted. The children were eight years of age (plus or minus 3 years). Eighty-eight percent of the children live in two parent families (86% married; 2% in a committed partnership). Seven percent live in homes with one parent who has never been married and less than 3% of the children live in divorced or separated families. Ninety-three percent of the fathers were employed full time, and 60% of the mothers stayed at home or worked part-time. The parents were generally very well educated. Over 70% have graduated from college. Over 30% have masters, doctorates, or professional degrees. Moms and dads/partners were very similar in their educations. The household incomes varied considerably with 15% having incomes below $50,000, 27% over $125,000 per year; and 58% of the families with incomes between $50,000 and $125,000.

An interesting finding from the surveys was that parents who did not have the referral reviewed by a medical professional were more likely to say the child had more medical problems than they were led to expect, compared to those who had the referral reviewed by a medical professional (23% vs.17%). 67% of parents reported that bonding occurred within a few days, and only 3% were still struggling after one year. (Even if you assume that the first number is high due to parental bias, this shows that bonding eventually occurs for most adoptions within the first year.)

Of the surveyed children, 7 countries accounted for 79%. These were South Korea (32%), Colombia (11%), China (10%), Russia (7.6%), India (7%), Guatemala (6%), and Romania (5.2%). The lowest instances of illness occurred in Korean children, and the highest were from Colombia, followed by China, Russia, Romania, Guatemala and India. Chronic ear infections were the largest medical problem, followed by vision, speech, behavior, anemia, hepatitis B and hepatitis C difficulties. Immediately after adoption to six months later, most problems occurred in sleeping, with children experiencing nightmares, followed by withdrawal, tantrums, hoarding, feeding difficulties, aggression, and crying. Medical issues were not the predominant issues facing parents after their children passed through the first couple of years. Most parents said their children were as healthy as their nonadoptive peers. Initial incidence of anemia, hepatitis C, elevated lead levels, and syphilis was reported by parents to be low. Hepatitis B was reported by 4% and no cases of HIV were reported. In contrast, speech, hearing, ear infections and vision problems (strabismus) were the most reported.

The age of the child at adoption and the care-taking environment prior to adoption had a major affect on school outcome. Children adopted at 2 years of age or older or who received poor or very poor care prior to adoption were 3 to 4 times more likely to be falling behind in some or all classes. If children were adopted at less than six months of age and were well cared for, they did better in school. Indeed, Dr Johnson concluded that children adopted at under 24 months with few risk factors were doing very, very well. Thirty-three percent of parents of the 1,483 school-aged children said they were excelling in most or all of their classroom subjects. Forty-four percent of the teenagers had at some time received an award for academic excellence, 20% had received awards for artistic endeavors, and 25% had received awards for athletics. 16% of the children are in gifted classes. School performance seemed to decline as the children became older and were more academically challenged. It has been noted in other studies that complex abstract thinking in the higher grades is more difficult for adoptive kids coming from an institutional environment and that sometimes tutoring or other special services are needed. These findings also show that children who spent less than 6 months in institutionalized care prior to adoption look similar to children who have lived in foster family settings.

Dr. Johnson makes the salient point that a child's condition does not depend on the country, but on the care. Thus, a blanket statement that Chinese or Korean adoptive children are better or healthier does not really mean anything per se. If you adopt a child from a terrible Chinese institution, then that child will need additional attention. It is the care that matters, not the country. If the children are being placed in foster care at an early age, if they are not being neglected in the orphanage or if there is no exposure to alcohol, that is what is important, not the country. He gave the example of a Russian child who is placed in foster care (and there are a few) as compared to a Korean child who may have FAE. While you can make generalizations, you have to also realize that it is child specific care that is critical.Dr Johnson broke down the risk factors into seven main areas. The risk factors were 1) a birthmother who was malnourished during the prenatal period, 2) prenatal exposure to alcohol or other drug exposure, 3) premature birth less than 37 weeks, 4) neglect of basic physical needs such as food, clothing or medical care, 5) neglect of basic social needs such as lack of love, affection, attention and cuddling, 6) physical abuse and 7) a child who was in an orphanage, baby home, or hospital for more than 6 months.

He summarized the results as follows:

	Europe	Latin America	Asia
Prenatal alcohol/drug exposure	44%	15%	9%
Prenatal malnutrition	50%	41%	24%
Premature birth	30%	14%	28%
Physically neglected	45%	26%	12%
Socially neglected	57%	22%	13%
Physically abused	13%	6%	3%
6 months or more in an orphanage, baby home or hospital	79%	17%	13%

He did find that children adopted over 24 months of age with a lot of risk factors did have significant behavioral and emotional problems and difficulties in school. The parents of these children will have a different parenting experience that those parenting a child without a lot of risk factors. They can still have a successful adoption, just that it is more work. These parents will have to learn to be advocates for their child and educate themselves on the special education system and how it works. Their child may need attachment therapy and may have more medical issues. Nevertheless, parents that are forewarned and forearmed do much better. They can set a level of expectations that is reasonable for their child and this in turn increases their chances of a successful adoption.

The problem with even this large study is that generalizations must be made carefully. There is no way to compare an adoption of a Romanian or Columbian child in 1990 with one in 1998, as the early care of these children has improved. Nor can you compare a 4-year-old Russian child with a 12-year-old Russian child. Further, many parents of Chinese children will tell you that their children have completely bounced back from their deprivations. So all generalizations naturally must come with plenty of caveats and footnotes.

Disabled Parents

The CCAA says it will not assign children to psychiatric disabled foreign adoption applicants. No one knows what that means. As to other disabilities, the CCAA says it will deal with each family on a case-by-case basis. In the past, parents have adopted from China where the father was in a wheelchair or where a mom had asthma. In 2003, moms in wheelchairs adopted infants from China. So it is possible. The key factors seem to be the U.S. agency's willingness to go to bat for you, a strong home study supporting your ability to parent, and most importantly, the CCAA's trust and relationship with your U.S. agency. If you are able to adopt from China, the Forbidden City is a nightmare for anyone in a wheelchair and the U.S. Consulate is also not wheelchair friendly.

To illustrate the CCAA's peculiar attitude toward disabled parents, their web site has a statement that "[f]or those disabled who can look after themselves and have the ability of bringing up and educating the prospective adopted children, CCAA shall identify appropriate adoptive referrals for them."

There is another option if the disability is not an obvious one and that involves nondisclosure. This option is outlined in the Home Study chapter and involves either not telling your home study agency at all or producing two home studies. One home study goes to the BCIS and details everything while the second is submitted to the foreign country and omits the disability. You can also have a doctor who is not treating you for the disability sign the medical clearance form, thereby producing a clean letter. This option is one that parents have taken.

Many parents have been treated for depression. If you choose to disclose, then the Chinese seem to be fine with a statement from your doctor that the depression is controlled with medication and does not affect your ability to parent a child.

If the wife has a serious physical disability, then India and Guatemala seem to be better choices. In India, the right judge is the key, and in Guatemala, a massaged home study helps. Guatemala has allowed wheelchair-bound and sight-impaired moms to adopt. Finding the right agency with experience in working with a disability is not easy. You have to keep searching and asking, but they are out there.

For information and tips on a disabled parent raising a child, see *http://www.lookingglass.org*. For an adoption story by a disabled parent see *http://www.oifamily.com/main/main.htm*. For a disabled adopter group see *http://groups.yahoo.com/group/disabledadoptiveparents/*

CHAPTER IV

American Paper Chase

Here is an important tip: If there is an opportunity to walk a document through then by all means do it. Each time you can have some gatekeeper take care of a document in front of you, the more time you will save. You can literally save months if you push hard enough.

BCIS Overview

In 2003, the INS was merged into the new Department of Homeland Security. The INS' immigration benefits function, which includes processing I-600As, was renamed the Bureau of Citizenship and Immigration Services (BCIS). Nothing has changed except for the name. There has been a great amount of disruption in regard to the border security side of the INS, with many employees leaving the Service, but this has not been the case with the immigration benefits side.

Whenever you deal with the BCIS you must remember that although you have paid your taxes, and your family may have come over on the Mayflower, you will not receive any special treatment from the BCIS just because you are an American. The BCIS does process the I-600A on an expedited basis, but do not expect them to answer any of your questions. There is no real hotline or ombudsman. They post a phone number for questions, but that is just for show. You have to wait in line like everyone else.

You truly begin your international adoption journey when you file for pre-approval to adopt with the BCIS. This is actually pre-approval of the parents, since you may not have accepted a child yet. The form is called the I-600A, the Application for Advance Processing of an Orphan Petition. It used to be orange. It is to be contrasted with the I-600, the Petition to Classify an Orphan as an Immediate Relative, which is the approval of the adopted child for a visa and which is filed at the time of your child visa request. The I-600 used to be blue. The BCIS offices and the various embassy visa units will now accept downloaded copies of these forms on regular white paper. At the moment the filing fee for the I-600A is $460. You will also need to include an additional $50 per person for fingerprinting. This fee is charged for each person living in your house over the age of 18. If you are only adopting one child or a sibling group, then no additional fee is required when you file the I-600 other than the $335 visa fee.

You can now download all of your forms from the BCIS and they should be accepted, even if they are not on the correct colored paper. You can download them at *http://www.immigration.gov/graphics/formsfee/forms/index.htm.* The BCIS web site states that…" [i]n an October 17, 2000 revised rule, these printing requirements were loosened to facilitate printing from the Internet. As a result, all BCIS forms may now be printed from the BCIS Website *without* any special printing requirements (such as head-to-foot, using specially-colored paper, etc.). However, using a dot matrix printer is not advised." The BCIS forms for the I-600A and I-600 are in Adobe Acrobat and are in "fillable" mode, which should make life easier. The I-864 form is not yet fillable. These forms cannot yet be filed electronically.

In March 2003 the BCIS changed the way they handled approving the I-600A by issuing a policy memo stating that you would not get your fingerprint appointment until after you filed your home study. This was such a ludicrous policy that the BCIS withdrew it in May and issued another policy memo saying that each of the dozens of field offices could make their own policy as to when they issued fingerprint appointments. By delegating authority, the Washington office was able to avoid any responsibility and any criticism. This means that the good field offices will go back to the way they did things and will fingerprint you sooner, while the bad offices will continue to jerk you around by delaying your fingerprint appointment until the last moment. The May 2003 policy memo is at *http://www.immigration.gov/graphics/lawsregs/handbook/FprntChks051303.pdf*

So depending on your BCIS office, you may be notified of your fingerprint appointment within several weeks of filing your I-600A or you may have to wait until after you file your home study. An "official" BCIS fingerprint person will take your fingerprints. The BCIS used to allow you to submit them from your local police department, but no longer. They claim they had too many bad prints. You no longer bring fingerprint cards with you. The BCIS provides these cards to you when you are fingerprinted. Do not use hand lotion on the day you are fingerprinted as this may cause a problem. Some offices, such as the Philadelphia BCIS, now use digital machines that take your fingerprints and send them out upon completion of your prints. No cards are needed.

On the I-600A at line 17 it asks you for the number of children you are adopting. You should put a number greater than you are currently considering. The same goes for your home study. The BCIS will actually go by the figure in your home study. Even so, both figures should be consistent. The reason for the higher figure is that many times people returning from overseas decide to increase their families by adopting again the following year. By already being approved for the higher number, you may be able to cut out a few steps the next year.

A confusing issue appears when you have filed an I-600A requesting approval for the adoption of more than one child, but have used the approval to only adopt one. I-171H approvals are only good for 18 months. You want to go back the following year and adopt another. Do you have to go through the whole BCIS process again? The answer is that it differs in each BCIS office and in each state. In North Carolina and in most BCIS offices all you have to do is file a brief amendment updating your home study, and as long as the adoption is within the 18 months you should be fine. However, in states such as Georgia and Florida you have to do the whole thing all over again, from start to finish.

You may file the I-600A and complete the home study later. Your home study agency will then get the state to approve the study and that agency will then file it with the BCIS. You can also file the I-600A even if you do not know which agency you will use or even which country. Just put down "unknown" or "TBD" (to be decided) and update the BCIS by letter later.

After the BCIS has received your I-600A, your home study and your FBI fingerprint clearance, you will, barring some home study agency brain drop or a crime against humanity on your record, receive official United States Government approval that you are eligible to adopt a child. That approval arrives in your mailbox on a form known as the I-171H. At the same time, the BCIS will send a Cable 37 to the U.S. Consulate in Guangzhou or Seoul notifying them of this approval. If you receive another form called a 797-C, this is a Notice of Action, and does not equate to an I-171H. It is the I-171H you need. As with all government documents make sure you double-check your I-171H for typos. Sometimes your I-171H specifies the number of children for which you are approved and sometimes not. That information is also located in the files at the local service office and at the consulate or embassy, which is why you should ask the embassy to confirm that information when you email or fax them. After you receive your I-171H you will need to verify with the U.S. Consulate or Embassy that they have received a cable (VISAS Cable 37) from the BCIS indicating that you are approved. You or your agency usually can do this through email or fax, although Seoul seems out of touch with the rest of the embassies and does not post an email address. Email and fax are the best methods, as you will then receive a paper confirmation, which you should take with you to China. The reason for taking the confirmation with you to China is that sometimes when your facilitator calls the embassy to set up the visa appointment, the embassy cannot locate your file. The paper confirmation will help overcome that little problem.

Generally speaking, the average time from filing the I-600A to receiving your I-171H is 4 to 6 months. If you have already completed a domestic home study and just need it amended to authorize adopting internationally, then the approval time should be shorter. Of course, delays can crop up. The FBI might lose your fingerprints. The BCIS might have a stack of applications and the only person handling them in that office gets sick or goes on vacation. Your home study might need corrections or be delayed because of the need for a document like a certified marriage certificate from Scotland. Or you might have to deal with the Gruesome Twosome, the two BCIS offices from hell, San Jose and Denver. When you receive I-171H notice of approval, it should have box #3 checked that "Your advance processing application has been forward to the consulate at Seoul (or Guangzhou)." Beneath it should be typed, "Notice of approval has been cabled to Seoul (or Guangzhou)." This is done in accordance with your designation of the consulate at question 16 on the I-600A petition.

This is how it generally works, except in Illinois. In Illinois there is an additional bit of red tape—the DCFS has to approve all foreign adoptions, and you will receive TWO I-171Hs. The second one is the one with "box 3" checked and it is only after the following additional steps that your cable can be sent overseas. In Illinois the additional steps appear to be that after you accept a referral you need to notify BOTH your home study social worker (through which you got your DCFS Foster Care license) AND Ms. Muriel Shaennan at DCFS in Springfield, IL. Her phone is 217-785-2692. You MUST provide her the following information after you accept a referral: Child's name (Chinese or Korean and new adoptive name), country of birth, and birth date of child. After reviewing your DCFS file, she will fax BCIS that they can release your final I-171H. BCIS will send you a second updated I-171H form with box 3 checked. Then you should e-mail or fax the consulate after you get your second I-171H to confirm receipt of your cable.

If you happen to have a picture of the child you are adopting, you may find that you receive quicker service from the BCIS if you attach a copy of child's picture to whatever document you need them to approve. People tend to care more once they see that an actual living child is involved. This also works for state offices when you are looking for a quick turnaround on a authentication.

BCIS Offices

The following is a list of some of the BCIS offices and a description of the kind of experience you can expect. The description is based on how fast you can expect to obtain your I-171H approval and how you are treated. This is not a scientific poll.

It is helpful if you understand how these offices generally operate. The BCIS does not really centralize any of their operations. They have established four service centers but they do not really affect the process, other than slow it down. There is no East Coast/West Coast regional adoption center like a regular business would have. Instead they have delegated the adoption petition approvals to each of their many regional offices. Usually there is no more than one person in each office who handles adoption petitions. This person may not necessarily be a federal employee, but may be a contract employee. The person may change every year or so, with the result that an office can be great for a while then suddenly go bad. Also, the executive branch of the government works on crisis mode. So if there is suddenly some hot issue of the month like refugees, asylum, or naturalizations, then the BCIS director will be told that suddenly this issue has become a priority and the adoptions person will be pulled off to help with that issue. The BCIS also undergoes "reorganization" and "streamlining" every other month to improve efficiency, which also slows things down. In 2003, the INS became part of the Department of Homeland Security. Except for the millions spent on changing their letterhead, you won't see any difference in their handling of adoption petitions.

Atlanta is rated as being in the middle of the pack. Not very fast, but not bad either. Takes about 4 months for approval of the I-600A. Since 2001, there has been a noticeable lengthening of the approval time.

Baltimore has generally been a terrific office. It has had some problems lately with losing files and fingerprints, but hopefully it will get back on track. Takes about 3 months for approval. Baltimore will accept a copy of the I-600A downloaded onto white paper. They don't care that it is not salmon colored (orange) They will not accept a personal check, but prefer separate money orders. They can give you a tracking number, and do fingerprints the same day. Parking is bad. Wednesdays seem to be the worse days to visit.

Boston has had a terrible reputation. They are difficult to talk to. Yet, their time for approval is not too bad. The best that can be said is that they receive mixed reviews. Unlike most other offices, they now require you to submit the home study when you file your I-600A. They fingerprint you two weeks after submitting the I-600A. If you have a question, the social worker has to call. They don't take calls from families.

Buffalo seems very much on the ball. You can file your I-600A before your home study is complete. Your fingerprints are optically scanned and take only 24 hours for FBI clearance. Once the home study is submitted, approval is in 10 days. Buffalo has gotten high praise for being very friendly. They answer questions and let you do your fingerprints at the same time as filing the I-600A.

Charlotte is pretty good. They do not take calls.
Chicago is not bad either. About 3 months. They have a pretty good reputation.
Cincinnati and Cleveland are not far behind Chicago.
Dallas is usually very fast and gets high marks. There have been a few problems recently.
Denver is next to last due to giving poor service.
Detroit did have a reputation for being slow, but recently they seem to have become more helpful and friendly.
El Paso is not very fast at all.

Ft. Smith, Arkansas office staff is rude to parents.

Houston, Texas is just great. Mary Chavez is just one of the nicest and most professional people you will ever meet. The BCIS is lucky to have her. The federal government is lucky to have her.

Jacksonville seems to be giving Baltimore a run for its money and is an outstanding office.

Kansas City, Missouri is pretty fast as is Wichita, Kansas. It may be that fewer people in the mid-west adopt internationally so the BCIS offices are not as overwhelmed as others.

Los Angeles is not very good. The wait for your fingerprint date is long although the I-171 seems to go smoothly. If you need help, you can call the Adoption/Orphan room at (213) 830-5122 and ask to speak to Marty, the Director. Be nice. It is really hard to get through.

Las Vegas is not very fast.

Louisville is very quick and gets high marks.

Manchester, New Hampshire is good and friendly.

Memphis is very good. Rated much higher than Atlanta. If you want to check on your status, the office phone numbers are 901-344-2300 and 901-544-0264. A human being always answers the phone. Officers Miller and Dockery are in charge of orphan petitions, so they're the ones who can help you. Memphis will fingerprint you the day you turn in your I-600A, if you ask. They are very courteous and helpful. In Tennessee, your home study first has to be submitted to the state ICPC, then the BCIS. It can take as long as 3 weeks to go through the ICPC, and then 4 weeks to get your I-171H, once the home study is received at the BCIS.

Michigan is in the middle of the pack at about 4 months.

Minneapolis is fast.

New Jersey is in the middle, although Newark has a tendency to lose documents and fingerprints. The New Jersey BCIS adoption unit phone number is 973-645-6309. Like all BCIS offices they receive lots of calls from people who have no idea what they are doing so they may be rather gruff sometimes, but you will get your questions answered. Call between 2 and 4 PM. Fingerprints are taken electronically in Newark, Philadelphia, and Hackensack, so their status is available to the New Jersey BCIS within 5 days. Once the file is complete

(I-600A, home study and fingerprints), New Jersey has been known to issue the I-171H within 2 weeks.

New York gets pretty high marks.

New Orleans is not bad.

North Carolina will not talk to you under any circumstances. The people in Charlotte do not seem to understand the big picture.

Philadelphia is fast. They send out fingerprint notices two weeks after the initial filing and the I-171H 10 days after the home study is submitted.

Pittsburgh is fast and friendly. They will even talk to you.

Portland, Oregon is dreadful—almost dead last.

Oklahoma has poor customer service.

Orlando BCIS office is fast and efficient. Once they have your home study they turn the I-171H around very quickly.

St. Louis office seems to have nice people working there and is fast.

The Salt Lake City office can be difficult because of one particular officer. If you have to wait any longer than 2 months for approval, call Senator Hatch's office.

San Antonio used to have problems, but it seems there has been a change as it is now very quick about arranging fingerprint dates and about sending out your I-171H after it receives your home study. It is even possible to be fingerprinted the same day if you hand-carry your I-600A with the required documents and a money order into the San Antonio BCIS office. The line is shorter after 3pm.

San Diego is poor.

San Francisco is a nightmare. Horrendous lines (you must be in line by 5 A.M.) if you have to visit and no one to speak to that has a clue about international adoptions.

San Jose is dead last as far as service is concerned. It has been dead last for years and years and this appears likely to continue. If you must use San Jose, then establish a relationship with Senator Feinstein's office. She is *very* responsive and her office cares about adopting parents. Forget about Senator Boxer— her office *never* responds. A suggestion in filing your I-600A with San Jose is not to leave any information blank. List your home study agency name where it asks "which agency" and as far as a travel date, you can write, "to be determined"—that will be an acceptable answer. If you leave anything blank, your documents will get shoved in a drawer or put in a box in an old restroom (yes, this is their filing system), and you'll never see them again. Another suggestion is to use a home study agency that has a good relationship with the BCIS office or orphan petition processing officer. You have to ask around, but it is well worth the effort. Regardless of which home study agency you use, try to make them work the San Jose office rather than you.

Always send your documents by certified mail or by FedEx or UPS, local delivery, since that is same day and much faster and is easier to track if it goes missing. (This is good advice for sending documents to any BCIS office). Watch to see when San Jose cashes your check. They almost always do that first, even if they have a "problem" with your documents. If they haven't cashed your check within 8 weeks, you might want to consider sending them a certified letter inquiring about the status of your documents, along with a copy of your certified mail postcard. Not that they will ever answer you, but you have created a paper trail to make it easier for the congressional liaison's office to intervene on your behalf (which you most probably will have to do at some point).Finally, good luck!

Sault Sainte Marie is wonderful—very prompt and courteous. Very well organized. Even can tell you how many people are ahead of you.
Seattle and St. Louis are pretty good.
Spokane takes about 6 weeks to issue the I-171H after receiving your home study.
Washington, D.C. is poor.

The BCIS field offices all have their own peculiar procedures. For example, Denver does not like personal checks, but will only accept money orders and certified checks. They also want in the home study the size of the child's room in your home and the distance to the nearest bathroom. Atlanta, on the other hand, will take personal checks and doesn't care about bathrooms.

The D.C. office in Arlington, Virginia accepts the downloaded version with one personal check including the fee and fingerprints. This office got good marks. In the Jacksonville, Florida office they do accept the form on downloaded white paper, but they don't accept personal checks. You can combine the form fee and fingerprint fees on one money order.

Here is one tip when dealing with the BCIS: If you have to go to an actual office, go as early in the morning as you can. If the doors open at 8 A.M., then get there no later than 6 A.M. The line will grow exponentially as the day goes on. For those who have the heartache of having to use the San Jose office, be forewarned—it is simply an abomination. Contacting the BCIS by phone in San Jose is impossible, instead one must stand in line from 5 A.M. to 9 A.M., hearing that the numbers of the day are gone and be told to come back tomorrow. IF (and only if) you are actually lucky enough to actually get "into" the building (your lucky outdoor lotto number is actually allowed in) you will enter the "inner sanctum" only to see 2 windows open and 200-300 people crammed into the building waiting to actually speak to one of the 2 people at the windows (not to mention the 50-100+people you have been standing with OUTSIDE). Most times, unless you are incredibly lucky to actually GET to the window, you are told the office is closing, and that you will have to "come back again tomorrow" to stand in line OUTSIDE again, and pray that you get another try at getting into the inner sanctum.

I-600A

Several documents must be included with your I-600A form. You need to include proof of U.S. citizenship. The best proof is a copy of the photo page from your passport. This can be a black and white copy, it doesn't need to be color. You will need a passport to travel so you might as well use the one you have or obtain one. (This is a good time to check on whether your passport needs to be updated.) The passport must be unexpired and valid for five years. If you do not have a passport you can submit a copy of your birth certificate. If married, also submit a copy of your marriage certificate. If divorced, they need a copy of the final decree. If the home study is not ready, explain in a cover letter that it will be provided at a later date. The $460 fee and $50 per person fingerprint fee can each be paid by regular check. (Write separate checks for these fees.) Indeed, this will give you a receipt that it was paid. You can pay by certified check, but that will not really speed the process along, as the BCIS must still wait for your home study and FBI fingerprint check before issuing the I-171H.

These document copies do not have to be certified, however, you will need to obtain certified copies of your birth and marriage certificates for your dossier and home study, so if you have an extra one, just send it with your I-600A. If you are adopting a second time, also include a copy of your previous I-171H. This will show them that you were approved before so they don't have to do any real checking on you. You should state in your cover letter, "Copies of documents submitted are exact photocopies of unaltered documents and I understand that I may be required to submit original documents to an immigration or consular officer at a later date." Sign it, print your name below your signature, and date it.

The form may say that the filing fee is $120 or $405 Ignore this. It is an old form. The correct filing fee is $460, plus a fingerprinting fee of $50 per person. Filling out the I-600A is not difficult and should only take a few minutes.

If you are married, then one of you becomes the petitioner. Don't fight over it! Make sure the petitioner is a U.S. citizen. Questions 1-9 are self-explanatory. As to question 10, regarding the name of your agency, you may not know this at the time of filing the I-600A. In that event, just put "Unknown at this time, will supplement." You can also leave it blank and just include in your cover letter that you will supplement this information later.

One result of the I-600A is a determination by the BCIS as to whether your child will be issued an IR-3 or an IR-4 Visa upon entering the United States. An IR-3 Visa means that both parents traveled overseas and saw the child before the actual decree or registration. An IR-4 means that the child was escorted to the United States or that only one parent saw the child and that re-adoption in the United States is likely necessary before the child can be eligible for citizenship. The I-600A asks at question 11 whether both parents are traveling. BCIS will confirm this at the time that you visit the U.S. Consulate in Guangzhou. If adopting from Korea, then your answer will be "no." For China, questions 11 and 12 on the I-600A should be answered in the affirmative, 14 in the negative, and 15 in the affirmative. The answer to question 16 is "Guangzhou, China" if adopting from China. For Korea, since the child will be adopted in the United States the answer to questions 11 and 12 is "no," and to question 14 is "yes."

For China, on question 13, just put down " unknown" for all three parts. You can also just take a guess at the month and year and the city in China you intend to visit. The BCIS does not hold you to these dates.

As to question 17, always put down one more than you expect and make sure you are consistent with your home study. If you decide to increase the number after you have received your I-171H then you will need to send in a revised home study or amendment to your local BCIS office with the approval paragraph noting that you are now approved for "whatever number of children." That's what the BCIS uses to decide how many you are approved for, not what you put on a BCIS form. You then fill out form EOIR-29 changing the number and send that to the BCIS with a check for $110 along with a copy of your original I-171H. The BCIS will then send you a new I-171H. This new I-171H does not change the original 18-month window.

Always express mail the package to the BCIS so you can have a trace receipt of its having gotten there. You must submit it to the office that serves your location. If you live in a large urban city, this is easy to determine. Otherwise ask your home study agency or your adoption agency to which office it should be submitted. This information is also located on the BCIS' web site. Write on the envelope, " ATTN: I-600A/Orphan Petition Section"

Once the BCIS issues you the I-171H, it takes a while for the applicant's dossier to arrive at the CCAA in Beijing. The date your dossier is registered with the CCAA is called the Dossier to China date or DTC. From the DTC date to time of referral the average has been about 12-14 months. Between referral and travel date, an average of 40 days elapses. The I-171H expires after 18 months and sometimes this can get dicey in relation to China. In the recent past this became a problem as the official China Center of Adoption Affairs (CCAA) was not able to keep up with the volume of adoption applications. The BCIS was asked to extend the 18 month I-171H validity period to 2 years, but it declined. The result was that many parents' I-171H forms expired and they had to start the whole process over. The CCAA has now said that the 2002 quotas reduced the number of incoming dossiers and that the expiration issue should no longer be a concern. The BCIS will send a Cable 37 to the consulate in Guangzhou notifying them that you are approved. Sometimes the consulate will confirm they have received the cable by sending a small brown envelope of instructions. Sometimes, however, this does not happen. It is always best to email the adoption unit in Guangzhou for confirmation that they have received notification of your I-171H approval.

I-600

The I-600 is the "Petition to Classify Orphan as an Immediate Relative" a/k/a the blue form. You file this form with the U.S. Consulate in Guangzhou, China when you are over there in order to obtain your child's visa. Both parents must sign. You will need to file one for each child you are adopting. Some fill out the form before leaving the States and then fill in those blanks for which they did not have the information once they are in China. Others wait to complete the form in China. Bring an extra blank form in case you need to make a change. You *must* file your I-600 with the U.S. Consulate before your I-171H has expired. If the I-171H will expire before you are able to file, then you have to begin the process anew. The BCIS does not grant extensions. An explanation of the I-600 is at *http://www.immigration.gov/graphics/formsfee/forms/i-600.htm.*

Because you both had to travel to adopt the child and the child is now with you in China, the form is easy to fill out. Questions 1-9 are the same as on the I-600A. You should ask your adoption agency regarding the answers to questions 16 and 17. Questions 17 b and c should be answered with "no." Question 18 should be "yes" to both parts, as China generally requires both parents to travel. Here are some other suggested answers. Question 20 should be "no" unless there is something obvious. The answer to question 21 is you, and to 22 and 23 none. Question 24 is your U.S. address. Question 25 is Guangzhou. Ignore the second 25 and for 26 give your name. The answer to question 28 is Guangzhou, China.

The U.S. citizen petitioner must sign the completed Form I-600 in the presence of the consular officer. If the petitioner is married, the other spouse must also sign the petition once it has been completed, although he or she does not have to sign before the consular officer. A third party may not sign the petition on behalf of the petitioner and/or spouse, even with a power of attorney. In the event that only one spouse travels abroad to file the Form I-600 petition, the consular officer is supposed to verify that the non-traveling spouse did not sign the petition before all of the information relating to the child had been entered onto the form. This is why many agencies advise you to fill out the I-600 once you have met the child, then fax it to the non-traveling spouse or call him so he can fill out the information. He then sends it by UPS or another carrier to your hotel in Guangzhou to hold for you. If Form I-600A, Application for Advance Processing of Orphan Petition, has been approved on behalf of a married couple, either spouse may sign and file the Form I-600—it does not have to be the same spouse who obtained the Form I-600A approval. The only exception is when the married couple consists of one U.S. citizen and one alien, since only the U.S. citizen may file the Form I-600 and the Form I-600A.

For Korean adoptions, the I-600 is filed with your local BCIS office in the United States once you have accepted your referral. Approval of the I-600 allows your child to travel to the United States.

I-864

Beginning in 1997, the BCIS began to require immigrants to file Form I-864, called the Affidavit of Support, in order to comply with the new federal law making it more difficult to bring immigrants into the United States. There is no exception for Americans adopting children overseas unless your child will be receiving an IR-3 Visa from the U.S. Most children from China receive the IR-3 and most from Korea do not. If your child will receive a IR-3, then you do not need to take any tax forms to the Consulate. If your child will be receiving an IR-4 Visa, then you have to file this form. The difference is that an IR-3 means that both parents saw the child before the Court hearing or decree registration. Usually an IR-4 is reserved for those adoptions in countries where the child was escorted to the United States or where only one married parent saw the child. Even if your child is receiving an IR-3, the State Department has decided that they will still apply the requirements of Section 212 of the INA. This section just says that the immigrant must have financial means to support the child. The State Department is interpreting that section as still requiring the parents to show some financial documents. Most consulates just want to see last year's tax return with schedules.

If you do have to file the I-864, then by signing the Affidavit of Support a sponsor (parent) is agreeing to repay the federal government for any means-tested benefits paid to your child. Your obligation ends as soon as your child becomes a citizen. You can get the form from the BCIS website or call 800-870-3676. To qualify as a sponsor, you must be at least 18 years old and a U.S. citizen or a legal permanent resident. The sponsor must have a domicile in the United States or a territory or possession of the United States. The form is not difficult to fill out. Where it asks for the name of your child, use the name she will have after the adoption.

If you have to file Form I-864, Affidavit of Support (and most parents of Chinese adoptees do not), then you should complete and notarize the form before you travel. The signature is good for 6 months. Gather copies of your last three years of filed personal federal tax returns, including schedules. Your state return is not involved, only your federal return. If you have not yet filed for the previous year, then bring the 3 years before that. If you have filed for an extension, you will need to bring a copy of that with that year's W-2s, in addition to the previous 3 years of filed returns. Make copies of all of this. The tax returns do not need to be notarized, just the signed form.

Have it notarized before you leave. If you can't find your last three years of tax returns, you can call the IRS at 1-800-829-1040. They will likely give you a one page summary transcript of your tax return or a letter called a 1722. Both of these are acceptable to the consulate. They take about 10 days to get and are free. If you filed electronically, then just print out the return and sign it. The I-864 serves as verification to the BCIS that you will be able to support your adopted child by demonstrating that your income is at least 125% of poverty guidelines. As an example, 125% of the poverty guidelines for 2002, except for Alaska and Hawaii, would require a family of four to have income of $22,625. You can find the most recent poverty guidelines at *http://www.immigration.gov/graphics/formsfee/forms/files/i-864p.pdf.*

Be sure to bring along a notarized verification of your employment and salary. If you are basing your Affidavit on documents other than tax returns, make sure you take those. Pack all of this in your carry-on, not your checked luggage.

If you rely on the income of your spouse in order to reach the minimum income requirement, your spouse must complete and sign a Form I-864A; Contract Between Sponsor and Household Member. If the spouse filed separately, then that separate tax return must also be attached to the sponsor's affidavit along with the spouse's employment verification. If you are not using the income of your spouse but filed a joint return, then you must include your W-2s to prove that your income alone qualifies you. The W-2s are not necessary if you filed jointly and are using both incomes to qualify. However, I would take them along if you have them, just in case. The 1722 is a substitute for your tax return so the rules regarding W-2s are the same. If you are missing your W-2s, ask your employer. By law they have to keep them for a few years. When filing the documentation with the consulate, place the I-864 on top, followed by the sponsor tax returns, evidence of employment, and the evidence of assets if these are used to qualify.

If you are adopting more than one child, you will need to file a second notarized I-864 accompanied by another (non-notarized) copy of your tax returns.

For information and forms see *http://www.travel.state.gov/checklist.html* and *http://www.immigration.gov/graphics/formsfee/forms/i-864.htm.*

FBI and Fingerprints

After you have your fingerprints taken by the BCIS they will travel to the BCIS Service Center in Nebraska. Then they will be sent to the FBI's fingerprint office in West Virginia. Once the fingerprints are logged in with the FBI, it takes them a very short time to actually run a check. Some offices are using digital fingerprinting, which theoretically should speed up the process. I believe this is the case in New York. After the FBI has processed your prints they send the results back to Nebraska, which sends them back to your local BCIS office.

The U.S. Immigration office in Lincoln, Nebraska is a regional processing office and does not deal directly with the public. They have two public phone numbers: (402) 323-7830 and (402) 437-5218. Be aware that BCIS phone numbers change frequently.

Approximately 2 weeks after the fingerprint appointment, you can call the FBI and ask them to check whether the fingerprints have gone through. To check on your fingerprint status, phone the FBI Liaison Unit at (304) 625-5590, and then push 4 on the menu. Hours are from 7 P.M. to 11 P.M. EST. You could also try (304) 347-5769. Voice mail is available from 7 A.M. to 11 P.M. EST. It is easier to get through later in the evening. They are now scanning in all fingerprints they receive on cards to make searches faster.

Just tell the liaison the date and city in which you had your fingerprints done and ask if he can give you a status. If they have been approved, then you can ask him to fax a copy of the approval to your BCIS office. It's most helpful if you can give him your BCIS assigned application number so he can put that on the fax. I believe this is called a LIN number. You can also call your local congressman's office and ask to speak to his BCIS liaison. His liaison can do some checking for you on your status.

Usually the FBI enters the status on Fridays. Thus, a whole week may go by before an updated status is available. Also, sometimes the FBI will tell you they can't locate your fingerprints and the next day you will receive BCIS approval. There is a certain amount of randomness in this process that defies understanding.

Sometimes fingerprints are rejected because your finger swirls are too light or they have damage from rough work or some other reason. It is advisable to refrain from using hand lotion the day you are fingerprinted and, if possible, to wash your hands right before being printed. The BCIS has gone to optical scanning in many offices. This was supposed to be more efficient, but instead it has caused more fingerprints to be rejected, thus delaying the process even more. Try to have the operator check your fingerprints while you are there in case there are any obvious imperfections.

If they are rejected twice, the BCIS is likely to ask you to go to your local police and obtain a record check and a letter saying you have no record. Most home studies require this anyway. You then give this letter to the BCIS. If you've lived in more than one place over the last 5 years, you'll need a letter from each jurisdiction. Just send a written request, the proper check, and a copy of your driver's license or passport for ID.

Asking what might show up in the FBI fingerprint check is like Geraldo asking what is in Al Capone's vault. You don't know unless you peek, but peeking is really not allowed. Generally speaking, the FBI runs an NCIC on you during the background investigation. However, any police department can (and frequently does) run one also. It is a nationalized reporting system. What that means is if you have been arrested in Iowa, assuming Iowa reports your arrest into the NCIC system, then it will appear on an NCIC report generated by the New York City Police Department (for example). Some states are horrendous for not reporting—Arkansas is a good example. The system is used by practically all city and county law enforcement agencies in the U.S. with sizable populations. If your local police department runs the report, it will be identical to the FBI report. The problem is getting your hands on it. If you need to know what will be in the report before you complete your home study, then you need to have someone local do you a big, big favor. In most states it is a criminal offense for that person to provide you an NCIC report if you're not in law enforcement. They are required to enter their own name, the subject's name, and the recipient's name on each report.

An NCIC report should show juvenile felony arrests, yet your state may or may not report them at all to the national database. The same goes for first offender dispositions. The state should not report those, but sometimes they do. Each state is different. If an item does appear, then you will know that you must disclose it in your home study and deal with it. If it does not appear, then you may want to consider not mentioning it. Just remember that even if an old (more than 10 years) arrest is out there, it will not likely disqualify you from adopting, but rather you will have to provide additional paperwork to the BCIS. A better check on what might show up is to send your fingerprints to the FBI before you hire a home study agency and ask the FBI to send you the report. This method is actually the easiest way of determining if an old arrest will appear. The FBI's web site has all the details on how you do this.

If you are pretty sure an old arrest will show up, then you should confess during the home study. The worst thing you can do is know it will appear and let the BCIS find out from the FBI and not from your social worker. Your social worker won't be happy either.

Your fingerprint check is only valid for 15 months, but your I-171H is valid for 18 months. If you plan to adopt during the "fingerprint gap," then you will have to redo your fingerprints. It is recommended that you begin the second fingerprint check at 12 months, since you can never tell if they will be lost or have some other disaster befall them.

Home Study

A home study is a document created by a social worker giving a snapshot summary of your life. This summary is based on interviews with you and from documents you provide. A home study is required by your state, the BCIS, and the foreign country, so there is no getting around it. It should take about two months to complete. It must be submitted to the BCIS within one year from when you filed the I-600A and must not be more than 6 months old at the time of submission. The home study should be 20% screening and 80% education. Sometimes it may feel that it is the reverse. There are very few absolutes in this world, but if you can have your adoption agency also write your home study, then you should have few problems. One of the most time consuming aspects of adoption is completing the home study. If you have completed a domestic home study then all you have to do is pay a little more money and get an addendum saying you are approved for international adoption. Unlike international adoption agencies, a home study agency usually must be licensed by your state. There are some states that allow independent social workers to conduct these studies, however, you need to check with your state to determine if this is allowed before hiring one. Also, some countries will not accept an independent social worker home study. Home studies by independent social workers are not accepted by China. A copy of the home study agency's license must accompany the home study.

When hiring a home study agency, make sure that the agency and the social worker have some experience with international adoptions. If they don't, don't hire them. A social worker that has adopted internationally can really be helpful to you. Also make sure that their state license will not need an extension any time soon. The home study agency should tell you the cost up front, approximately how long it will take, how many visits, and if the price includes postplacement visits or if they are extra. They should have a working relationship with the BCIS and know who to talk with there. If you have a first meeting with the social worker and she makes offensive comments or you are not comfortable with her, just fire her and hire another home study agency. It's completely your decision. Your goal is just to get the document and move on. The cost is generally $1,200+, but it can be less. In Utah it can cost as low as $400 and in California as high as $2,200. Do shop around.

If you want to do anything "out of the ordinary" such as adopting out of birth order, adopting a large sibling group with no prior parenting experience, adopting two unrelated children at once, or if you are very young, or older, or have multiple divorces, then talk to the social worker about this before you pay the agency any money. Some agencies rarely approve certain types of people to do certain types of adoptions, and if they have any "secret guidelines" it is better to find out about them before you waste your time and money.

China and Korea do not really want to know about your extended family and their troubles. They do not really want to read about your entire emotional life story. They do not care about your relationship with your mother, father, brother, or uncle. Nor do they care about the trauma caused when your childhood dog Skippy was run over by a submarine. So why are you asked these sorts of questions? It is certainly invasive. Just remember that it is up to you how much information you want to give beyond the basics. No one forces you to tell your entire life story. It is up to you how much information you wish to disclose. The best policy is not to offer more than what is asked. Keep explanations brief. The home study is just another document to check off on your list of things to do.

This advice is especially important if you are asked to write your "autobiography." Be careful about what you spill on paper. You don't want to write anything that could be used against you. Use positive language. Think about the questions and do not put down anything negative that could be unfavorably misinterpreted. Stick to factual information, do not write a novel, and leave your doubts and problems for your verbal discussions with the social worker or your day on Oprah.

One negative item that should be openly discussed (but not put into writing) with your adoption agency and home study agency is if there are any problems with an ex-spouse. If the divorce was a bad one and the relationship is icy, then it isn't unheard of for the ex-spouse to write a letter or call the agencies and bad-mouth the other spouse. So be upfront with the agencies in case this happens. You want them to be prepared, not surprised.

The BCIS regulations at 8 CFR 204.3 (e) require answers to some questions. The Service requires at least one personal interview of the couple and one home visit. They want the home study preparer to check your physical, mental, and emotional health. They want an assessment of your finances and whether you have a history of sexual or child abuse, substance abuse, or domestic violence. You will need to disclose any history of arrest or conviction. They want a detailed description of your house or apartment. The home study must include the specific number of children you may adopt. If you are adopting a special needs child, then the home study must include a discussion about your preparation, ability, and willingness to properly care for the child. Your state may also require some of the questions asked by the social worker.

The CCAA also has its list of required questions, which tend to overlap with the BCIS requirements. They want to know that you met with the social worker at least 4 times and the locations. They want to know your reason for adopting from China and that you understand the risks of international adoption. The home study must include some family information such as your education level, work experience, financial status, number of children and their ages, relationship with parents and siblings and health status, some statement regarding a parenting plan (like there really is one!) and guardianship plan in case you both die. The social worker must inquire into any criminal record and abuse history and assess the suitability of the residence. Singles living with a partner of the same sex shall submit a statement that both of them are not homosexuals.

A good social worker can be of great help to you. She can ask questions that relate to parenting and cause you to think things through. For example, questions dealing with disciplining your child. You and your spouse may have generally talked about it, but this question can focus you on the issue. The discipline issue is one where the social worker will eventually require you and your spouse to agree never to spank your child. You may even have to sign a piece of paper to that effect. Just do it and move on.

Yes, the corporal punishment police are out in force and you must give them what they want. They want to hear that when you discipline your child you will use time outs, logical consequences, thinking chairs, grounding, holding time, taking away toys, or canceling play dates, but you would never ever spank your child. The reality is that all decent parents try very hard to use anything but corporal punishment, but sometimes, under certain circumstances, your child will do something serious where a swat on the rear is the only educational tool that may work. A child who puts their finger in the light socket or their head in the microwave or runs out into the street to bite tires, may need more than a time out to prevent him from becoming an early Darwin Award winner. Contrary to what is taught in academia, a tap on the leg or diaper bottom does not immediately turn your child into a psychopath. A 1996 special conference by the American Academy of Pediatrics concluded that there was no evidence to suggest that spankings per se are harmful. Just know the answer the social worker is looking for and give it to her. The truth is that producing a well-behaved child probably results more from a parent's consistency in meting out consequences than in the punishment itself.

Each state has it owns rules about the corporal punishment issue. In Virginia, adoptive families are required to sign a statement saying that corporal punishment will not be used, although there seems to be some discussion on ending this requirement. One of the reasons the corporal punishment statement exists is primarily due to foster care laws. In cases where children have been physically abused by their biological parents and subsequently removed from the home, it is rightfully felt that the foster parents should not be allowed to use corporal punishment. After all, that was the reason why the children were removed from their parents' custody in the first place. However, as most of us can agree, there is a big difference between swatting a child's behind every now and then and severely beating him with a belt. Children have died from that kind of abuse, and in two cases, one in 2001 and another in 2002, young Russian children adopted by Americans became such victims. The law does not really distinguish between those two extremes, though, and so we are left with the poor social worker having to throw out common sense in order to satisfy what is required of her.

The other problem with the corporal punishment statement, at least in Virginia, is that it is only "valid" until a Final Order of Adoption is issued. So in other words, you cannot use corporal punishment on your child until after he is officially adopted. So what is the point of having parents adopting internationally make such a statement?

Finally, depending on how things were handled in the children's home, your child may not be so different from the kids in the U.S. foster care system. A foster child who has been physically abused often cannot distinguish between different kinds of hitting, and this is why corporal punishment is so ineffective. The reality is that you will be like all parents and have to undergo trial and error in determining what action on your part conveys to the child the message and lesson that the behavior was improper or unsafe and will not be tolerated. If authority of the parent and consequences are not understood early on, it is much more difficult to gain that authority later. Again, consistency of consequences, not the type of punishment, is the key.

Because of the transracial aspect of adopting from China and Korea, a lot of time will be spent exploring your attitudes and beliefs about parenting a child of another race (if you're not of Asian ancestry yourself), and the effects of becoming an interracial family on your extended families.

Your social worker may also ask about lead paint, fire extinguishers, guns, fire alarms, childproof locks, prescription medicines, insecticides, cleaners, pets, and other potential hazards in the home. She will ask where the child will sleep and want to see the room. If you live in an older home, she may ask about updated electricity and plumbing. She may want to see if you are using an older crib where the slats are too far apart, or have older window blind cords that still have loops. Since 1995, window blind cords have been manufactured without loops, which can strangle a young child. She may ask about guns in the house and how they are stored. All of these questions are not necessarily bad questions to ask. These questions may have little to do with adopting a child, but they have a lot to do with creating a safe environment in which to parent that child. When the social worker visits, she is not looking to do a "white glove" test so do not clean every speck of dirt. Nor are milk and cookies necessary. She just wants to see that the house is in decent shape and where the child will sleep. It isn't even necessary to have the child's room completed. Indeed, many times on a social worker visit parents are in the middle of a remodeling effort and the place is a wreck.

Other ideas regarding childproofing your home are to take electrical cords and tack them to walls rather than placing them under a rug. Place bumpers on sharp edges like fireplaces and coffee tables. Your fireplace will need a hearth gate and a strong screen. Place nonskid pads underneath rugs. Look out for dangling appliance cords. Put plastic covers over electrical outlets, and safety gates at top and bottom of stairs. Secure your entertainment unit and bookcase to the wall so the child cannot pull it over. Place smoke and carbon monoxide detectors in hall. Put safety latches or locks in the kitchen where dangerous utensils or chemicals or poisons are stored. Use the back burners on the stove whenever possible and turn the pot handles toward the back. Lower your hot water heater temperature to no more than 120 degrees or perhaps install anti-scalding devices on faucets. Use a toilet lock to prevent drowning. When bathing your child, bring the cordless phone in with you so you do not feel the need to run out to answer the phone. Put a bath mat in the tub to prevent your child from slipping and hitting her head on the back of the tub. (This one happens a lot!)

BCIS regulations require that a home study amendment be submitted if there has been a "significant change in family circumstances." This generally means that people have moved, and it doesn't matter whether it is next door or many countries away. The reality is that if the move will take place after the adoption or close in time, then just leave everything alone and don't volunteer anything. If it will take place while you are still waiting for a referral, then you should made the change, which is usually accomplished by a one-page amendment from your home study social worker.

One exercise that only a few home study agencies require, but which would be of great help to you in preparing for your international adoption, is to meet at least two families who have adopted from the country in which you are interested. You will learn far more from them than from reading or listening to a social worker. You will learn first hand about adoption language, grieving, medical issues, the process, parenting, etc.

After the home study is completed, the home study agency will obtain your state's seal of approval. Then it will be sent on to the BCIS by your home study agency. This is generally how it works. No doubt there are exceptions. Do not be afraid to call your home study agency and follow up as to when the study was sent to the BCIS. Your social worker should allow you to see a copy before she sends it, in order for you to review it for minor errors like names and birthdays and matching the number of children with the figure placed on your I-600A. You should also receive a final copy of the home study once it is signed, sealed, and delivered. If the home study agency does not agree to give you a final copy, don't hire them. The reason your state must give approval to the home study is that the state department is not allowed to issue a visa to your child unless you meet state pre-adoption requirements.

Make sure you put in your home study that you wish to adopt one child more than you really mean to. As previously mentioned, it is very common for a family to adopt one child then go back the next year to adopt a second. By already having the approval in your home study for more children, you may be able to shorten the process. If you find your child has a sibling and you need to increase the number of children then have your home study amended and write a letter to the BCIS amending your answer to line 17. Also, make sure you add a couple of years to your expected child's age. For example, if you want to adopt a child under 2, then put that you are looking for 0-4. The reason is that during the process of adopting that 2-year-old, he may turn 3. This has no bearing on how specific you actually tell your adoption agency to be and what referral you accept from the foreign country. This only has to do with the problem of showing up at the embassy with a child outside the age for which the BCIS approved you.

The social worker will likely want the following documents from you, so begin collecting them:

1. Certified copy of your marriage license and birth certificate

2. Copy of the deed to your house or apartment lease

3. Copy of your passport and copy of your latest tax return or W-2

4. A fingerprint clearance letter from your state or county

5. Medical form to be filled out by your doctor

6. Criminal record clearance letter

7. Some states require a child abuse clearance letter

8. Letters from friends saying that you will make great parents

She will likely ask you the following questions, so prepare your answers. Remember that the questions are her problem, but the answers and what follows are yours. Elaborate answers just lead to more questions.

1. Why do you wish to adopt a child?

2. How do you feel about adopting a child of a different race?

3. What do you consider to be acceptable methods of disciplining a child?

4. How might you facilitate your child's learning about her birth culture?

5. What values would you like to pass on to your child?

6. What are your hopes and dreams for your child?

7. What was it like growing up in your family?

8. What are the strengths and weaknesses in your marriage?

9. How do you and your spouse resolve disagreements?

10. If you are single, what extra challenges do you anticipate facing as a single parent?

If you have been arrested in the past like for an old DUI, it will likely show up on the FBI fingerprint check. Although it is possible that if it occurred in a small town, then it might not have been reported, the odds are against you. The BCIS may send you a "J" letter asking you to submit original or certified copies of any court dispositions and proof of completion of court requirements. The BCIS is now looking for any criminal record, no matter how small. There is no logic to it. They may also ask you to supply an affidavit explaining the situation and any extenuating circumstances. If documents are not available, the BCIS will want the police station or court to sign a letter stating that no records exist. If you know an arrest is going to turn up, you might as well begin to collect these documents and submit them with your home study. The BCIS will be unhappy if the arrest shows up on the FBI check but not in the home study, so be careful if you decide not to disclose.

Some other issues that might arise include multiple marriages or depression due to infertility stress. Multiple marriages should not be a problem unless they were recent. However, occasionally you will run into a social worker whose bias and inexperience cause them to give you a hard time. If you have settled down into a long relationship, your ancient history should be just that and no more. You will not likely run into a judgmental social worker. Try to find one who has some years of experience. Stay away from the less experienced ones who are fresh out of school.

Many people have taken anti-depressants to cope with infertility. However, there are two schools of thought about whether to disclose it to your social worker. The first school says they will find out anyway and if they find out and you haven't told them then you will look bad. That school of thought is non-sense. This isn't nursery school and the social worker is not your mother. If you do not tell them, it is unlikely they will find out. It will not show up on any medical report or test unless your doctor hates you. If the social worker sees a bottle on the home visit, then maybe she will find out, but that is about it. Actually taking an anti-depressant will not likely affect the home study. Depending on your social worker, it will be glossed over or discussed then dismissed. For example, your social worker might put, "well controlled with medication." So what can happen is that your social worker will minimize the issue or issue two home studies, one for the BCIS containing everything and one for the foreign country that is sanitized. This is another reason to use a home study agency that is used to doing reports for international adoptions. You don't want an inexperienced social worker making a big deal about it.

If you are unsure from which country you will adopt, all you have to put in your home study is "Asia." The BCIS will issue the I-171H without a specific country. You will have to return to your social worker to get some added paragraphs to comply with the specific country when you do decide. Also, the BCIS will have to be notified so they can send the Visa 37 Cable to the correct embassy, but meanwhile you will have received your I-171H. If you decide after receiving your I-171H, then you will have to pay $140 and file Form I-824. If you decide before receiving the I-171H, then when you send in your home study just add a short note on top of the submission telling the BCIS from which country you intend to adopt.

The full BCIS home study checklist is as follows:

1.   *Personal interviews and home visits*
- conduct at least one interview in person
- conduct at least one home visit
- state number of interviews conducted
- state number of home visits
- interview in person with any other adult member

- discuss whether post-adoption counseling is offered
2. *Assessment of ability to properly parent the orphan*
- initial assessment of physical, mental, and emotional
- assessment of potential problem areas
- referral to licensed professional, if appropriate
- copies of any outside evaluations
- any recommended restrictions
- apply all to any adult members of household
3. *Assessment of the finances of the prospective adoptive parent(s).*
- description of the income, financial resources, debts and expenses
- describe evidence that was considered in the assessment
4. *Screening for abuse and violence*
- statement regarding results of appropriate checks
5. *Inquiring about abuse and violence*
- response from each prospective adoptive parent regarding history of substance abuse, sexual or child abuse, or domestic violence, even if it did not result in an arrest or conviction
- response from any additional adult members of the household regarding history of substance abuse, sexual or child abuse, or domestic violence, even if it did not result in an arrest or conviction
6. *Information concerning history of abuse and/or violence and/or criminal record*
- information concerning all arrests or convictions for substance abuse, sexual or child abuse, and/or domestic violence and the date of each occurrence
- certified copy of the documentation showing final disposition of each incident, which resulted in arrest, indictment, conviction, and/or any other judicial judgment or administrative action
- signed statement from the prospective adoptive parent giving details including mitigating circumstances, if any, about each incident
- apply all to any additional adult members of household
7. *Evidence of rehabilitation*
- discussion of rehabilitation

- evaluation of the seriousness of the arrest(s), conviction(s), or history of abuse
- number of such incidents
- length of time since the last incident
- any counseling or rehabilitation programs which have been successfully completed
- evidence of rehabilitation by an appropriate licensed professional
- all facts and circumstances which were considered
- reasons for favorable home study
- apply to any additional adult members of the household

8. *Previous rejection for adoption or prior unfavorable home study*
- adoptive parents' response to whether rejected or a previous unfavorable home study
- if rejected or unfavorable, the reason for such findings
- copy of previous rejection and/or unfavorable home study
- must be applied to any additional adult members of household

9. *Living accommodations*
- detailed description of the living accommodations
- assessment of the suitability of accommodations
- determination whether space meets applicable state requirements, if any

10. *Handicapped or special needs orphan*
- discussion of preparation, willingness, and ability to provide proper care

11. *Summary of the counseling given and plans for post-placement counseling*
- statement that there was a discussion of the processing expenses, difficulties, and delays associated with international adoptions
- any plans for post-placement counseling

12. *Specific approval of the prospective adoptive parent(s) for adoption*
- favorable recommendation for proposed adoption
- reasons for approval
- number of orphans that may be adopted
- any specific restrictions such as nationality, age, or gender of orphan
- approval for a handicapped or special needs adoption, if any

13. *Home study preparer's certification and statement of authority to conduct home studies*

- statement certifying authorization to conduct home studies

- for parents residing in the U.S., a statement should include authorization under state of orphan's proposed residence, license or authorization number, and expiration date of such authorization

- if prospective adoptive parent(s) reside abroad, and the orphan's adoption is finalized abroad, a statement identifying the authorization by the adoption authorities of the foreign country where the child will reside or the authorization by any state in the U.S., including authorization or license number if any, and expiration date of such authorization, if any

14. *Review of home study*

- review by state authorities if prospective adoptive parents reside in a state, which requires such review

- if prospective adoptive parents reside abroad, appropriate public or private adoption agency licensed or otherwise authorized by any state to place children for adoption, must review and recommend

15. *Home study updates*

- must accompany a home study that is more than six months old or if at any time, there have been any significant changes including, but not limited to:

- residence of prospective adoptive parent(s)

- marital status

- criminal history, substance abuse and/or history of abuse or violence

- financial resources

- addition of one or more children or other dependents

More information on the BCIS' home study requirements can be found at *http://www.immigration.gov/graphics/services/bopreq.htm* and at *http:// www. immigration.gov/graphics/services/homestud.htm.* Information on Chinese requirements can be found at *http://www.chinaconnectiononline. com/Guidelines. htm.*

CHAPTER V

Chinese Paper Chase

Overview of Chinese Adoption Procedure

Chinese adoption law underwent a revision in 1999, however, the core provisions remained the same. The major feature of Chinese adoption law is that the CCAA gives priority to childless families and next to those having 1-2 children at home. Adoptive families who have 5 children living together with their parents will not get a referral from the CCAA. All parents must be 30 years of age or older. Singles cannot be over 50 years of age. A family can get expedited processing by applying to adopt a special needs child or an older child above 6.

Another change added a new medical requirement for all adopters. Adopters must also "not suffer from diseases considered medically unfit for adopting children." A new medical form was also required.

Adoptions no longer need to be notarized in China, although the Notary Department is required to do so if any of the parties request it. It may be better to go ahead and do it as notarization has a legal effect not unlike an administrative court order here in the U.S. Since mandatory notarization has been eliminated, the effective date of the adoption is now the day of registration of the contract.

Children available for adoption must be under the age of 14 who have been orphaned (parents deceased) or abandoned or whose parents are unable to raise them due to unusual difficulties. Children 10 or older must consent to the adoption.

Independent adoption is not allowed in China so U.S. couples must work through agencies. An agency collects 8 to 10 dossiers from several parents and then sends them on to the CCAA in Beijing for processing. It is easier for the agency and for CCAA to track the dossiers if they arrive in a group. In addition, this reduces the travel costs since one guide/translator can work with multiple families, which allows the costs for guide services to be shared among the group rather than being paid by just one family. Some agencies do not group families either for sending dossiers or for travel. This speeds up the process a little, but means increased travel costs and requires the family to travel by themselves to China.

Once the CCAA has your dossier you must wait, and wait some more. Generally only one child can be adopted at any one time. There have been rare cases of twins or siblings being adopted simultaneously, but that is extremely rare.

In Beijing, the dossiers are entered into the registry and then translated or the translation done in the U.S. is checked. The documents are checked that all of the legal requirements have been met. At the same time, the Children's Welfare Institutes (orphanages or children's homes) in various provinces have assembled a dossier on each child available for international adoption that includes a photo and medical report. These are also sent to CCAA in Beijing. Finally, the two sets of dossiers come together and a child is matched up with a family. The referral package, including a medical report and a very small photo, is sent back to the adoption agency in the U.S., which passes it along to the family. There is no video of the child. The family either accepts the referral or not. After some more waiting the CCAA sends a permission to travel document back to the adoption agency and you are on your way.

The CCAA will expedite dossier processing if you fall into one of the following categories: 1) adoption of medical special needs children; 2) adoption of children 4 and up by parents under 45; 3) adoption of children 7 and up by parents between 46-55 years old; 4) adoptions where one or more parents are Chinese or of Chinese ancestry; and 5) adoption by people who have been living in China for more than 1 year for work or study.

After your acceptance of the referral is logged in by the CCAA, the CCAA notifies the orphanage and the province officials that a family has been identified for the specific child. The officials will notify the CCAA that the child is still available for adoption. All of these back and forth notifications are usually handled by mail rather than fax. This is part of the reason it can take so long to receive permission to travel from the CCAA. Once all of this paperwork is completed the permission to travel document is prepared and signed by one of the vice directors of the CCAA. This is sent to your agency, which then notifies you. It would speed things up if the CCAA would use fax or email for these internal notifications, but alas they do not.

It is common for several families to travel at the same time. The trip usually lasts between ten days and two weeks. The group may travel together from the U.S. or meet in China on a specific date. Since this is a *hard* trip, not a vacation, you should leave your elderly parents and anyone under 5 behind. If you are single, a parent or friend is a great help. Otherwise, reserve your energies for your new child. Lastly, this is not a sightseeing trip, it's work!

After meeting your child you must complete additional paperwork that varies depending on the province. The final adoption paperwork may be completed in the local town where the child resides or may require travel to the provincial capital city. It used to be that a notary finalized the adoption. In China, the notary is a substantial government official with significant authority. He has the authority of a judge. When the notary finalizes the adoption, both China and the U.S recognize the adoption as final. There has been a recent change in these rules and the adoption need no longer go through a notary. However, it may still be the better practice and your agency should be able to guide in this regard. After finalizing the adoption, your child needs to obtain a Chinese passport and exit visa. You may have to go to the provincial capital for these.

After completing the provincial and local paperwork, the family travels to Guangzhou, China to the U.S. consulate for processing of the state department documents and the issuance of a visa allowing the child to legally enter the U.S. This usually is completed in two to three days. There are three tasks: the medical exam, the interview at the consulate, and picking up the visa for your child.

The medical exam is quite simple and short, usually taking no more than 15 minutes. The interview at the consulate is also relatively quick with the wait being much longer than the actual process. The next day you return to the consulate, pick up the visa for your child, and you are free to go home!

A video showing the Chinese adoption journey called *Good Fortune Video* is available at *http://www.celebratechild.com/videos/index.htm*. You can also buy "Big Bird in China at this site as well. (You must buy this video!) Another good video is called *Made in China*.

The U.S. Consulate's web site has an excellent review of the Chinese adoption procedures at *http://www.usembassy-china.org.cn/guangzhou/*.

Changes in Chinese Adoption Law

The CCAA was inundated with applications in 2001. This may have been a result of the changes in Russia, which slowed adoptions considerably during 2000. As a result of the large increase the CCAA issued certain restrictions for 2002. It limited the number of applications per U.S. adoption agency to the average of an agency's Chinese adoptions during the 3-year period of 1998-2000. This quota system has been suspended for 2003, but if a backlog develops do not be surprised to find it reinstated. The CCAA also began to strictly enforce its post-placement reporting requirement of two reports within a year of the child's adoption. This is a reasonable request.

In a negative development, the CCAA now only allows agencies to make 8% of their placements to single moms (single dads are not allowed). This figure was increased from 5% in 2002. However, it is in sharp contrast to the estimated 30% of previous placements that went to single parents. Because of this restriction, agencies have placed most singles on a long waiting list. One of the questions to ask agencies is about the length of their singles list. This is one of the few occasions where if you are single, going with a large agency might be an advantage.

The CCAA has also begun to enforce age guidelines. Parents between 30-45 years of age have first priority for infants. Parents between 45-50 may adopt infants if they are available, but more likely will be matched with a toddler. Parents between 50-55 will likely get children aged 4 and up and a parent over 55 is likely not to qualify. Multiple divorces are also frowned upon by the CCAA. If you have had three or more divorces, then you are likely not to qualify. A single woman must be under the age of 50 to qualify. Homosexuals are not allowed to adopt.

Another major change in 2003 has been the CCAA's implementation of the Hague intercountry adoption rules. These do not affect you as much as your agency. These provisions will eventually cause the cost of an adoption to increase by only allowing large agencies to adopt from China. They also require that American agencies become licensed by some U.S. governmental agency. As of yet, the State Department is still working out its regulations including licensure. It is unfortunate that China is beginning to implement the Hague. It will be even more unfortunate when the U.S. does.

Fees

Here is a list of some of the fees an adoption might entail from the Chinese side:

1. Fees for authentication of documents by the Chinese Embassy or Consulate in the United States: $10.00 per document. (A document may be a single page or multi-paged, the fee is for authentication of the seal.)

2. The China Center for Adoption Affairs (CCAA) advises that its initial fee is U.S. $365.00, plus U.S. $200.00 for translation of the documents. (The translations can be done in the United States or China; however, the China Center for Adoption Affairs (CCAA) will "rectify" any errors, which could lead to some extra cost above the initial $365.00.)

3. Fees for the issuance of the registration of the adoption by the Civil Affairs Bureau. U.S. $100.00.

4. Fees for issuance of the Chinese notarized certificate approving the adoption. This fee varies on a case-by-case basis. Since the notarized certificate is no longer required, this fee is optional.

5. Fees for the Chinese passport: Approximately $12.00 for normal ten-day issuance. (An additional fee for expedited issuance.)

6.   Children's Welfare Institutes may charge from $3,000 to $5,000 as a combined donation to the institution and a fee for having raised and cared for the child prior to the adoption.

Authentication

The following discussion primarily involves China, not Korea. The United States is a signatory to the Hague Convention on legalization of foreign public documents. By this convention, some countries will accept as authentic, documents that have been "apostilled."

Some countries, like China, only accept documents that have been "authenticated." This is a different procedure than "apostilled." In the "authentication" procedure the notarized document is taken to that state's secretary of state where the notary's signature and stamp are essentially certified by the state. Make sure they do a "regular certification" not an apostille certification. Tell them it is for China. If you have documents notarized in a different state, then it will have to be certified in that particular state. For example, if you live in Georgia, but were born in Arizona, then your certified birth certificate will have to be certified authenticated by the Arizona Secretary of State. In some states, like New York, the notary is first certified at the county level then by the New York Secretary of State.

If your documents originate in Virginia, Maryland, Washington, D.C., West Virginia, Delaware, Kentucky, Tennessee, North Carolina, South Carolina, North Dakota, South Dakota, Nebraska, Montana, Idaho, Wyoming, or Utah, then they are sent to the State Department of the United States for authentication before they move to the Chinese Consulate or Embassy for final authentication. The state department charges $5.00 per document. No more than 15 documents can be certified per day on a walk-in basis. On the Chinese Embassy's website, their Visa Office has instructions for notarization, certification, and cost. The Visa Office/Embassy for the People's Republic of China in Washington DC is located in Room 110, 2201 Wisconsin Avenue. N.W. Washington, D.C. 20007 Tel: (202) 338-6688 Faxback: (202) 265-9809 Fax: (202) 588-9760 Email: *chnvisa@bellatlantic.net*.

If your documents originate from New York, Rhode Island, Pennsylvania, Connecticut, Massachusetts, Vermont, New Hampshire, Maine, Ohio, or New

Jersey, then they are authenticated by the New York Chinese Consulate. They do NOT go through the U.S. State Department. The address of The Consulate-General of the People's Republic of China is 520 12th Avenue, New York, NY 10036 Phone: (212) 330-7409.

If your documents originate from Illinois, Indiana, Wisconsin, Iowa, Missouri, Kansas, Colorado, or Michigan, then they are authenticated by the Chicago Chinese Consulate. They do NOT go through the U.S. State Department. The address of the Consulate-General of the People's Republic of China is 100 West Erie Street Chicago, IL 60610 TEL: 312-803-0098 FAX: 312-803-0122 Recorded Message: 312-573-3070 Office hours: 9–12 and 1–2:30 Monday–Friday.

If your documents originate from (Northern) California, Oregon, Nevada, Washington, or Alaska, then they are authenticated by the San Francisco Chinese Consulate. They do NOT go through the U.S. State Department. The address of the Consulate-General of the People's Republic of China is1450 Laguna St. San Francisco, CA 94115 Tel: (415) 674-2900 Fax: (415) 563-0494.

If your documents originate from Southern California, Arizona, New Mexico, Hawaii, or the Pacific Islands, then they are authenticated by the Los Angeles Consulate-General of the Peoples Republic of China. Its address is 443 Shatto Place Los Angeles, CA 90020 Tel: (213) 807-8088 Fax: (213) 380-1961. They do NOT go through the U.S. State Department.

If your documents originate from Texas, Louisiana, Mississippi, Alabama, Florida, Arkansas, Oklahoma, or Georgia, then they are authenticated by the Houston Consulate-General of the People's Republic of China. Its address is 3417 Montrose Blvd. Houston, TX 77006 Tel: (713) 524-4311 Fax: (713) 524-7656. They do NOT go through the U.S. State Department.

At the end of this process, a paper trail exists that provides official assurance to the examiners at CCAA that you signed the documents. This process must be done for all components of the dossier that are sent to China. There is an aging rule that you must keep in mind as you jump through the authentication hoops. When documents are authenticated at the Chinese Embassy or a Consulate, a six month clock begins on the validity of the notarial stamps. The clock stops when the documents are logged in at CCAA, but resumes when a referral is sent. The clock stops ticking on the date of adoption. As long as there is less than six months of clock time, there is no problem. Under normal circumstances, this should pose no problems. One tip is to have all your documents authenticated at the same time and not piecemeal. Also, have your agency send your documents quickly to the CCAA after the agency receives your completed dossier.

Some families have used a dossier courier group called Pata Group to make the rounds. Their address is: 617 K Street NW Washington, DC 20001 and their telephone number is: (202) 789-1330. Another one is Jeff Doyle, P.O. Box 3239, Arlington, Virginia 22203-6134; phone is (703) 298-2382; *jaydoy@starpower.net*. A courier that some families have used is Patti Urban at *http://www.Legal-Eaze.com*. Her email address is *Patti@Legal-Eaze.com* and her phone is (914) 362-4630; fax: (914) 362-4637. Another courier service is Laura Morrison, also an adoptive mom. Her email address is *laura@asststork.com* and she has a great website at *http://www.asststork.com*. The Plachtas (also adoptive parents) are at *http://www.special-deliveries.net* and finally Denise Hope at *www.theres-always-hope.com* has a good handle on the procedures at the Chicago Consulate. Laura Morrison's web site has a lot of good information on the authentication process. The couriers keep a pretty good eye on your dossier and can help you if there are mistakes. Usually they can tell you where your dossier is at any given time.

You can find a list of each state's secretary of state at *http://www.corban-consulting.com/adoption/states.html*, Here is a sample of some states' addresses:
VIRGINIA:
Secretary of the Commonwealth
Capitol Square
Old Finance Building
Richmond, VA 23219
Tel: (804) 786-2441

NEW YORK:
(New York City)
Department of State
Certification Unit
123 William Street, 19th Floor
New York, New York 10038
Hours: 9:00 a.m. to 3:30 p.m.
Phone: (212) 417-5684
The closest subway station is Fulton on the green line.

Note that in New York State, after you have your signature notarized the county in which he is registered as a notary must certify the notary's signature. It is only after completing that process that you then go to the secretary of state for the Authentication. When having all of this done, make sure that all of the seals are raised. Do not remove certifications to make copies and then try to re-staple.

NEW JERSEY
State of New Jersey
Business Services Bureau—Notary Division
225 West State Street, 3rd Floor
Trenton, NJ 08608-1001
Main: (609) 292-9292
or
State of New Jersey—Dept of Treasury
Business Services Bureau—Notary Division
PO Box 452
Trenton, NJ 08625
Ph: (609) 633-8258 or (609) 633-8257
For expedited service, you must deliver your package by hand or use a commercial carrier like FedEx. You can't use U.S.P.S. Express Mail because they don't deliver to the West State Street address.

A recommendation is that you express mail your document with a return prepaid express envelope and indicate your name, address, phone number. In your cover letter you should tell them that it is for an adoption in China. One way to avoid high fees is to take your documents to a nearby state that has lower fees. This does not apply to state-specific documents such as birth certificates or marriage certificates. There is a website with all of the addresses of the offices of vital records in all 50 states at *http://www.asststork.com/pages/myvitalrec.html.*

A trick with state specific documents that are not located near you is to ask the clerk to send the certified document on to the state's secretary of state's office. This will save time. In order to do this you need to enclose a stamped pre-addressed envelope to the state and then a second one that the state can use to send the document back to you. You will need to include all fees and the usual cover letters. Sometimes the state's Bureau of Vital Statistics will simply send you an authenticated version for an additional fee. South Carolina is one such state. In some states, like Georgia, the process has been delegated to another office rather than the state's secretary of state.

Like everything in life, always call ahead to make sure of the correct procedure and fee. And always double-check your notary before and after she signs the documents. Make sure the expiration of her license shown on her stamp is at least a year away. Make sure she signs using the exact name on her seal and stamp and puts the county name on the document. No abbreviations are allowed. Different states have different rules.

A good tip is to open your own FedEx account. It only takes a few minutes and does not cost anything. You can do this over the phone or if you live close enough to a FedEx branch you can also do this in person. This allows the return express mail to be billed to your account, saving much time.

Dossier

Your Korean dossier is basically just your home study. It is hardly a "dossier" at all as that term is used with other countries. So the following discussion pertains primarily to China. What is a dossier? It is all your paperwork that you have gathered in the States. It is your home study, your birth certificate, marriage certificate, form for this, and form for that. It is all of those documents, notarized and authenticated. Your agency compiles all of this into your "dossier" and has it translated. It is sent to China and reviewed by the CCAA. If you were born in the United States, your birth certificate is likely located at some division or bureau of vital statistics that may be connected to the Department of Health of your birth state. They will send you a certified and authenticated birth certificate upon payment of the usual fee.

The dossier will likely contain some of the following documents:

1. Application for Inter-Country Adoption;
2. Birth Certificate;
3. Certificate of Marital Status;
4. Certificates of Profession, Income, and Property;
5. Certificate of Health Examination;
6. Criminal Clearance letter;
7. Home Study;

8.   I-171H;

9.   Copy of each parent's passport; and

10. Two 2-inch bareheaded passport photos each of the parents and 6
     photos reflecting their family life. These family life photos should only
     be of you and the people who live in your home. Do not include
     friends, relatives or the cabana boy.

While you are making passport photos, consider taking an extra 2 sets to be
attached to your visa application and 1 set to carry with you to China. Except
for items 9 and 10, the above should be authenticated by the State Department
and by the Embassy or Consulate of the People's Republic of China.

If you were born overseas as a United States citizen, then you can either get
someone over there to obtain your certified birth certificate or you can order a
certified copy of your Certification of Report of Birth (Form DS-1350) from:
Correspondence Branch, Passport Services, Department of State, 1111-19th St.
NW, Suite 510, Washington, D.C. 20522-1705. The phone number is (202)
955-0308. Call them first to determine the correct procedure and fee.

For China, the Application for Inter-Country Adoption is signed by the
parents and in the case of a couple, the application shall be jointly signed by
both of them. It shall include the names of the parents, their dates of birth,
places of birth, nationality, the reason for adoption, the definite desire and
request for adopting Chinese children, the adopters' statement of assurance
that they shall not abandon or abuse the adopted child, and statement of
assurance that the adopted child shall be entitled to enjoy the equal rights as
their biological children and be educated and brought up healthfully.

Single adopters for China should submit documents attesting to single status.
The unmarried shall submit a statement that they are unmarried and are not
homosexual. The divorced shall submit their divorce decree. In the case of the
death of a former spouse, the adopter shall submit the spouse's death certificate.

When your dossier lands at the CCAA, it is initially reviewed in the
Registration Department for the technical requirements of notaries and
authentication. This can take 3-4 months. Then your dossier goes to
Department 1 for a content check. This is where they discover your husband
was raised by apes and his name is Tarzan. Then your dossier travels to

Department 2, or the Matching Room. This is where your dossier is matched with a referral.

Financial Status Form

For China, parents need to submit certificates of profession issued by their employers. These certificates should include the profession, position, the duration of employment, the annual income and the prospect of continuous employment. Self-employed adopters shall submit certificates of profession and annual income issued by a certified public accountant. They also need to submit a certificate of financial status and property on this form:

CERTIFICATE OF FINANCIAL STATUS

APPLICANTS' NAMES

	This year	Last year
Annual Income: self/husband:		
Self/wife:		

Other Annual Income: self/husband:
                Self/wife:

Life Insurance: self/husband:
                 Self/Wife:

Assets: Value
   Personal Property (vehicles and others)
   Real Estate (Residence and others)
   Stocks and bonds
   Savings Account
   Checking Account
   Other Investment

Total Assets (Not including annual income & insurance):

Liabilities:	Monthly Payment	Total Owed
Credit Cards		
Home Mortgage		
Other Liabilities		

Total Liabilities:

Net Worth:

I/We attest that the above-mentioned financial statement is an accurate summary of my/our assets, liabilities and others.

Signature   Signature

Health Form

Parents need to submit a health certificate form issued by a doctor. Please tell your doctor to write legibly. If it can't be read, it is no good. The CCAA has a particular form they want you to use. The CCAA wants to know if you are on any long-term medication, what kind, and the dosage. They want to know if you suffer from a serious illness or had an operation and if so then a special medical report shall be made by your doctor. The medical report should include the date the patient suffered the illness or had an operation, what kind of illness or operation, course of treatment and its result or that of the operation, whether the patient has recovered from illness, whether the patient needs further medication to place his condition under control, and whether the applicant is suitable for adopting a child. Unless you have had a serious operation in the last year or two, have your doctor just put down "none." The point is not to give a full medical history since the day you were born, but just fill out the document and move on. The health report is valid for 12 months from the date of examination.

The format of the certificate is below:

**CERTIFICATE OF GENERAL PHYSICAL EXAMINATION
FOR ADOPTION APPLICANT**

TO EXAMINING PHYSICIAN:

Your medical report is of paramount importance to the China Center of Adoption Affairs in its examination of the adoption qualification of the adopters. You are kindly requested to fill in all the blanks. Thank you for your cooperation.

Applicants' Names: _____ DOB: _____

Address:_____

MEDICAL HISTORY:

Have you ever had Tuberculosis?	No/Yes
Tumor?	No/Yes
Heart Disease?	No/Yes
Liver Disease?	No/Yes
Sexual Disease?	No/Yes
Neuropathy?	No/Yes
Mental Disease?	No/Yes
Other Communicable Disease?	No/Yes
Alcoholism or Abuse of Substance?	No/Yes
Any Genetic Disease?	No/Yes
Any Operation?	No/Yes

PHYSICAL EXAMINATION:

Height:_____m Weight:_____kg Blood Pressure:_____
Vision: L_____R_____
Hearing: L: Normal/Abnormal; R: Normal/Abnormal
Heart: Normal/Abnormal Liver: Normal/Abnormal
Lung: Normal/Abnormal Lymph: Normal/Abnormal
Thyroid: Normal/Abnormal Nerve System: Normal/Abnormal
Blood Test (Date of Test):
    Routine Blood Test: Normal/Abnormal HbsAg: Negative/Positive
    Liver Function: Normal/Abnormal
Urinalysis (Date of Test):
    Routine Urine Test: Normal/Abnormal
HIV Test (Date of Test): Negative/Positive
Is the patient taking any medication? For what purpose?_____

PHYSICAL TEST RESULT:

Is there any physical, mental or psychological unfavorable elements of the adoption applicant, which will affect the upbringing of the child?

Is the adoption applicant's state of health suitable for raising a child?

Physician's Signature: Date:
MD License No.

Don't expect your doctor or your doctor's staff to have a clue about filling out these forms. Make sure they understand that if the question is on the form, then that means your agency wants a test result or a definitive answer like "no." The words "Not tested" or "Not done" are not good enough. It must say normal, negative, or have some other appropriate value. You should fill out as much of the form as you can before giving it to the staff or have the doctor fill it out in front of you so he does it correctly. Some offices do not have a notary, so you will need to provide for one. Be prepared to be stern with the staff or doctor. Your form has a low priority with them. Remind them that this is for a child. This is when it helps to have a friend for a doctor.

Some insurance companies might not pay for the exam or tests. If you have doubts, check beforehand. An alternative that might be cheaper could be your county health clinic.

Holidays

Holidays can interfere with the process of having your dossier approved and your child's visa issued. In China, the U.S. consulate is closed on American and Chinese holidays. This can delay the visa appointment at the consulate and your return. The CCAA is closed for Chinese holidays. These are the Chinese Lunar New Year, International Labor Day and Chinese National Day in October, the anniversary date of the founding of the People's Republic of China. The Lunar New Year can really jam things up, as a third of China's population fills planes, trains, and buses to visit home. Knowing when these holidays occur can help your planning. The trade show in October in Guangzhou is also a problem and hotel rooms are hard to find. The complete holiday schedule is posted at *http://www.usembassy-china.org.cn/beijing/holiday.html.*

CHAPTER VI

Korean Paper Chase

Overview of Korean Adoption Procedure

One major difference between adoption from Korea and China is that babies from China are mostly girls, while a Korean adoption is more likely, though not exclusively, to result in the adoption of a boy. The yearly numbers are about 60% male and 40% female. You have to wait a little longer for a girl than a boy. If you are childless, you cannot specify your gender preference with Korea.

Another difference in the two country's programs is that in China many, but not all, of the children are cared for in foster homes, while in Korea, all are in foster homes. In Korea, the children receive excellent medical attention and are rarely malnourished. Korea provides the adoptive parent with updated medical reports after referral and before arrival. They also provide some social history on the referred child, unlike China where usually there is little or no social information known. The Korean program is usually faster than the Chinese program with the whole process taking about 12 months from application to adoption.

One huge difference between the two programs is that Korea is one of the few countries that allows your child to be escorted the U.S. You do not have to travel to Korea to adopt your child. There are many reasons why it is better if you can travel, but it is not necessary. Also, Korea does not allow single parent adoptions, while China places limits on the number. The cost of adoption ranges from $18,000 to $22,000.

American adoption agencies are only allowed to work with four licensed Korean child welfare agencies, to wit:

1) Eastern Social Welfare Society

    493, Changchun-Dong, Sudaemun-Ku, Seoul

    Tel: 82-2-332-3941/5

    Fax: 82-2-333-1588

    www.eastern.or.kr and *http://www.eastern.or.kr/eng/htm/home.htm*

2) Social Welfare Society

    718-35, Yuksam-Dong, Kangnam-Ku, Seoul

    Central Post Office Box 24, Seoul, Korea

    Tel: 82-2-552-1015~8, 552-6227

    Fax: 82-2-552-1019

3) Holt Children Services

    382-14, Hapjong-Dong, Mapo-Ku, Seoul

    Tel: 82-2-322-7501~4, 322-8102-3

    Fax: 82-2-335-6319 or 334-5440

    www.holt.or.kr/holt/main8/main.htm

    Also see *http://www.geocities.com/koreanadoption/index.html* for a family's experience with Holt in Korea.

4) Korea Social Services

    533-3, Ssangmun-Dong, Dobong-Ku, Seoul

    Tel: 82-2-908-9191~3

    Fax: 82-2-908-3344

An American agency will work through one of these agencies on your adoption. The Korean process will be handled by the foreign agency. American agencies are approved to place children only in specific American states. This doesn't make a lot of sense (Belarus does the same thing), and appears to exclude Americans living abroad except for military families. Agencies are allowed to place special needs children in more than just their "assigned states."

Harry and Bertha Holt started Korean adoptions when they adopted eight children from Korea in 1955. In 1956 the Holts established an adoption program, Holt Children's Services of Korea, which later became an independent organization. Today Holt International Children's Services in the United States and Holt Children's Services of Korea continue as partner agencies. Holt-Korea places children with adoptive families throughout the United States and several other countries through umbrella or joint programs with other agencies, of which Holt International is just one. In all, there are 23 U.S. agencies approved to place Korean children.

The Korean requirements are not unreasonable. The requirements vary slightly depending on the agency. They want couples to have been married at least 3 years. You are each allowed one divorce. You must be no more than 45 years of age and they may not allow an adoption if you have more than 4 children. The age difference between husband and wife should be less than 15 years (some agencies say 9). There is a minimum financial requirement of an annual income of $25,000 (some agencies say $35,000). This is a Korean, not a U.S., requirement. For U.S. requirements see the I-864 and poverty guidelines. Unlike other countries, Korea will place your adoption on hold if you are pregnant.

Eastern Social Welfare agency and the Social Welfare Society (SWS) have a very peculiar requirement regarding a parent's weight. If weight is a concern, then before paying any money you should certainly query your American agency whether they work with Eastern or SWS and if weight will be a problem. If so, simply move to an agency that works with one of the other two Korean licensed agencies.

The Korean foster system is a very good one. A social worker might receive a phone call from your child's birth mother and counsel her. If the birth mother is not married, she is at risk of being disowned by her family and usually becomes estranged from her boyfriend. The social worker might be told some personal history. Learning this information for your child is one reason to make the trip to Korea. The child will then be placed with a foster family. The child will have many medical checkups and be in pretty good health. The child's medical record information is extensive and generally reliable. You are provided with the background of the birth family, if available. The children are from age 5 months to 2 years. The average age of children when they come home is 6 to 10 months. While domestic adoption is on the rise in Korea, Korean culture and its emphasis on genetic ties and family name continue to slow acceptance of adoption in the home country.

An interesting development in the Korean programs has been in post-adoption services. Birth family searches by adoptees have become common. These occur as the adoptee enters adulthood and desires to know more about his or her origins. It is a common desire. In the past the Korean adoption agencies hid or destroyed records, but after strong criticism and the rise of Korean adoptee advocacy groups, these agencies now have come full circle and will assist an adoptee. Usually trips take place during the summertime and the adoptee spends time meeting their old foster mothers, visiting their birthplaces and various historic sites, and sometimes reuniting with their birth family. In contrast, China offers little in the way of a paper trail, as most children enter the system as abandoned infants.

The state department provides a summary of the adoption rules in Korea at *http://travel.state.gov/adoption_korea.html* and *http://usembassy.state.gov/seoul*. Another good site is *http://www.adoptkorea.com*. A video showing the Korean adoption journey is *Born Journey: Korean Adoption Documentary* at *http://www.celebratechild.com/videos/bornjourney.htm*.

Adoption Today

The Korean process works similarly to other countries with the main difference being that it is focused on adopting the child in the United States rather than in the home country. Even the enactment of the Child Citizenship Act is not likely to change this process. According to the State Department's summary, finalizing an adoption in Korea entails the parents staying in-country for a month or so. Thus, most parents will continue to finalize in their state. If you are a military family, you have some additional steps. See this web site for more information: *http://www.anewarrival.com/military.html*.

Once your dossier is submitted to Korea you can anticipate a two- to three-month wait for a referral. At time of referral you will be provided a photo and medical. You will not get a videotape. You can decline the referral or sign a child acceptance agreement. It takes approximately another 3-4 months before the child is ready to be escorted to the United States.

In Korea there are more boys than girls available, so there is a gender policy in place. If you are childless, you will be referred a boy. If you have two children, a boy and girl, an agency might only refer you a boy. If you have only boys, you can request a girl. Agencies differ slightly on their gender policy. If an agency restricts your choice, be sure to research other agencies. Korea has no one-child policy like China. However, it has the sonogram. Most couples in Korea try to have only two children, a boy and a girl. The problem arises when the first-born is a girl and the sonogram informs the couple that the second is to be a girl, too. This second may be aborted, and if the third fetus is also not a boy, she is in as much danger as was her aborted sister. If the first and second children are boys, the couples are satisfied and stop reproducing. In Korea in 1993 there were 115.6 boys born for each 100 girl babies. (The normal ratio is about 105 males to 100 females.) In 1995 only 47.9% of primary school children were female, which meant an extra 200,000 6- to-11-year-old boys. It is estimated that by 2010 there will be 128 men to every 100 women in the 27-to-30 year cohort.

Even though Korean adoptees are generally considered healthier than those from other countries, you still need to have the child's medical information reviewed by an IA doctor or pediatrician and you also need to be educated on the usual adoption medical issues. This is especially true if you are adopting a special needs child. You cannot simply rely on the fact that it is a Korean adoption and neglect your own education. Korean birth mothers are part of the world culture and have access to alcohol and the usual vices.

The initial report will include his medical history, lab tests results, any medical complications or medications given. There will be a section on his or her Korean name (usually given by the social worker who works with the birthmother) and its meaning, age/religion/education/occupation/marital status of the birthparents, description of the baby's birth, and some background on the birthparents (how they met, circumstances by which the baby was placed for adoption).

If you are planning to have your child escorted to the United States, in a few weeks after your acceptance you will be sent your child's "legal documents."

These are:

1) Certificate of Acknowledgment from the American Embassy

2) Extract of Family Register showing your child's name, birth date, etc.

3) Certificate of Appointment to Guardian of Minor Orphan in Orphanage attesting that the Korea agency has been granted guardianship

4) Statement of Consent to Overseas Adoption which shows the agreement of the child's guardian to have the child adopted overseas

5) Copy of baby's Korean Birth Certificate

You attach these documents to the I-600 and send it in to your local BCIS office. The I-600A was filed when you did not have a referral. The I-600 is sent when you do. The BCIS should send you approval within a month. You will also need to file the I-864, since your child will be traveling under an IR-4 Visa as you have not seen him yet.

A few weeks after your I-600 is approved you will get a phone call saying that your child will arrive in a few days. This is when you panic. The most important item is to make sure your insurance company is covering your child the minute he is in your arms. The second most important item is to have diapers in the house. Your agency will give you some sort of official form to be given to your health insurance carrier or HR department confirming that the child lives with you and your family and that you accept full responsibility for the child's medical care.

The Korean agency is appointed guardian of the child and this guardianship is transferred to the American partner agency before the child travels to the United States. Once a child is placed with an adoptive family, a social worker visits the adoptive home after the placement to see how the adjustment is going. Even though a child is physically in the adoptive home, the legal guardianship of the child is still with the adoption agency until the adoption is finalized. Once the adoption is finalized in court, the adoptive parents become the legal parents of the child.

Your child will have a Pre-flight Report on his general health and condition as well as his/her immunization chart and other pertinent medical data. Take these and any other medical information you receive and give copies for his file to your pediatrician. Your agency will also give you an authorization letter giving you permission to treat the child. Give the pediatrician a copy of this as well. Your pediatrician will need some standard growth charts for Korean children. These can be found at *http://www.adoptkorea.com/childgrowthchart.htm.* You should also educate him on the nature of Mongolian Spots.

Let your new child show you what he needs. Bonding and trust come from his understanding that you will provide what he needs. Sometimes Korean children are ready for solids sooner than usual. If so, just go with the flow and provide soft foods along with a bottle and let him dictate his wants. He may also need some transition to a crib or to sleeping alone. Many parents keep the crib in their room for several months until the child is comfortable. Place your child in a Snuggli and let him stay near your skin around the house. Rub his feet and put the same lotion on you and the baby. All of this promotes healthy bonding.

Korea requires three post-placement reports, a post-placement medical report and pictures of the child and the family in the six months following placement. This is generally required before the adoption is finalized. State law governs adoption so you have to look to your own state as to what is required before the adoption petition can be filed. Some states want you to wait 3 months and others 6 months.

Traveling To Korea

As previously stated, you do not have to travel to Korea. However, even if only one parent travels, the experience and knowledge is well worth it to you and your child. You will learn much about your child from his social worker and foster parent, which you will later be able to share with him/her.

South Korea is characterized by mountainous terrain in the north and east and broad plains in the south. It's densely settled, with a majority of its 46 million population concentrated in the southern section, although about a quarter of the South Koreans live in Seoul, thirty miles south of the Demilitarized Zone. South Korea is the size of Mississippi and 70 percent of it is covered with mountains. Women constitute nearly 40 percent of the labor force, about a third of who work on family farms. The rest work in services, health care, and textile and electronics manufacture, whose work force is 70-90 percent female. South Korea is one of the

20 richest countries in the world, an astonishing achievement over a mere three decades. Its GDP per capita is eight times India's, 15 times North Korea's, and already even with the lesser economies of the European Union. Because of the Asian crisis, Korean growth in 1998 was sharply cut, but now it has bounced back. Before you travel pick up a copy of *Lonely Planet's Guide to Seoul* and look at these great web sites: *http://www.visitseoul.net/english/*and *http://www.geocities.com/koreanadoption/compilation.html.*

Korea is hot in the summer and cold in the winter. Unlike China you will want more than one nice outfit. Think business casual not vacation casual. Otherwise the same travel and packing advice applies. Expect to stay about 5-7 days. You do not need a visa if you are staying less than 30 days and since your stay is usually no more than a week or so, one should not be necessary. Korea has both 110 and 220 outlets so make sure you have an adapter.

Use the usual prepaid phone card when calling from Korea. Do not use the hotel phone unless it is an emergency. It is extremely expensive. If someone from home is trying to call you in Seoul, they should dial, 011 822 and then the local 7 digit phone number.

The trip to Seoul is about 13 hours from the West Coast. Many parents fly Northwest, Singapore Air, Korean Air, or Asiana. Seoul switched from Kimpo Airport to the new Inchon Airport as its main international airport in April 2001. When you arrive in Seoul, there are many ways of getting into the city from the airport. A cab will cost about $40 from the airport to your hotel. You may have to haggle some. The cab will want you to pay the tolls. Taxis come in two colors; black and yellow. Yellow are regular taxis and black are deluxe. If you absolutely, positively must be somewhere at an exact time and the address is complicated, then choose a black taxi. Otherwise, the yellow ones are fine.

Try to stay near City Hall, which is in a main downtown area with great subway connections. Some parents have stayed at the New Seoul Hotel. There is also the SeoSeoul Hotel, which is closer to Holt, but not as nice. Holt, Eastern, and SWS also have guest houses at which you can stay and these might be your first choice.

The Seoul subway is very easy to use. With one ticket, you can ride anywhere in the same zone, as long as you stay underground. A good web site on the subway is at *http://soback.kornet.net/~pixeline/heeyun/korea/subway.html.*

When you meet the social worker and foster mom, make sure you have written out all your questions. Let your spouse be in charge of taking notes as you will be busy with the baby. Give gifts to foster mom and staff as described in the gift section.

Your child's airplane ticket should be in his Korean name, since you have not yet adopted him. On your return home the spouse not carrying the child will have to pay an exit tax. The carrying spouse will have their tax waived. If you want a layover, then try Tokyo. The Tokyo airport is very transfer-friendly, and there is a great parent and child room for taking a break. Just follow the signs to "main terminal," and then to "parent-child" room. Of course, most parents want to just gut it out and get home, but Tokyo is an option.

CHAPTER VII

Agencies

You should interview adoption agencies just like interviewing a pediatrician or a home study agency. Although you may feel intimidated, remember that they work for you. Your agency should give you references of families who have adopted through them and who have agreed to be references. They should (but not all do) include some families that have not had a great experience. All agencies, no matter how wonderful, will have situations that did not turn out where everyone was happy. It may have been just one of those things, or something beyond the agency's control, or the agency may have dropped the ball. You are entitled to hear it all before making your choice. After all, this is your life and family you are talking about. Remember that you should never have to pay an agency anything but a small registration fee ($100-$200) before reviewing their contract and set of program fees. Most agencies have web sites where you can find a lot of information about their various programs. Here is a web site with a list of agencies that work in China: *http://www.fwcc.org/internetsources.html#china.*

One issue that is usually not very important is your geographic proximity to the agency. Phone, fax, mail, and e-mail work fine. Your agency does not have to be in your state for you to use them. Of course, if you feel more comfortable with actually seeing their offices and people then by all means make that a consideration. Another issue that is not too important is the actual size of the agency. A larger agency will likely have a permanent staff in China and everything over there will go like clockwork. However, the size of the agency has no bearing on how fast your American BCIS paperwork is processed and no bearing on the ultimate outcome of bringing a loving child into your family. If you are very concerned about the health of your child, then working with an agency that has a doctor on site to monitor the children before adoption may be the best answer.

You can always do some general searches for information on an agency that you are investigating. You can search using paid services like Lexis/Nexis, *www.knowx.com* or Westlaw. These may be available at your local library. The ICAR pamphlet is also helpful.

Here are some questions you might ask:

1. Does the agency have an 800 number? You don't want to pay for your calls.

2. Will the agency tell you how many other "customers" they have? You want to know where you will be in the "line" and how many children are they currently referring. This will help you figure out how long you will have to wait.

3. Will the agency help you with the paperwork, or do they expect you to do it all?

4. How knowledgeable is the office staff? How long have they been with the agency? Can the person who will be assigned to your case answer questions about China, or do you have to wait until they get back to you? Find out who will you be dealing with on a regular basis, answering questions, etc. Find out their qualifications and experience with the China program. It is not important that they have a social work degree or some other degree. It isn't relevant. Have they lived in China or traveled there? Talk to her. Ask yourself if you can work with her.

5. When was their last Chinese adoption? (If it was more than 2 months ago, then you have to wonder how well run their program is.)

6. Does the agency provide a snapshot or a video of the child?

7. They should also give you a good explanation for where your money goes.

8. What medical records and family history will you receive? If you have medical questions about the child, can the agency get answers from the Chinese?

9. If you give me a referral, and I do not accept, when will I receive the next referral? In other words, do I lose my place in line?

10. How many successful adoptions has your agency performed in the past year? In the age group that I am interested in? How long have you had a China program? How many families have you taken to China?

11. If there is a facilitating agency or individual in China with whom you work, how long have you worked with him/her? The longer the agency has worked with a facilitator the better. You want someone who is reliable.

12. Where will we stay while in (adoption city) and in Guangzhou?

13. Will we travel with a group or will we travel by ourselves? How many are there in a group?

14. What support will we receive while in China? A guide and driver?

15. What if I decide not to continue with your agency, for whatever reason, what will it cost me? What is your refund policy? (It is very important to see this in writing)

16. Who obtains the foreign visa?

17. Does the agency require your health insurance company to sign a letter stating they will cover the adopted child? If you have an individual policy versus a group policy, obtaining this letter may prove difficult.

18. Does the agency have rules about how long you have to be married, or the age of the child you can adopt, or do they restrict you from choosing the gender? Some agencies have such rules. Most do not.

19. Are post-placement reports free or do they charge you for processing? They should be free or included in the cost.

20. Does the agency have rules about adopting while pregnant (some don't allow it) or adopting within a year of adopting the first child?

21. What is the agency's timeline from DTC to referral and referral to travel date? Compare that to what you read on the APC.

22. If there is dissolution of the adoption, how will the agency help?

23. If things go wrong when you are in the foreign country, what resources and commitment does the agency have to getting the adoption back on track?

24. If you plan on taking other family members with you to China, such as a child or parent, make sure the agency agrees to allow that before you pay them any serious money. Get them to confirm that in writing. You do not want any surprises immediately before traveling.

25. Does the agency do any screening of the children? If so, how? If they say they have doctors who review these children, are these Chinese doctors? Chinese doctors have a propensity to say that the child is fine, and that he'll catch up. While that may be true, it is also true that many times there are medical and developmental issues and you would like a little notice. Rely on your own IA doctor and just add the agency doctor's opinion to your growing pile of medical information. I am not suggesting you dismiss the agency's medical opinion, just weigh its credibility along with the doctor's training and incentive.

26. What provinces do they work in? You may decide you only want to go to certain places based on what other families have said.

27. What are all of the expected fees and costs related to the adoption? What specifically is included/excluded in the agency's fees?

28. How are problems/disagreements handled between agency and client?

29. Does the agency have a guide/translator familiar with English medical terms? The problem with some agencies is that if you have a medical problem or your child does in-country, the translator does not know enough English medical terms to tell the Chinese doctor what your doctor in the States has recommended. This is a question to ask the references as well.

30. Select an agency that will send someone to travel with you and advocate on your and your baby's behalf if a medical situation or some other problem arises. You need an agency representative either with you or close by. This is the job the agency is supposed to do, but some agencies do not.

An agency's refund policy is very important. It may be triggered by a "stalled adoption." This term is rarely defined. You should ask for the agency's policy as explicitly as possible, including dates. If you have to wait six months or a year from the date the dossier was submitted, does that trigger the refund clause? You don't have to be Perry Mason, just be aware that the ability to walk away with your money and your dossier becomes increasingly important the longer you have to wait and the longer you are not getting straight answers from your agency.

The underlying thrust in an international adoption is that *you* are ultimately responsible for the adoption, even if your control is limited. You have to understand that principle or allow yourself to be surprised. The BCIS is not responsible, the State Department is not responsible, your state children's department is not responsible, and your agency is not responsible. Just to make that last point even clearer, agencies have been including exculpatory clauses in their contracts and even gag clauses. These exculpatory clauses have been litigated with results in favor of the agency. See <u>Ferenc v. World Child, Inc</u>. 977 F. Supp. 56 (D.D.C.1997); <u>Sherman v. Adoption Center of Washington, Inc.</u> 741 A. 2d 1035 (D.C. 1999) and <u>Regensburger v. China Adoption Consultants, Ltd</u>., 138 F.3d 1201 (7th Cir. 1998). A more recent case is discussed at *http://adoption.about.com/library/weekly/uc031102a.htm.* Contrast these cases with <u>Commonwealth v. Stephen R. Walker</u>, 653 N.E. 2d 1104 (Mass. 1995) and you have to ask whether parents who adopt internationally are being treated differently than domestic adoptions.

Some agencies include gag clauses in their contracts. They want to deny you the right to post questions (and criticisms) on the Internet. One choice is to agree and then simply post anonymously on the listservs or email privately to other listserv members. It is difficult to respect these sorts of adhesion clauses or the agencies that have them. Another choice is simply to ask for changes in the contract before you sign it. Again, the refund and return of the dossier is the place where most changes are requested.

The Internet and lists like the APC allow adopters to compare experiences, warn others of rough spots in the road, and become more prepared parents. Lists like the APC provide a prospective from parents going through the exact same thing as you. Confidentiality agreements allow bad agencies to hide poor performance and unethical acts, and they also hurt good agencies that use them by not allowing clients to publicize their good performance.

Some agencies impose religious, age, marriage, and other restrictions beyond the Chinese requirements. Others do not. Some insist that you use their affiliated and expensive home study or travel agency and do not allow you to shop around.

Some of these questions may not matter to you. You must decide which questions are important *to you.*

You can also review a non-profit agency's balance sheets (including assets, revenues, and operating expenses) at *http://www.guidestar.org.* You can call the International Concerns for Children office at (303) 494-8333. Ask them for whatever information they might have on the agency. Call the Department of

State at (202) 647-4000 and talk with the "desk officer" for the country you wish to adopt from. What do they know about the agency or facilitator you are working with or wish to work with? Call the Office of Children's Issues at the Department of State at (202) 647-2688. What do they know about the agency? Call the Consular Officer at the U.S. Embassy in the country in which you are interested. What do they know about the organization?

Things that some agencies do that are positive is telling clients beforehand what kind of post-placement support services they offer, telling clients that the agency will call them when they are settled in, and for the client to definitely call if they have any post-adoption questions. Good agencies send information on re-adoption, applying for citizenship, and requirements for post-placement reports.

A few agencies are very large and many are very small. A smaller agency will return your calls quickly, while a larger agency may be too busy. For every argument in favor of one type of agency over another, there is a counter-argument.

The cost of adopting from China varies with each agency. Most families complete their adoptions with total costs in the $12,000-$18,000 range. When asking an agency about costs, it is important to get a specific breakdown of expected fees. Some agencies may include travel in their estimates, but others will not. Some agencies handle a lot of the dossier paperwork, and others leave it to you. (If you are halfway organized and do the paperwork shuffle at work, then collecting the dossier stuff is not that difficult.)

If you know someone who has a lot of frequent flyer miles, ask if they will donate them for your trip. Ask agencies if they will allow you to travel separate from the group so you can make your own travel arrangements. Some agencies won't allow this, some require it. If you have enough frequent flyer miles, you will save a lot even if you have to leave a day or two earlier and return later than your travel group.

Travel costs make up a large part of the cost of adopting from China. Ask agencies specific questions about travel costs, who makes the arrangements, and if they have a tour package. Consider finding an agency that books a total package including in-country travel, food, lodging, translators, guides, and baggage transfers. This is an area that many agencies are vague about, and costs can be higher than you expect. Many people don't investigate travel costs prior to choosing an agency, and you don't have a lot of choice after you have the referral and are ready to go. Ask the hard questions. Ask references if travel costs were as predicted. The most expensive way to travel in China is to pay as you go and the least is with a package. As an example, the fee for the U.S. medical exam should be about $10, but some agencies add a surcharge for no particular reason.

Be sure to compare total costs, not just the agency fees. Make columns by agency to see what the fees include. With agencies that charge a flat placement fee you need to ask what the fee includes and where the funds actually go.

Some agencies will have you pay a $250 registration fee then afterwards tell you that you will receive no referrals unless you pay an additional $3,000. Make sure that before you pay an agency a single dime they fully disclose to you at what stage of the game you will receive referral information. You should not have to pay thousands of dollars up front. There are many agencies that only require an application fee before entering you into their program. Large fee payments should come at the time you accept a referral or just prior to traveling.

The fee paid to the agency does not cover your out-of-pocket expenses while in China. The better agencies will give you an estimated, but itemized, list of expenses.

Your agency may help you with some of the paperwork (although the authentication legwork is more often than not on you) and serves as a liaison with the CCAA. It retrieves the photographs from China and sends them to you. You are responsible for having a medical review of the picture and dealing with the BCIS.

One thing to remember when researching agencies is that not all fee quotes are alike. One agency's fee may be less than another, but it also may not include some services that another agency includes in its "higher" fee. Indeed, you can easily find yourself paying more "a la carte," than for a flat rate arrangement. Some parents have found setting up a spreadsheet helpful in order to make useful comparisons. The difficulty in writing about agencies is that there are some very good ones and some very bad ones and a lot in between.

My final advice is to know what risks you are willing to assume and which you are not. Do not be afraid to speak candidly with your agency. The better they know you, the better they can match your referral request.

Reference Families

When interviewing reference families for an adoption agency you should ask them some of the same questions asked of the agency. This way you can compare answers. Be sure to inquire as to the year they adopted, since significant procedural changes have occurred in China since 2001.

Some questions to ask are as follows:

1. Does the agency have good contacts in China? Find out everything you can about an agency's contacts in China. Was the process in China smooth and quick? Any hitches? Were they able to overcome any obstacles? Do they help you through the entire adoption process? What are the arrangements for housing and travel while you are in China?

2. How long did the agency give you to decide on a referral?

3. What is the health and developmental condition of the children placed (with the families you talk with)? Be specific as to which children's home, province, and age of child.

4. If a family was uncomfortable with a referral, was the agency cooperative in having the CCAA find another child within a reasonable amount of time, or did they try to pressure you?

5. Did the process work as the agency said it would?

6. Was the agency supportive and helpful during the process?

7. Were you informed, in advance, of all the costs involved in the adoption, including travel and incidentals?

8. What is the agency's policy about returning a portion of what you paid if the adoption doesn't work out? For example, if China closes or has a moratorium, or you withdraw because of a long wait, the agency encounters problems, etc.

9. Did the agency seem to be familiar to the children's home director and other officials? (If the agency has hosted the CCAA people or the director in the United States, then you can assume that they have a good working relationship.)

10. Was the agency organized? Returned phone calls timely? Supportive?

11. Did the family think the agency was more an advocate for the child rather than your family? A few agencies are such advocates for these children (whether for humanitarian or monetary reasons) that they forget that it is really your family's well being that comes first. This issue should be explored with the reference families.

12. Make sure you compare apples to apples. Do not compare the same agency's program in Korea with its program in China. So when you speak with families make sure you categorize the country program and the year of adoption.

13. If a reference family had a bad curve thrown at them in the foreign country, find out how the agency handled it. Some agencies will move heaven and earth for you and others will leave you high and dry.

14. Ask the families if you should talk to anyone else. You may find that a family that is not on anyone's list has some interesting information.

15. What services does the adoption agency offer after the adoption? A lot of agencies feel that once you return, you are on your own. While post-adoption services are not necessary for the majority of Chinese adoptions, if you run into an issue it would nice to know what help is available from your agency.

16. Ask about the waiting time. A family that has just recently adopted will give you more accurate information than an agency with its rosy view.

18. Ask about the age of the children referred by the CCAA.

19. Were the costs and timing in line with the agency's estimates?

20. Would they use the agency again?

Keep in mind that sometimes when you hear from a reference family that there was a problem with an adoption, it may not have been the fault of the adoption agency. Because of client confidentiality, agencies are limited in the information they can release that might either explain the situation or make it very clear that the accusation is unfounded. Nor can you always say that the fees are too high when there are many dedicated people working long hours trying to put you from Little Town, USA together with your Chinese or Korean child 10,000 miles away. They worry about the children (that is why they work at an agency) and the delays (over which they have no control) to which they can give you no rational reason. This is not a defense of all agencies; just a desire to see that the debate is kept fair.

CHAPTER VIII

Assessing Children's Information

Referrals

After choosing an agency and giving them your paperwork and a portion of their fee, you then wait for a referral of a child. Good agencies will refer you a child that is within the parameters you have set. They will also give you some time in which to decide and should not rush you. By the same token, this child is waiting for a "forever" family and a family is possibly waiting for this child, so time is of the essence.

The referral comes by way of a phone call from the agency saying that a photograph and medical summary of the child is on its way to you. They will describe the child over the phone. Sometimes an agency will send a referral to you that is outside your parameters. Give the agency the benefit of the doubt in this regard. Many times a child whose age or gender is different than what you initially requested will captivate you. If the referrals you see are far outside your parameters and you ask the agency to stop sending those kinds of referrals to you, then the agency should honor your request.

Families sometimes turn down referrals. It may be the child has issues that the family does not think it can handle successfully. These issues may be medical for which the family has no insurance coverage or simply the family is not in position to deal with certain issues. Your agency should not try to pressure you. It is your decision and your marriage and your family. Instead, the agency should try to obtain another referral. Quite often what is an overwhelming medical problem to one family is perfectly acceptable to another. Indeed, it is the unknown that causes the most fear.

There have also been cases where a couple arrives in China and is shown a child who has an obvious serious medical problem and the Chinese will then immediately offer a different child. This emotional situation is hard to imagine, yet it has happened.

You really need to look at your family and decide what you can handle. If you are a young couple with no children, then maybe adopting a child under three is best. If you are a couple with three teenagers (let's say 13, 15 and 17), then an older child could work for you. Families wanting an older child who already have a 10-month-old, 3-year-old and a five-year-old need to stop and think some more. Older children take a lot of work initially (new language to learn, educational delays, learning to live in a family, etc.). Dealing with all of this will take a lot of your time and energy away from your other children. You must choose the right child for your family and be realistic about what you want. Your first priority is your existing family and not an image of a child you saw on the Web late one night. There is no shame in admitting that you do not have the resources to deal with a particular issue or that you are not the right family for a specific child. Not every family is right for every child. If because of your personal schedule or personal health issues you will not be able to give the necessary attention to a certain special needs child, admit it without guilt and choose a child that will be a better fit.

Once you are reviewing a referral, you may want to contact those reference families who adopted in the province you are now considering. By checking with those who have adopted from that province, you can gain a precise knowledge of your agency's program in that area.

You may wonder if you have been given all the information that there is on your child. The Chinese, unlike the Koreans, do not feel any great need to develop information. They give you the bare minimum. The fact is, you will never know everything about your child's history. You just have to do as much research as you can, and then take that leap of faith. But it should be faith based on the knowledge that comes out of doing your homework first.

Information you would like to have with the referral is anything pertaining to maternal history, the child's birth history (prenatal care if any, birth weight, height, and head circumference, gestational age, Apgar scores), medical examinations, tests, and hospitalizations. Ongoing measurements over time are extremely helpful to assess growth. Current developmental milestones (vocalizing, sitting alone, eating semisolid food, strong eye contact) are also helpful. Sometimes statements are available from the caregivers about the child's personality, demeanor, and skills. It's very helpful if the orphanage doctors give an opinion about whether the child has any signs of fetal alcohol syndrome. Descriptions of the child's verbal abilities and determination of the child's ability to hear are also extremely valuable.

It is not unusual for parents to turn to their agency and ask, "What should we do?" Be careful if you do this. Look out for responses like, "That's just something they write to make the kid eligible for adoption; or, "We've had lots of kids adopted with that diagnosis. They're all fine;" or "He just needs good nourishment and love. You're just what he needs to thrive," and "Many other people have adopted children in worse shape and they've turned around with proper attention and care." Agencies have even said to parents who were struggling with the decision, "You should decide to adopt the child soon or risk losing him," and "If I were into gambling, he's a good one."

If you want to gamble, you'd go to Vegas. What you want is to make an informed decision knowing that adoption comes with risk. You want advice from professionals like the international adoption doctors and information from your preparation classes and materials. There is always the chance that what you receive from an agency is marketing, not reliable advice. On the other hand, by you asking them that question you have placed them in a difficult position. Do not use the agency as a substitute for your research and preparation. You have to put in the time. There are no short cuts. Remember that the credibility of any information is affected by the motivation of its source.

At some point you will have all the medical information and medical expert reviews you can obtain. There will come a time when you must decide whether to accept this child or not. You will still have doubts. You will not have answers to all of your questions. You will have plenty of facts about this child but not the answer to the ultimate question of "what should I do?" Yet, it is time to either take that "leap of faith" or decide against. Only you can make that decision. Just remember that when a child is born to you it comes with both good and bad. As a parent you just accept them and love them. Make the same conscious choice in your adoption and make the best of this wonderful gift of this child that you will care for and love.

Finally, fight against the natural desire of wanting "the perfect child" or the "Gerber baby." Parents sometimes forget that life doesn't give guarantees and the child whose referral they turned down because she was a little short or had an ear infection, might have become a loving child and a concert pianist in contrast to the "perfect" child they adopted that ran off with the rock band. Have realistic expectations. Raising children, whether adopted or biological, is not a fantasy experience. It's real and it's a lot of work.

Photograph

A photograph is important to a medical evaluation. A video would be better but, unlike other countries, neither China nor Korea provide a video. You should ask the agency for the approximate dates of the photographs. This is important in order to evaluate the child's development. If the child is an infant, you will want to see the child unclothed, but the Chinese and Koreans are not very helpful about providing this. It does allow you can see all the fingers, toes, hands, arms and legs.

Here are some questions to ask:

1. How does the child respond to people in the room?

2. Does the child move and bend her arms and legs in a normal fashion? Normal movement can indicate that cerebral palsy is not a concern. Is muscle mass and fat on the arms and legs approximately equal and symmetrical indicating the baby is equally coordinated and developed on both sides? Also, when the baby moves is there any expression of discomfort?

3. Do her eyes follow the camera or some other toy? This indicates responsiveness and is a slight indication of the condition of her eyes. Does she track sound in the room?

4. Does she roll over, sit up, play with toys and move them from hand to hand? These are milestones to look for. Does she show emotions? Even crying is a good sign.

These are questions the IA doctors would like answered. The problem with China and Korea is that they are not very forthcoming with answers. This is one disadvantage of these programs. Of course, an advantage with the Korean program is that you receive a lot of additional medical information and with the Chinese is that the children are infants and can overcome most developmental delays.

Medical Review

What drives the desire for better medical records and knowledge about children's health is the fact that international adoption works best when prospective adoptive parents know as clearly as possible what sorts of challenges a specific child may bring to the family. Some parents believe they can care for a child with many medical challenges. Other parents, including some who already have children with special needs in their families, believe they can only cope with an additional child if the child has minimal or no health problems. Good preparation before making the decision to adopt internationally includes understanding and accepting that no child, whether born in a family, adopted domestically, or adopted internationally, comes with any "guarantees" or "warranties." Just look around your neighborhood. All children have challenges and gifts that cannot be anticipated.

Listed below are some of the medical specialists available to provide pre-adoption and post-adoption assessments to adoptive parents and children. This is by no means an exhaustive list. The procedure is that you mail a copy of the video (if you have one) or photographs and the medical report to the physician, and after she reviews the material, you speak with the doctor by phone. The doctor will likely call you within a few days of receiving the material, probably in the evening or at night. You should have a list of questions prepared ahead of time so the maximum amount of information is exchanged. You may wish to ask the doctor if you can record the conversation in case a spouse is unavailable or you want to keep better record of what was said. These doctors all have jobs and families, and receive many requests a week, so take that into account if you pressure them to expedite a review. Most of these doctors are adoptive parents themselves, which is how they got into the field.

Generally if you request the review of pre-adoptive medicals, you should include a donation. From $100 to $350 is customary, but always inquire as to the suggested donation amount. The information you receive is far more valuable.

Jerri Ann Jenista, M.D.
551 Second Street
Ann Arbor, Michigan 48103
Phone: (734) 668-0419
Fax: (734) 668-9492

Web site: *http://www.comeunity.com/adoption/health/jenista.html*. This web site has a lot of good information about the medical health of the children from China. Most is positive. She was the editor of *Adoption Medical News* and has a long history in the international adoption medical field.

International Adoption Clinic
University of Minnesota
Dana Johnson, M.D.
420 Delaware Street SE
Minneapolis, Minnesota 55455
Phone: (612)-626-2928; Fax (612) 624-8176
Donation: $150

Dr. Johnson is one of the founders of the international adoption medical field and runs a very well known clinic. His web site is at *http://www.peds.umn.edu iac/default.html*.

Andrew Adesman, M.D.
Schneider Children's Hospital
Division of Developmental and Behavioral Pediatrics
269-01 76th Ave.
New Hyde Park, N.Y. 11040
Phone: 718-470-4000 Fax: 718-343-3578

Dr. Adesman takes a direct approach and concentrates solely on the child he is reviewing. He is a night owl and likes to schedule phone conferences late at night (after 11p.m.). This can be helpful for people who have a lot of other commitments during the day or who do not live on the East Coast. He is very thorough and nice. Like a lot of these doctors, he really cares about you and the children.

Julia Bledsoe, M.D.
Pediatric Care Center
University of Washington, Roosevelt Site
4245 Roosevelt Way N.E.
Seattle, WA 98105
Phone: 206-598-3000, 3006 Fax: 206-598-3040

If you have a child who you think might have the signs of FAS, Dr. Bledsoe has a real expertise in that area and you may want to consult her for an opinion. She is head of Adoption Medicine at University of Washington and charges $350 for a video and medical review.

International Adoption Clinic
The Floating Hospital for Children at New England Medical Center
Laurie Miller, M.D.
750 Washington Street Box 286
Boston, Massachusetts 02111
Phone: 617-636-8121 or 617-636-7285; Fax: 617-636-8388
This clinic is associated with Tufts University Medical School

She charges $100 for a video and medical review. She has a great manner. Some call her the Marcus Welby of adoption medicine. Her web site is *http://www.nemc.org/adoption/*

Dr. Aronson
151 East 62nd Street Suite 1A
New York, New York 10021
orphandoctor@aol.com
Phone: 212-207-6666
Fax: 212-207-6665

Dr. Aronson charges $350 to review a video and medical information. Her web site is at *http://www.orphandoctor.com/*.

The Rainbow Center for International Child Health
Adoption Health Service
11100 Euclid Avenue, Mail Stop 6038
Cleveland, OH 44106-6038
Contact: Adele, Center Coordinator
Phone: 216-844-3224

Rainbow Center's web site is *http://www.uhrainbow.com/International_Health /page14.html*.

Rainbow's approach is to spend time determining what you know about the process and then to conduct an educational session. It is child specific, but it also encompasses more. Many families like Rainbow's approach. The review costs about $265.

Ira Chasnoff, M.D.
Chicago, Illinois
Tel: 312-362-1940

Dr. Chasnoff has an $8 developmental booklet he sells called "Across the Seas." You can buy it at *http://www.childstudy.org/crtstore.cgi/bkt-002.html.* "Across the Seas" is a booklet checklist designed to be completed in country and then used to consult with Dr Chasnoff or any IA specialist. The guidebook provides a structured assessment parents can perform while at the orphanage with the child. This assessment helps parents appraise the child's growth, development and attachment status.

Texas Children's Hospital International Adoption
Heidi Schwarzwald, M.D.is the Director
6621 Fannin St.
Houston, Texas
832-824-1038
Toll free: 866-824-5437
Fax: 832-825-1281
Email: *internationaladoptions@texaschildrenshospital.org*
Website:*http://www.txchildrens.org/CntExe/IntAdopt/IntlAdoption.pdf.*
This Texas IA program charges $250 to review a video.

A list of clinics and hospitals in China where traveling parents might find medical services including doctors or staff who speak English can be found at *http://catalog.com/fwcfc/ChinaMedDirectory.*

In general, the older the child, the easier it is for an expert to identify potential problems. Also, doctors are going to err on the side of caution since they are not able to examine the child or run any tests so expect cautious optimism at best. I would also talk to other parents who have adopted children of the same age as the referral and also from the same province or children's home. Do not discount other parents' experiences.

Finally, there are lots of things you and the doctors cannot see such as learning disabilities, developmental delays, speech delays, sensory integration issues, and so on. I remember a doctor who said that premature children from an institution would always have to pay some price. By that she meant that in school the child will likely be delayed in an area, you just do not know which one. Look around your neighborhood though, there are plenty of children who are physically healthy and are wonderful kids but who have one or more of the above issues. Many of the conditions are ones you cannot see for years.

When you begin this adoption journey you have to ask yourself, "Am I prepared to deal with the unknown?" This is a question that most biological parents do not have the chance to ponder; it is just thrust upon them. Just because a child has rickets, or a cleft palate, or some other "identifiable" physical ailment doesn't mean that this child will be more of a health risk than that supposedly perfectly healthy child who comes home and has attachment issues.

Finally, there is a limit to the information that any doctor can give you, based upon a child's health records and a few pictures. You can only be prepared up to a certain point. You can guide your agency about what you think you are capable of handling, study all the medical information, read all the books, but in the end you must accept that there are no guarantees in life or in international adoption. Sometimes you just have to follow your intuition and your heart. A doctor's opinion is good thing to have, but the final decision is yours.

Children's Medical Questions

At the beginning of the adoption process local authorities in China complete a medical report for each child, whose information is then forwarded to the CCAA. The medical report contains limited, very basic information concerning the general health status of the child at the time of examination. This information is months out of date by the time a family receives a referral and much more so by the time a family arrives in China. Families often feel that the medical information is insufficient to provide complete confidence about the health of the child. Adoptive parents may have had only a single photograph and no more than a one-page summary of medical information. The normal leap of faith that exists with any adoption is more like a long jump. Yet, because most of the children are infants, the negative impacts of institutional care and malnutrition have not yet had their severe cumulative effect.

Here are some of the questions that you might ask, if you are able. Just realize that, unlike Korea, the Chinese adoption process does not engage in a broad flow of information and you will likely obtain few answers.

1. Current information: current head circumference, height, weight; developmental milestones appropriate for the child's age, rolling over, sitting, crawling (what can the child do). You really want to get a range of measurements over time in order to gauge the velocity of growth. Don't accept just one set of measurements taken at just one point in time.

2. Emotional development of the child (attachment evidence).

3. History of illnesses, fevers, hospitalization, surgery, etc., and outcomes.

4. What do you know about her birth parents? Their medical history and medical history of siblings? Any history of alcohol use by the birth mother?

5. What was the prenatal history? (Less relevant for older children.)

6. Why was the child put in the orphanage?

7. Does the child have a favorite caretaker?

8. Does the child have any special friends?

9. What are the child's likes and dislikes?

10. What seems to comfort the child?

11. What kinds of foods will he eat?

12. What is the routine at the orphanage?

13. What is the child's ethnic background?

14. Does the child smile or laugh?

15. What should I know in caring for this child?

16. How is she doing healthwise?

17. What do they know about the birth mother? Age? Number of pregnancies? Physical description? What do they know about the birth father?

18. What are the lab results for HIV, HEP, and syphilis?

19. How does the doctor think she compares to other babies her age at the orphanage?

20. Child's Apgar scores and at what minute intervals?

21. What inoculations has the child had?

22. How many children are in the home and in his sleep area? How many caregivers does he have?

23. What toys does she play with?

24. Does she use a spoon or bottle?

25. Does she use both hands?

26. Does she pass a toy from hand to hand?

27. Will he be able to go to a normal school?

28. What is her age of development?

29. Results of any eye examination and hearing exam.

30. Result of any ultrasound of the brain.

31. What antibiotics has she been given? (Certain ones given to preemies may cause deafness.)

32. What future assistance might this child need based on the doctor's experience, i.e. physical therapy, speech, or developmental help?

33. Does the child have floppy muscles or stiffened limbs?

34. Has the child had any convulsions? If there is a notation in the medical record of the child being given barbiturates, you will want to know what these were for and if they were related to a seizure condition.

35. Is there anything else the doctor would like to add about the baby or give advice about? How does this child compare with other children the doctor has seen?

You may wish to review the *normal* developmental milestone timeline of a child in order to gauge how delayed your child may be. One set of guidelines can be found at *http://www.health.state.ny.us/nysdoh/eip/earlydif.htm*. Another good site is at *www.kidsgrowth.com*. This site goes beyond just plotting on charts. It gives information on daily, weekly, monthly, and yearly growth. The *What to Expect* books are good as well. Just remember, these children are delayed by a month for every 3 months in the children's home, so you must consider that in your analysis of what is normal for these children. Of course, foster care kids will have better milestone results.

Generally a 6-month-old infant *not in a children's home* should be able to:
Follow moving objects with his eyes
Turn toward the source of normal sound
Reach for objects and pick them up
Switch toys from one hand to the other
Play with her toes
Help holding the bottle
Babble
A 12-month-old should:
Sit without support
Pull to a standing position
Crawl
Drink from a cup
Play peek-a-boo
Wave bye-bye
Put objects in a container
Stack two blocks
Know five words
An 18-month-old should:
Like to pull, push, and dump things
Follow simple directions
Pull off shoes, socks, and mittens
Like to look at pictures
Feed himself
Make crayon marks on paper
Walk without help
A 2-year-old should:
Use 2- to 3-word sentences
Say names of toys
Recognize familiar pictures
Feed herself with a spoon
Identify hair, eyes, ears, and nose by pointing
Build a tower of 4 blocks
A 3-year-old should:
Walk up steps alternating feet
Put on shoes
Open a door
Turn one page at a time
Repeat common rhymes
Use 3- to 5-word sentences
Name at least one color correctly

Older Children

Adopting older children is a great experience. Older children bring their culture, their language, and their history with them. They are interesting and fun right from the start. Their medical reports are probably more accurate than an infant's, simply because most symptoms will already have appeared and be present. The psychological issues are a little more risky. With an infant, the risk is reversed. Like everything else, you need to do your research and talk to parents who have adopted older children. If you are older, it may be that parenting an older child is better. You don't have to go through the whole diaper and baby experience, but can jump right in with children who will interact with you. You also don't have to wait 18 years until they go off the college to reclaim your life!

Some keys to assessing older children is to find out how long they have been in the children's home, if they ever lived with a family, and if they are attached to a particular caretaker now. These questions relate to attachment. You need to find out about siblings and where they are located. Siblings who are attached to each other are more likely to be able to attach to their new family. A good predictor of being able to attach to someone new is being attached to someone already. (This is why foster care helps with attachment in infants.) In addition, siblings give each other a lot of comfort and support. These are just a couple of the good reasons to consider adopting siblings if you want more than one child. Find out as much as you can about their life before she was placed in the children's home. The most important factor in assessing attachment isn't how long a child was in an institution, but the care received before and after entering. A child who was in an institution for a long period of time but was cared for and loved, and had stability will be better prepared than a child who was in for a much shorter time but who was abused, neglected, unloved, and moved from place to place (like in the U.S. foster care system). Also, talk to other parents who have adopted older children or from foster parents. You will learn more from them than from any book.

If you discover that parental rights were terminated, push to discover the real reasons. You may not be able to do this until you are in-country and even so they may not open the records to you, but finding out the reasons for the termination of rights can greatly help in any post-adoptive therapy that the child may undergo. Push to get the child's medical records translated and sent to you ahead of time, including a translated parental termination of rights document.

Some older children may have sensory integration issues such as Central Auditory Processing Disorder (CAPD). CAPD is sort of like dyslexia, but it's about what you hear getting mixed up rather than what you see. Many times what happens is that in a classroom, for example, there are so many auditory stimuli that the child cannot focus on the teacher's words and therefore misses the lessons and the homework. This condition may arise if the child spent several years in the institution. This can take a toll, as they may be deprived of the stimulation that comes from normal nurturing and loving. You may have to help him reclaim his right to parental love. There are professional language programs such as Fast Forward or Earobics that are available. Then there are those older children who will suffer no ill effects from institutionalization. It may be that they were in a family for a while and had normal attachment experiences. They may not have been in the institution for very long or were a favorite of a caretaker. If you do accept a referral of an older child, send him a photo album of his forever family, future friends, and pets. This will allow him to become accustomed to his new life while you all wait for a court date, and will give him a reason to believe that a new and happier life is just around the corner.

There are many questions that surround adopting older children. Indeed, by the time you wade through all of the medical and family advice you are guaranteed to be thoroughly confused. Just remember that there are plenty of stories of very happy older child adoptions. Good stories are just not news. Still, being prepared through education is the best medicine, even if it's painful. Gain the knowledge, file it away, and hope you never have to use it.

One of the risks adoptive parents take when adopting a child who comes from a background of abuse is that the child will perpetuate the abuse. Thus, younger siblings may be at risk. This is one reason that when an older child is placed, it may be better for her to become the youngest in an established family or be an only child. The other reason is that an oldest child has a firm sense of identity, based on birth order, and it is often traumatic to him to be displaced. Sometimes families with several children adopt a child who becomes the third or successive number because the youngest children aren't affected as much by having one more older sibling. It is the first 2 children in the family who have the strongest sense of their position.

Some believe this birth order issue is an artificial one created by academics just looking for a problem where none exists. In many families, adopting out of birth order is not a problem at all, although your U.S. social worker will be against it. Definitely do some research before deciding if this is right for your family.

If adopting an older child 3 or older, you should ask additional questions, particularly if the child will be older than existing children in your house:

1. How does she treat the other children in the orphanage in her age group?
2. How easily is she disciplined?
3. What is her temperament like?
4. Does she show aggression?
5. What is her personality like?
6. Has she bonded with a caretaker in the home?
7. What do they know of her background?
8. Why is the child in the home?
9. Height and weight. If the child is in the 5th percentile that means that of all American children who have been charted for height and weight at that particular age over a certain period of time, your child fell in the 5th percent, meaning that your child is on the low side. If he is at 50% (percentile), he is at the bell curve where most American children of that age fall. If he were in the 95%, then he would be much large than most children that age.

When you are at the children's home, watch her around the other children in her group and how she plays with them and how she treats them. If she is very loving and helpful while playing with them then she is likely to be loving and helpful to her new siblings. You do have to ask a lot of questions about their mental state and what you can get about their past and do your homework. Compare what your agency and the children's home have told you with what you actually observe.

Don't misunderstand. Not all older children were abused, and there are many, many happy "forever" families with adoptive older children, but you do have to be careful and get as much information as you can about the child's past and mental state. Before you travel you should look inside yourself and be prepared to have the courage to walk away. Do not overestimate your parenting skills. Love and good food are not cures for everything.

Infants and Wobblers

The general rule is that children are delayed a month of development for every 3 months in the children's home. Physically, the children tend to run on the small side as well. The reason for this is that in addition to factors such as prematurity, undernourishment, and sickness, a child's development, both physical and mental, depends in large part on how much affection they receive. It is a common story that when children are brought into a loving home with lots of cuddling they suddenly grow like weeds. So it is important not to overemphasize the weight or size of a child, as the child could very well be perfectly healthy, just small. This is not to say that when the higher cognitive abilities like abstract thinking are required in the third or fourth grade the child might not need some extra help, but that is true with any child.

A small head circumference that is not proportional to the body may be a red flag, as it could indicate that the brain is not growing. On the other hand, a small head circumference that is proportional may not be cause for alarm. If the child is born with a head circumference below the charts, then you begin to look for problems in utero that caused growth retardation and those can often be more serious (birthmother's drinking, drugs, poor pre-natal care). Of course you can also just have a baby who is tiny because of genetics or because she was premature. After looking at the birth statistics you will want to see a 'curve' on the chart with growth in head circumference, height, and weight. You may be less concerned with a small head circumference if the rest of the child is small also. If you see height and weight gains, but no head growth, then that is a problem. The head only grows if the brain is growing. Remember that microcephaly (which has many negative associations) is a small head size compared to the rest of the body and is different than simply being low on the charts. Not all doctors make that distinction, so if they use the word make sure you are all discussing the same condition.

One mitigating factor is if the child comes from a poor region where a lack of food is a real possibility. This can cause small growth all the way around. Also, if the child has a cleft palate it is possible she is having difficulty getting enough food. If malnutrition is a factor you should see weight and height gains fall off first, but head circumference continue to increase. This means that the body is sending what nutrients it has to the brain for growth. Do not base a whole referral on head circumference alone, but look at the whole picture and see if the rest of the child is small, talk with others who have adopted from this orphanage/province, check where the child is developmentally, and see if there are other contributing factors to the small head circumference like small birth parents, lack of food at the orphanage, etc.

Most international specialists focus on the head circumference measurement, as that can be indicative of mental development. The average head circumference for a full term infant is 35cm. Doctors worry about full term children born whose head circumference is less than 31cm. The general theory is that big heads equal big brains. The larger the head the greater the number of neurons and the more neurons you have the larger the bandwidth. Heads grow because the brain grows, and this mostly occurs in the first few years of life. Be aware that some of the experts are now saying that many children are demolishing the medical community expectations and heads are growing when adopted after the age of 3 years. While head size may be an objective medical evaluative tool, it should not be the only factor to take into consideration when assessing a child's cognitive potential. Indeed, Dr. Keenan of Harvard Medical School has questioned the connection between overall birth size and higher cognitive ability. He believes a family's expectations about a child's intelligence and ability have more of an impact than birth weight.

Usually the head circumference is plotted on an old 1979 American growth chart developed by the National Center for Health Statistics. The CDC has recently published an updated one that is available on their web site at *CDC.gov* under National Center for Health Statistics. For older children, the Nelhouse curves are commonly used. These were published in 1968 and were based on a compilation of 14 studies of head growth published in the 1940s, 1950s and early 1960s. This is widely accepted by pediatricians. In his original paper,Nelhouse said that these curves should be applicable to all children regardless of ethnicity and geographic location. However, in looking into the basis for the curves it was found that they rely primarily on studies of American Caucasian children so there is a question about whether the curves are really applicable for children from other countries. Measurements of native Chinese children are available at *http://catalog.com/fwcfc/growthchart.html.*

There have been many studies of head circumference in children and what it means. None have specifically targeted adoptive children. Head circumference studies of large groups of children were published in the 1960s and 1970s using already at-risk populations of children. Using children who have other issues puts a question mark on the credibility of the findings. The findings from these studies were that children with a head circumference 2 standard deviations and greater below the mean are of lower intelligence. You might call this the generic finding. In 1977, 1,000 children in the Seattle school system were studied. No difference in IQ between small heads and big heads was found, but there was a difference in truly microcephalic kids.

Two standard deviations below the mean is the 3rd percentile. The mean is the 50th percentile. Think of the mean, or the 50th percentile, as the top of a bell curve where half the people fall on one side and half on the other. Standard deviation (SD) is how far one travels along the bell curve away from the top peak, or how far away one deviates from the 50th percentile. One SD from the 50% is the 16th percentile on one side and the 84th percentile on the other side. Two SD from the 50% is the 3rd percentile and the 97th percentile. For whatever reason, many growth charts show a "normal" range as from the 5th percentile to the 95th percentile. Most experts prefer a "normal" range of from the 3rd percentile to the 97th percentile, or 2 standard deviations. The experts see the risk going up below the 3rd percentile. There is a further differentiation between those children that are within the normal range at birth (3rd percentile to 97th percentile) and fall below this over time versus those that are consistently below the 3rd percentile (the latter group carrying a higher risk of long term neurological problems).

The conclusions about head circumference are truly mixed, as there are no definitive studies concerning adoptive children. There are some general findings that head circumference tends to drift down the longer a child is in the children's home, even where head circumference was normal at birth. This is not at all unexpected, due to factors such as malnutrition and lack of love and stimulation. Children in general (not just adoptees) who have suffered an early brain insult because of these factors tend to show residual effects even where the insult is resolved such as where nutrition is improved (the Barbados Study). The residual effects that appear later at school age may be language delay, impaired sensory inputs, and higher incidence of ADD. Nonetheless, a supportive new environment greatly improves the outcome for an adoptive child underlying the importance of early intervention, whether it is speech therapy or occupational therapy, or simply love, good nutrition, and lots of parent-child interaction. A clear finding by the adoption medical community is that there can be a remarkable recovery in head growth in adoptive children. What they are reluctant to conclude without a proper study, however, is that some sort of residual effect will not appear in a child later during the school years.

In summary, cognitive abilities are mainly determined by genetic factors, therefore the effect of a low head circumference in adoptive children cannot be interpreted in isolation. The IA doctors will want to know the gestational age of the child and other risk factors. The longer the insult to the brain the more profound the deficit. A healthy post-adoption environment has a profound positive influence on outcome, yet a residual effect cannot be ruled out. Keep in mind that head circumference is but one data point to consider, albeit an important one. There are many other factors to consider that might either minimize or increase the risk profile of a child.

Here are some issues to investigate in regard to infants:

1) If the head circumference is proportional to her body, the growth rate may be proportional as well. In other words, if the body were growing slowly then it would not be surprising to find that the head was likewise. If the body and head do not match, that may be a concern.

2) How is the child developmentally? Is she close to her milestones after deducting for the usual institution-caused delays? Does she crawl, walk, babble, and have good social interactions? Is there evidence of early-handedness? Infants usually do not choose which will be the dominant hand until they enter toddler stage and begin to use tools such as spoons or crayons. Early handedness may be an indication that one side of his body isn't functioning properly.

   Dr. Aronson has developmental checklists on her site at *www.orphandoctor. com* that you can print out. Another developmental list is at the site *www.kidsgrowth.com*. Some parents also like the lists in the *What to Expect* books. Just remember that generally these children lose one month for every three months in an orphanage.

3) Was her mother young and was it a first pregnancy? There seems to be a correlation between alcoholism and a mother who is older and has had numerous pregnancies.

Small head circumference means that you need to look at the total picture in order to assess the risk.

The World Health Organization defines low birth weight as less than 2,500 grams or 5 pounds, 8 ounces. 10% of infants born in the United States are low birth weight. Infants have low birth weight if they are born premature before 37 weeks, or because they failed to grow inside the uterus.

There are two types of intrauterine growth retardation (IUGR): one is asymmetric and the other symmetric. Asymmetric, as its name suggests, is where the effect on the three measurements (height, weight, head) is not the same. The weight is affected the most, followed by the height some and the head little. This occurs in a situation where the fetus must make a choice and starves the rest of the body, saving the most important parts—the brain and heart. It is typically seen in mild malnutrition situations. In symmetric cases the insult is even across all three factors. The head is not spared. It is thought it comes from an early insult as from an infection in the first trimester or severe malnutrition. Where the head circumference is the most affected of the three factors, then serious pre-natal alcohol abuse or early infection is generally the cause. Other toxins like lead and mercury can also affect fetal growth. Maternal smoking does affect weight, although not brain development. In the United States IUGR is closely associated with maternal hypertension. A problem with assigning an adoptive child to one of these categories is that the birth weight may not be accurate, the gestational age may not be accurate, and pre-natal history of the presence or absence of alcohol may not be available.

A smaller than normal infant is always a concern, but there are studies supporting catch-up growth. There was a study published in the *Journal of Pediatrics* in June 1998. It described adolescent growth of 32 extremely premature children from birth through 12-18 years of age. All weighed less than 1,000 grams at birth (<2.2lbs) The study found that by 12-18 years of age, only 6% of the children were below the normal range for height, and these children had mothers who were short themselves. This study did not discuss the ages at which small children landed on the growth chart, but did state that 45% of all children grew faster than normal between 8 years and 12-18 years. The conclusion was that catch-up growth continues well into adolescence. Here is a web site that discusses growth and the premature infant in more detail: *http://www.comeunity.com/premature/child/growth/catchup.html*.

You may also notice that some infants have their hands clenched. While this can be a sign of cerebral palsy, most times it is not. They clench their hands because it provides stimulation and touch. If they had had a lot of toys to play with, they probably wouldn't do this. It goes away after a month or so. Just give them toys to hold and massage the fingers.

You might also see some rocking back and forth by an infant or toddler who comes out of an institutional setting. This can be mild or severe. Rocking is a pretty typical comfort behavior. They rock for comfort or when they are upset or under stress. It is probably better to just let it be. In most children it will eventually diminish after a few months and then stop.

Medical Measurements

Most of the world uses the metric system, which means that all road signs are in kilometers and speed limits in kilometers per hour. Drinks come by the liter (mostly 0.5 or 0.3) or in hundreds of milliliters (usually 330 ml for a can of soda). The exception is shots of vodka (and other liquors), which are generally served in 50- or 100-gram measures. Food is weighed in grams or kilograms. There are 10 millimeters in a centimeter, 100 centimeters in a meter, and 1,000 meters in a kilometer.

In order to read the medical summary you will need to have a metric conversion table handy. To convert kilograms to pounds, multiply by 2.2:
2.8 kg x 2.2 lb/=6.16 lb

If the weight is in grams, convert it first to kg by moving the decimal point: 2800 gm=2.8 kg.
Length will be given in centimeters. Some conversions are as follows:
30 cm=11.81 inches
35 cm=13.7 inches
40 cm=15.7 inches
50 cm=19.7 inches
70 cm=27.5 inches

The actual formula is to multiply the cm figure by 0.3937. Therefore, 45 cm would be equal to: 45 x 0.3937=17.7 inches.

And you thought you were through with 7th grade math!

CHAPTER IX

Medical Conditions

Medical Information

Families should not presume that adopting a child from China or Korea is a guarantee of a "better baby." Yet you will hear this from both prospective adoptive families and Chinese and Korean government officials. There are no guarantees in life or adoption.

Medical information from China on the children is minimal and often outdated or inaccurate. Typically, a medical report consists of a physical examination form in which every space is filled out, "Normal." Usually, a single set of growth measurements is given, often many months or even a year old. Children are usually wearing many layers of clothing when weighed. Currently, medical reports also include results of hepatitis B surface antigen testing and liver function tests. Generally, the information given parents is simply not very complete. Chinese designations of "Normal" or "Special needs" have little meaning, unless the disability has a physical manifestation. Dr. Laurie Miller's survey results give a good picture of what you can expect. You can find her report at *http://www.pediatrics.org/cgi/content/full/105/6/e76.*

Because the Chinese use leaded gasoline and their cities have high pollution indexes, it is not uncommon to find elevated lead levels in these children. They should be tested and treated as soon as they get home.

The saving grace is that the children are young and many have had foster care, so there is less of a chance for emotional problems such as attachment disorder or Sensory Integration Disorder. Indeed, most Chinese adoptees turn out fine as illustrated by this small survey report at *http://catalog.com/ fwcfc/medicalcondition.html.*

Fetal Alcohol Syndrome or drug exposure do not appear to be factors with these children. Further, any parasites, lead problems, or rickets are easily treatable and disappear. The greatest health effect is in developmental delays, both in motor skills and cognitive/language. Yet, even in this area the children catch up quickly, typically within six months. However, let me quote from Dr. Jenista, "…apparent good condition is *never* a reason to skip any or part of the standard evaluation recommended for all international adoptees. This protocol was developed by the American Academy of Pediatrics based on decades of research and experience."

Apgar Score

An Apgar score is an index used to evaluate the condition of a newborn infant based on a rating of 0, 1, or 2 for each of the five characteristics of color, heart rate, response to stimulation of the sole of the foot, muscle tone, and respiration with 10 being a perfect score. This score enables medical personnel to identify babies that need routine care and babies who may need further assistance. The baby is evaluated and scored at 1 minute after birth and then again in 5 minutes. The second score is more important than the first one, as many infants may have a brief period of being "stunned" and need help initially adjusting to life. The Apgar score is important to identify babies *at the time of birth* who need help and to observe whether the help that has been given has had the desired effect.

The scoring is as follows:
HEART RATE/PULSE: 0 points for absent heart rate, 1 point for heart rate below 100, 2 points for heart rate over 100.

RESPIRATORY EFFORT: 0 points for absent, 1 point for weak cry and hypoventilation, 2 points for good crying.
MUSCLE TONE/ACTIVITY: 0 points for limp, 1 point for some flexion of extremities, 2 points for well flexed.
REFLEX/RESPONSE TO STIMULATION/GRIMACE: 0 points for no response, 1 point for grimace, 2 points for coughs, sneezes or cries.
COLOR/APPEARANCE: 0 points for blue or pale, 1 point for body pink, extremities blue, 2 points for completely pink.

An Apgar score will typically be stated in the form of two numbers with a slash between. The first is the one minute score; the second is the 5 minute score. The scoring ranges for the Apgar score are:

1. 7-10: Active, vigorous infant; routine care
2. 4-6: Moderately depressed infant; requires stimulation to breathe and oxygen
3. 0-3: Severely depressed infant; immediate ventilatory assistance required

Because the Apgar score is subjective and only taken at birth, its importance after birth should not be overemphasized. It will primarily tell you that your child had a stressful birth or a non-stressful one. It is just a snapshot of how the baby was one minute and five minutes after birth. Don't accept or reject a referral on that alone. Indeed, most children with developmental disabilities have excellent Apgar scores when born and most children with poor Apgar scores do well. How the child is today and what your medical reviewer says regarding the medical information and any conversation you have with the orphanage is far more important in evaluating your child.

Fetal Alcohol Syndrome

One of the issues usually discussed in relation to intercountry adoptions is the risk of your child having Fetal Alcohol Syndrome (FAS) and Fetal Alcohol Effect (FAE). Unlike Eastern Europe, n Chinese and Korean adoptions this is not much of an issue.

Fetal Alcohol Syndrome (FAS) is always a risk in any child where the birth mother drank alcohol during pregnancy. Its effects vary widely. Some birth mothers can drink heavily and there may be no effect. In others, just a few glasses can cause damage. FAS occurs in every country including the United States. It is almost impossible to detect with certainty before the age of 2. If you believe your referral might be affected, have one of the adoption medical specialists give you an opinion. Of course, remember that a brief video and a few still shots make any precise diagnosis of any medical condition difficult at best.

An FAS diagnosis usually is made based on impairment of growth and development plus a characteristic pattern of facial features including short eye openings (palpebral fissures-small width of the eye), short, upturned nose, low nasal bridge (sometimes noticed as a broad nasal bridge), flat vertical groove (almost absent) between upper lip and nose (philtrum), and thin upper lip and simply formed external ears. Another minor facial anomaly is epicanthal folds (which can be either unilateral or bilateral) and which are also representative of certain ethnic groups, just to make things harder. Other anomalies are ptsosis-muscle drooping of the eyes; clown eyebrows—eyebrows that are laterally arched; hyperterlorism; and flat mid-face. Since an infant may have some of these characteristics by just being a baby, it is very hard to make any diagnosis at a young age. Dr. Bledsoe has also suggested that an isolated cleft is more worrisome than a cleft/palate combination.

Since so many young children have developmental delays and poor growth due to neglect and malnutrition, many children will have some of the features of FAS or FAE. It is difficult to figure out when a child is delayed because of just general children's home experience or due to alcohol. Also, children with an Asian background can appear to have some slight FAS facial characteristics when in fact it is just the way they look.

Another example of how difficult a diagnosis can be is that some young toddlers will not have well-developed earlobes and this can be as a result of FAE. But if the child has no sucking instinct her facial muscles will be very underdeveloped. Once home and actively sucking, earlobes will begin to grow. Of course, you won't know that until after the fact. This is another reason to look at the whole picture. Webbing between the 2nd and 3rd toes is also a trait, but this too can occur naturally.

A good article written by Dr. Aronson on FAS and international adoption can be found at: *http://www.russianadoption.org/fas.htm.* She writes that children born to women who drank alcohol excessively during pregnancy appear to be at increased risk for ADD with hyperactivity, fine motor impairment, and clumsiness as well as more subtle delays in motor performance and speech disorders. In the absence of physical features and abnormalities, this is called Fetal Alcohol Effects, or Alcohol Related Neurodevelopmental Effects. FAE is usually not apparent until children are school age. Behavioral issues will surface in preschool and cognitive difficulties around third or fourth grade. The term Fetal Alcohol Effect has been used to describe conditions that are presumed to be caused by prenatal alcohol exposure, but do not follow the exact configuration of the three characteristics used to identify FAS. Typically, children with FAE are of normal size and have some, but not all, of the facial anomalies and central nervous system (CNS) dysfunction associated with FAS. Family history is important. Without the telltale facial features, identification of CNS damage as a result of prenatal alcohol exposure can be difficult. Dr. Bledsoe's clinic specializes in FAS/FAE, and if you suspect that your referral may be subject to the condition you may wish to contact her for a second opinion.

Dr. Bledsoe is a primary care pediatrician who practices pediatrics at the University of Washington's Pediatric Center and has an emphasis on adoption. The University of Washington is one of the top centers on Fetal Alcohol Syndrome. According to Dr. Bledsoe, FAS is a birth defect expressed by a child having four characteristics: 1) below 10% for height, weight, and head circumference; 2) specific set of facial anomalies; 3) structural or functional evidence of brain damage—very small head or abnormal results from neuropyschometric testing; 4) history of alcohol exposure in utero. True diagnosis of the syndrome requires careful measurement in each of these areas. In the United States about 5,000 infants a year are born with FAS. Infants are most vulnerable in the first trimester. Alcohol exposure is dose-dependent. The higher the level of exposure the more damage to the brain. Damage lasts a lifetime. Prenatal alcohol exposure does not always result in FAS. There are other factors— both individual and maternal, such as placenta blood flow—that can influence the amount of alcohol exposed to the brain. Dr. Bledsoe now believes that infants below the age of 2 can be evaluated for FAS by doing a "computer mapping" of a child's face and then comparing this child to their database of FAS characteristics.

The behavioral consequences of a child having FAS/FAE can be hyperactivity, ADD, lack of inhibition, learning disabilities, or mental retardation. They have trouble with habituation. They can't tune out stimuli and are easily overwhelmed and distracted. They demonstrate inappropriate perseverance in that they will continue maladaptive behavior despite negative consequences, as they do not absorb normal cause and effect lessons. The detrimental cognitive effects can include lower IQs, lower achievement test scores, poor comprehension of words and grammar, poor word recall, and lower math skills.

Children with FAE are routinely misdiagnosed as being rebellious, uncooperative, lazy, or stubborn rather than as disabled. They have difficulty learning from experience, lack remorse, and are vulnerable to peer influence. They can be emotionally volatile. Doctors are reluctant to diagnose FAE for various reasons. Toddlers and young children with FAE are described as requiring high maintenance, being manipulative, being very loving, a danger to self and others as they do not understand cause and effect, unable to engage in normal sequential learning so they lack proper reasoning, judgment and memory, being difficult to manage in public, having no fear of danger, and commonly misdiagnosed as their IQs appear normal. Pre-adolescents are impulsive, manipulative, have no sense of fairness or empathy, need a lot of stimulation, have mood swings, are isolated and lonely. Adolescents are described as having no moral compass, still a safety concern to themselves and others, obsessed by basic primal instincts like fires and sexual activity, very vulnerable to peer structures like gangs, impaired judgment and reasoning, vulnerable to ideas in movies, music, and on television, mood swings, and are unable to take responsibility. Young adults with FAE are described as being without a moral center, vulnerable to anti-social behavior, not following safety rules, unable to manage money, emotionally volatile, and being vulnerable to mental problems. While some of these traits occur in non-FAS/FAE people, in these children the behaviors are exaggerated and do not respond to normal modification techniques.

Intervention with FAS/FAE kids should begin as early as possible and continue throughout their lives. The keys to appropriate early intervention are developing and maintaining realistic expectations, thinking long-term, learning to reframe child behaviors, and keeping an open mind about goals and strategies. Early intervention is necessary in order to prevent or lessen secondary consequences. These consequences are problems such as depression, disruptive school experiences and problems with the law. Lack of inhibition controls lead to inappropriate sexual behavior. Jobs are difficult to keep. Alcohol and substance abuse is also higher. To an outsider FAS children seem slow and are criticized for just nor "getting it" when the truth is that they are trying as hard as they can, but their body is letting them down. Expectations must be realistic and may need to be reset at a lower level. These children can learn, just in a different manner. They benefit from early specific motor and mental stimulation, loads and loads of structure, classrooms with minimal stimuli, and concrete learning methods. Abstract thinking is very difficult for these children. They learn through seeing, feeling or touching. Instruction should be given one task at a time. Change should be kept to a minimum and advanced warning of what is to come next should be given. Focus on teaching them vocational and life skills.

These children benefit from living in a stable and nurturing home, not having frequent changes of household, not being a victim of violence, receiving developmental disability services, and receiving a diagnosis before age 6. They benefit from moderate stimulation rather than over stimulation and concrete instructions and consistent limited rules. They need structure both at home and at school.

Life with a fetal alcohol child can be very difficult. Respite care to prevent caregiver burnout may be necessary. Get as much knowledge as you can, and decide what you can honestly handle. The outcome cannot be guaranteed, but if your referral is suspected of having FAS/FAE, the probability of a lifelong involvement with these issues is great. You might read Ann Streissguth's book, *Fetal Alcohol Syndrome: A Guide For Families and Communities* (1997). She gives a lot of very good, detailed information based on 25 years of research. She even includes pictures, which is helpful.

Strabismus

Strabismus is a vision problem in which the eyes are misaligned, meaning they do not look at the same point at the same time. For example, while one eye looks straight ahead, the other may look up, down, in, or out (deviate). Strabismus is sometimes called cross-eyes, walleye, or squint. Strabismus may also be called "lazy eye," but this term is more commonly associated with poor vision resulting from amblyopia. If you are told your child has the eyesight of 1.0 then he has perfect eyesight. 1.0 right eye and 1.0 left is equivalent of 20/20.

Normally the six muscles surrounding each eye work together to move both eyes in the same direction at the same time. An infant's brain learns how to control the eyes' movement with these muscles by 3 or 4 months of age. The brain then merges what the two eyes see into a single image. When the eye muscles do not work right, the eyes may become misaligned. Because misaligned eyes look at different points in space, they send two different images to the brain. The brain cannot merge what the misaligned eyes see into a single image.

In a young child with strabismus the brain is able to avoid the confusion of two images by ignoring (suppressing) the image from one eye. Before age 7 to 10 years, the visual system is still developing and the brain is still learning to use both eyes to see, so it is easy for it to ignore the image from one eye. Once the visual system in the brain has completed its development, however, it cannot ignore the image from one eye. A person who gets strabismus after this development is complete will therefore have double vision (diplopia).

A newborn's eyes may be misaligned, but the eyes should become aligned by 3 to 4 months of age. Any child older than 4 months whose eyes are not aligned all of the time should have an eye exam by an ophthalmologist. A child will rarely "outgrow" strabismus once it has developed. Without treatment, strabismus can cause permanent vision problems. For example, if the child is not using one eye because it is misaligned, it can lead to poor vision in that eye ("lazy eye" or amblyopia). Also, seeing with only one eye instead of two limits how well a person can perceive depth and distance.

Strabismus may affect vision all of the time (constant) or some of the time (latent or intermittent). The eye may turn the wrong way (deviate) only when the person is looking in a certain direction, or it may deviate the same amount no matter which way the person is looking. The eyes may become more misaligned when the person is tired or in bright sunlight. Without treatment, strabismus that initially comes and goes may become more constant.

Usually the cause of strabismus is benign, such as a muscle imbalance or uncorrected farsightedness. Rarely is the cause more serious, such as an underlying neurological condition. In some cases, children with signs of FAS or CP will also have strabismus, which is why you should always evaluate the whole child and not just an individual condition.

Children with strabismus can appear clumsy, as they have limited depth perception. Double vision is not uncommon. Depending on the case, the solution is glasses, patching, or surgery. If left untreated, it can cause developmental delays. Surgery is usually done before the age of 7 and is generally a 45-minute outpatient procedure. The surgery "relaxes" certain muscles so they can orient in unison. It is not painful. The eyes heal very quickly and the child should be able to go back to school in a day or so. Toddlers may need to wear arm splints for a few days to keep them from rubbing their eyes.

The surgery is done everywhere. The most serious issue with this surgery is the anesthesia. You should research and find out who is a good pediatric anesthesiologist. In a small percentage of children the pre-medication causes a reaction and the child is miserable when he wakes up. Try to stay with your child as long as possible, even through the pre-medication stage. Adoptive children tend to react to separation very strongly, as you might expect, so try to be with him when he wakes up. Don't let the hospital treat this as just another case. Explain to them that unless they want a possible hysterical child in the recovery room they should allow you to go to him as soon as he awakens. Your child probably won't have any of these reactions, but if it is his first surgery, you do not know.

There are many articles on treating strabismus. One is in the *American Orthoptic Journal*, Volume 48, 1998.

Syphilis

Sometimes a child will test positive for syphilis at birth because of the mother's umbilical cord blood. Syphilis is treatable, and penicillin is cheap. Usually the child will be tested again and the test will come back negative, however, you will see the positive test in the history.

Have another test performed in the states by your pediatrician. Dr. Aronson has reported on a study of 478 adopted children from various countries. Of this number, eleven children were positive for syphilis; nine from Russia, one from Moldova, and one from Vietnam. None had an acute infection. This is good news. It shows that syphilis is not a concern among Chinese or Korean adoptees. Here's a good web link: *http://www.orphandoctor.com/medical/ 4_2_1_6.html.*

HIV

HIV-1 and HIV-2 are zoonotic infections thought to have originally crossed over in the 1930s. HIV-1's primary primate reservoir is the chimpanzee sub-species *P.t. troglodytes* and for HIV-2, the *sooty mangabey*. Although HIV is spreading rapidly within the Chinese population, most Chinese children do not have HIV. It is not widespread in that population. It is almost impossible to accurately test a newborn for HIV. Many of the babies who test positive do so because they are carrying some of the HIV antibodies from their (HIV+) mothers. As the baby gets older the mother's antibodies die off, allowing for an accurate HIV test. Thus, the presence of HIV antibodies at birth usually only reveals the mother's status. This is similar to hepatitis.

If you are told that a child has tested positive for HIV, try to find out exactly when the test was done and what type of test it was. Ask for a re-test and always consult with an IA doctor. Since children under 18 months may still have maternal antibodies, HIV ELISA, Western Blot, PCR, p24 antigen, or HIV cultures are needed. Note that the Western Blot (WB) is a more specific test that allows one to visualize antibodies directed against each viral protein and is a confirmatory test for a positive HIV ELISA. PCR, or polymerase chain reaction, extends the capacity to identify, manipulate, and reproduce DNA, while the p24 antigen is not a very sensitive test. It will only appear as positive if there is a huge amount of viral replication going on.

This is not to say that there are not some HIV-positive babies in China or Korea. There are bound to be. It's hard to know the epidemiology of HIV in China as widespread screening is not practiced. However, for the vast majority of Asian adopted children HIV is not an issue. The only known highly epidemic areas in China are the provinces bordering India, Myanmar (Burma), and Vietnam.

Dr. Aronson has reported a study of 490 adopted children with only two Chinese children HIV ELISA positive and these were PCR negative, so they were not actually infected. In the May-June 2002 issue of *Adoption Medical News* it was reported that out of 7,299 children tested in 17 centers in the U.S. since the early 1990s, only 12 children were found with the HIV infection (0.16%); four cases each from Cambodia and Romania, two from Vietnam, and one each from Russia and Panama. Excellent information can be found at *www.thebody.com* on infant HIV.

Cleft Palate/Lip

Some children have a condition called cleft palate and/or cleft lip. These conditions are entirely treatable. A cleft lip is a separation of the two sides of the lip. The separation often includes the bones of the upper jaw and/or upper gum. A cleft palate is an opening in the roof of the mouth in which the two sides of the palate did not join together as the unborn baby was developing. Cleft lip and cleft palate can occur on one side or on both sides. Because the lip and the palate develop separately, it is possible for the child to have a cleft lip, a cleft palate, or both cleft lip and cleft palate. Dr. Bledsoe has suggested that an isolated cleft is more of a sign of FAS/FAE than a cleft combination.

Surgery will most often correct the condition, and is done in stages. As a general rule, you can expect one surgery to repair the lip and a second surgery to repair the palate during your child's first year home. Both surgeries generally involve a 1-2 night stay in the hospital. Sometimes the lip and palate can be repaired together in one surgery if the cleft is not that wide. You want the palate fixed sooner so you can start on speech therapy. The child might have a third surgery (bone graft) when she child is 7-10 years old to "fix" the gum line so permanent teeth have a place in which to anchor themselves. Almost any other surgeries are outpatient cosmetic. There is some postoperative pain, like with tonsils, but it is of short duration. The end result is just a small scar on the lip.

There is an organization called Operation Smile. It helps children all over the world who are born with facial defects. Operation Smile will assist families whose insurance will not cover the entire surgery. If you have a referral of a child with a cleft palate or lip, you should contact them for more information. Their website is at *http://www.operationsmile.org/*. Another is at *www.widesmiles.org*.

Cerebral Palsy

Cerebral palsy (CP) is the general term used to describe the motor impairment resulting from brain damage in a young child. The more severe the case, the earlier a diagnosis can be made. Severe cases can be diagnosed in the first few weeks or months of age. If a child is able to walk normally at 14-18 months, it is quite unlikely that the child has CP. The problem is that for most children CP cannot be diagnosed until a child is at least 18 months old. The etiology of CP is still not well understood. It seems derived from a prenatal condition and preceded by a perinatal inflammatory condition.

Many of the normal developmental milestones such as reaching for toys, sitting, and walking are based on motor function. If these are delayed, CP might be a reason. Indeed, your reviewing doctor will be looking for just these sorts of milestones. Yet, developmental delays are expected in these children because of the institutional environment, which makes the diagnosis difficult. A delay in walking or a child's problem with her limbs may have various causes, such as malnutrition or being swaddled too tightly (common with Chinese children), and not just because of CP.

A diagnosis of cerebral palsy cannot be made on the basis of an X-ray or blood test. An Apgar score of less than 3 at the 5 minute mark is one of the few possible indicators, but even this is not always so. The most meaningful review of cerebral palsy is examining the physical evidence of abnormal motor function. An abnormal motor function may be spasticity, which is the inability of a muscle to relax, or athetosis, which refers to the inability to control the movement of a muscle. Infants who at first are hypotonic, wherein their muscles are very floppy, may later develop spasticity.

Of course, the problem is that a medical report or photograph cannot substitute for a physical medical exam, An observation of delayed motor skills, which could simply be based on poor nutrition and environmental factors, is hardly an adequate basis for a CP diagnosis.

Hip Dysplasia

Hip dysplasia is sometimes caused by asymmetrical hip ball joints. Ultrasound of the hip is the most important imaging study and will demonstrate hip deformity. A hip X-ray (joint X-ray) is helpful in older infants and children. If the dysplasia is picked up in the first few months of life, it can almost always be treated successfully with bracing. In a few cases surgery is necessary to put the hip back in joint. The older the age at diagnosis, the worse the outcome and the more extensive the surgery needed to repair the problem. It is considered a mild special needs attribute if everything else looks good.

Post-Institutional Issues

Research on children adopted abroad is now just starting to emerge. The earliest studies (from 1990-1991, like the Ames Study) were done on kids from the terrible Romanian orphanages that came out in the first flood. You have to keep in mind that Russian, Romanian, and Chinese institutions (to name a few) are not all the same. However, that doesn't mean you should just discard the early studies, just that you should not automatically assume that the conclusions are equally valid in regard to your child in her particular children's home. Of course, good foster care in China and Korea practically eliminates the risk.

Your child's particular situation and the particular children's home that are the most important factors in judging whether your child is at risk for post-institutional issues. First, the majority of adoptions from China and Korea turn out just fine. Even among older child adoptions you will find many happy families and many situations that defy the general view. Yet there are some children who will have serious psychological issues. These are not developmental or speech delays. Almost all of the children have at least a mild case and it is to be expected. Rather, serious issues such as reactive attachment disorder (RAD), post-traumatic stress disorder (PTSD), and sensory processing disorder are always possibilities although found in only a minority of all foreign adoptions.

The age of a child at adoption is not directly linked to attachment issues, although the roots are always in the early years. The key factor is quality of care. You can have a 24-month-old who lived in an orphanage where there was a low child/staff ratio and a loving, nurturing environment. Likewise, you can have a 10-month-old who had little contact with caregivers beyond being fed and changed. This child is at far greater risk for attachment issues than the 24-month-old in a loving orphanage. As long as a child has learned how to bond and attach, he can do it again. It is when a child has never learned to attach and bond that attachment issues arise. Remember that you are, at a minimum, the child's third placement after her birth mother and the children's home or foster care.

Layering is a common practice in cold climates due to the lack of adequate heat. Because of this, a child's limbs might not be able to extend and flex due to the bundling. If a child is unable to bring her hands and fingers to her mouth she will not learn to get pleasure sucking her fingers and hands like most new-borns, resulting in an inability to move her tongue, make noises, put food in her mouth, or chew. She will be very quiet. Without the experience of sucking and chewing on her fingers and hands, a child has no reason to move her tongue much, resulting in the delayed speech. However, with simple exercises from a specialist a child can soon discover the joy of babbling, chewing, and putting food and other things in her mouth. Each child's circumstances reflect the specific delays that might result, most of which can be easily treated with the help of skilled professionals. This is why it is important to request a referral to an early intervention program if you have concerns about your child's development.

Transracial Issues

Only a handful of studies have been done on the success of transracial adoptions, but most show that the adopted children generally are well adjusted and comfortable with their families. In a recent study, the Search Institute found that a sample of 199 Korean-born adolescents scored as well as same-race adopted counterparts on 4 measures of mental health and were more likely to be highly attached to both adoptive parents. Sharma said 80% of Korean adoptees said they get along equally well with people of their own and different racial backgrounds, though 42% said they're occasionally ashamed of their race.

Older studies of Korean adoptees focused on the adaptation of the child to the American family. Smoothness of adaptation equaled success. A positive outcome was the child's identification as an American, not as a Korean. No one ever asked how well the family adapted to its new identity as one with a diverse membership and diverse cultural connections.

There is no doubt that transracial adoption introduces a layer of complexity into the child's life, but so does illness, divorce, and everything else that goes with living. Sharma also noted that any family that adopts transracially, "becomes inherently a transracial family, not a white family with a child of color."

For most adoptive parents, the important information is that these studies on intercountry adoptees paint an optimistic picture. The general impression from reading the studies of specifically Korean adoptions is that of good outcome based on positive indicators such as educational achievement, good relationships with families and peers, and a general feeling of positive self-worth and confidence enjoyed by the adoptees.

The question of connection with cultural heritage and racial identity is considered in all the studies. The commonly held position is that, "pride in cultural identity is essential to reducing the crisis of adolescent identity and resolving role conflict." Studies describe parents eagerly providing cross-cultural experiences for children until adolescence. At that point, the children's interest seems to naturally wane as they become involved in teenage pursuits that require "fitting in" to their mostly Caucasian peer group. A group of Korean adult adoptees cautioned parents to be sensitive during this period. They advise parents to be responsive to their children's reactions to cultural activities native to the child. Interactions with Asian-Americans may be awkward for children of this age, as the thoroughly American behavior of the adoptee may perplex and disappoint the Asian-American. Other studies emphasized that such factors as self-esteem are more important than cultural identity for successful adoption results.

While growing up, adoptees do not want to be differentiated by other children in the society. They want to have blue eyes, blond hair, and fair skin, so they may not be happy about their Korean or Chinese middle name. When they reach college age, they begin to appreciate their ethnic background. On one survey of Korean adoptees 45% of the male respondents considered themselves Caucasian and 34% of the female respondents viewed themselves Caucasian while growing up. Once adoptees go to college, they are exposed to a diverse of races on campus and this gives them the opportunity to seriously consider their ethnic identity.

The positive outcome from intercountry adoptions surprises some researchers, though probably not adoptive parents. Why does intercountry adoption work as well as it does? Some researchers' explanations build on David Kirk's belief that adoption works best when there is openness about the adoption and acceptance of the difference between parenting biological and adopted children. The researchers suggest that parents of ethnically different children approach the inherent difficulties of adoption in an open and accepting fashion.

Some suggestions on achieving this openness are interacting with people of your child's race; finding mentors or role models for your teenager that are of her race; confronting racism openly and discussing it with your child; and creating a positive cultural environment at home. There is no formula for success. The most you can do as a parent is try hard and hope it all turns out.

The vast majority of Korean adoptees show positive self-esteem and a good sense of integration into their nuclear and extended families. Most intercountry adoptive parents said they would definitely "do it again" if given the choice.

CHAPTER X

Waiting and Waiting

While You Wait

You may be waiting for the day when you are told you can travel to unite your family or perhaps you are waiting for your child to arrive from Korea. If you have received your I-171H, then you might be waiting for your dossier to be approved. Or your agency might be delaying your departure so as to bundle several families together (it's more convenient for them). There are lots of reasons for delay.

You also may have already accepted a referral and that child is now yours. But you can't have him yet; you must wait. Any delay is as frustrating for your agency and as it is for you. Your agency should be able to tell you where the kink is in the chain. Still, everything is really out of your hands, you have done all you can do, and *your* child is there and you are here. Here are some suggestions as to what you can do while you wait:

If you are close to the holidays, go to the Salvation Army or some other organization and support a family with a child around the age you are adopting and give that child a gift.
Learn child CPR while you are waiting.
Gather social security and citizenship application forms.

Study up on the federal adoption tax credit rules.

Interview pediatricians.

Begin your hepatitis vaccine shots and any other shots you need.

Begin to pack your suitcase and your child's.

Check into the school system or day care centers in your area. Ask your neighbors.

Write your will so it includes your adoptive child.

Discuss with spouse about parenting styles, discipline styles, and which relatives get to raise the child in case you both predecease her.

Learn about your state's re-adoption requirements.

Childproof your house. Have friends with kids come over to review.

Install plug protectors, edge protectors, cabinet locks, and toilet locks.

Practice with the Diaper Genie.

Diaper your dog or a furry doll for practice.

Do lots of nice things for yourself. It will be your last time. Go away for a long weekend with your spouse.

You should also ask your agency in which children's home or province your child is located. With this specific information you can then post on the Internet and find someone else who has traveled to the same home and who can tell you exactly what to expect.

Study some Chinese phrases.

Go to some Chinese restaurants and practice with chopsticks. (The larger cities and hotels will have forks but the smaller ones may not.)

Start your child's lifebook.

Fix up the baby's room.

Buy the crib, car seat, and the usual baby books. Read the books.

Post poison control and children's hospital phone numbers on the fridge.

Begin thinking about what kind of adoption notices you want to send out, if any.

Write a letter to your child telling them how you are feeling while you wait for them. Give it to them when they turn 18 or some other special time.

File an application for Title IV non-recurring money if your state allows it.

Get your passport ready.

Check out your county's early intervention programs if appropriate. Ask your pediatrician for some recommended evaluators.

Clean your house like it has never been cleaned before.

Take a parenting class.

Find out the dates for children's consignment sales and plan to attend.

Make an effort to go out with your friends, as you will not have time later.

Take that swing dancing class you've always wanted to take.

Nest, nest, nest—it's your time! This waiting time will be the slowest weeks of your life. Just fill your days.

Choosing a Pediatrician

Most parents choose a pediatrician based on recommendations from friends and family. Find out if the doctor has worked with international children and has any as patients. If she has not, then you can expect to have to educate the pediatrician. Indeed, if the doctor just works in a middle class community you are likely to find that he is not knowledgeable regarding the issues faced by an international child.

Is she willing to review the referral photo? Since this child might be a patient of hers soon, she should be. On the other hand, if you are not used to giving a medical conclusion based on a skimpy medical report and one photo, giving such a conclusion is against a pediatrician's standard training. Also, remember that any local pediatrician's review is in addition to the adoption specialists' review and not in place of it. Bringing the local pediatrician into the referral review process allows you to lean on that doctor for advice as to what medicines you should take over to your child.

The pediatrician should allow you to make an immediate appointment as soon as you return from China or Korea. You should not have to wait a week to have a thorough examination and screening. You should emphasize to the doctor that the examination needs to be thorough and longer than the usual visit. If you can, you should try to make the appointment before you leave.

You should raise the issue of reimmunization of your child. Even if your child has been immunized, the vaccines may have been out of date, not given in the same dosage as in the states, or not refrigerated as necessary. You should not accept any resistance regarding your desire to reimmunize.

Is she familiar with hepatitis B and C in children? What about parasites such as giardia and other international medical issues? Middle class doctors do not have patients with parasites and may be resistant to testing for them. Any resistance is unacceptable.

Standard questions would be to find out if the doctor has a particular area of pediatric interest, the hours of the office, and the hospitals in which the doctor practices. Check out the waiting room, as you will likely spend quite a bit of time there over the next few years. Are there things to keep the child occupied, like toys, books, fish tank, that sort of thing? Do you like the nurses and staff?

Lifebook

Some families create what is called a "lifebook" for their child. It is an illustration of the adoption journey and can serve as the baby book they never had. The lifebook might include a section on the history of your life before the child became part of your life, such as where you grew up, lived, work, went to school, etc.

You might have a section on the adoption process itself including pictures of the agency people and the referral picture, then a section on your child's life showing where she was born and lived and why you chose her name and what it means to you. Copies of her social security card, court petition, and decree and citizenship certificate could be included, then a section on your home and fixing it up for her arrival, include pictures of her room.

There might be a section on traveling to China or Korea including copies of receipts and ticket stubs, pictures of the plane, hotel, tourist spots, and homestay families. Include maps, money, and brochures. You could even include a small vial of dirt or a rock from the children's home. Some families have their children's caregivers or foster parents write a letter to the child, which you can have her open at whatever age you see fit. This letter could be part of the book.

If there is a baby shower, you could include the invitation, photos from the baby shower, and a piece of the gift paper. You could have a section regarding your return with ticket stubs, description of the travel with the child, and passport photos. If people met you at the airport you could include pictures of the celebration and pictures of your house when you returned. Include the adoption announcement. Include your child's own section with her favorite toy and book. Include what you found out about her immediately such as her sleep and nap patterns, favorite foods, and bathing and nighttime rituals. You may (or may not) have a medical section with information from the children's home, a report from your pediatrician when you returned, hand and foot imprints, and birth statistics (such as height and weight).

You could have a section on what was happening in China (Korea) and the United States at the time. (This is a good reason to buy some English language newspapers while you are there.) You could include movies and songs that were playing in the United States at the time.

The White House will also send you a welcome card for your child if you ask them. (It's a little hokey, but cute.) Better yet is the flag they will fly over the Capitol the day your child becomes a citizen. They run these up and down the flagpole very five minutes all day long. Just ask your congresswoman.

If you adopt an older child, you might consider sending a copy of the lifebook to her in order for her to get used to the idea of joining your family and leaving her country. It should be a picture book, which might include actual photographs of the child, your family, your dog or cat, home, her new school, extended family, friends, the city she will live in, and the places you and she will go. It might include magazine cutouts and notes from family members. If possible, the book might include both English and foreign captions/translations.

Here is a sample outline:

1. Introduction: including the child's picture and how you and your family feel about her.

2. An explanation of things to come: This portion can include a lot of magazine cutouts. Include pictures to indicate the in-country travel; acknowledge her feelings—understand she'll be sad to leave her friends; see a doctor; get her picture taken; take an airplane ride to the U.S.; pictures of friends and the house.

3. An explanation of the first few weeks home and the normal routine for both weekdays and weekends. Include an explanation of her being taken to the doctor and dentist visits. Pictures of her classroom, explaining the purpose of each area; the playground; daily routine (get up, brush teeth, get dressed, drive to work/school; eat breakfast/lunch at school; come home cook dinner; a large variety of after-school/dinner activities; take a bath; brush teeth; set out clothes for next day; say prayers; give hugs and kisses; go to sleep); our weekend routine (clean

house, other chores like laundry/shopping, go to church. List potential activities and sports.

4. Spring/Summer events: pictures of friends who she will meet; pictures of family who will be visiting; magazine cutouts of the beach and pool, Fourth of July fireworks, etc.

Some families create an audio "Lifebook" for their older child. They make the tape in the native language before leaving the States or in-country with the help of their translator. The tape explains what a hotel is and that they will fly on several large planes to get home; what a city is; that there will be lots of cars and people in the larger cities they will be stopping at on their way home; that their new mama and papa love them and it will take time for everyone to get use to being a family; all about the household pets; all about his new home and that he would have his own bed; who his new relatives would be; school; routines and house rules. This kind of tape can really help an older child understand the whirlwind adjustments to his life that he is undergoing. It can become his story.

An adoption-oriented lifebook or "keepsake" book can be found at *http://www.adoptshoppe.com/lifebooks.htm*. It has removable pages and appropriate sections for you to fill in, such as "Tell me about the day you adopted me," and "Tell me about the first time you held me," etc. Tapestry Books also has one at *www.tapestrybooks.com*, called *This Is Me: Memories To Gather And Keep*. Other places sell them as well.

Learn Your Child's Language

You do not have to learn any language for your adoption. It will go just as well if you do not know. However, it is like traveling in any foreign country— knowing the native language broadens the experience.

If you are adopting an older child or even one as young as 4, you should consider learning some basic phrases just to help with the bonding process and to make the trip less stressful. Bring a phrase book and point. Everyone can read the characters, no matter what they speak. If you are adopting a toddler or older child, be sure to learn words like mommy, daddy, potty, eat, sleep, yes, no, etc. Even infants under 1 can recognize when you speak a few words to them.

For Chinese, while it is helpful to speak a few tourist type phrases (where is the bathroom, hotel, etc), it is even more critical is to be able to recognize a few characters. Try to be able to recognize the characters for your child's name, and things like "birthday." You'll be getting documents in Chinese and English and, although you probably won't be able to read them, if you can at least recognize a few key characters that could be useful. Chinese writing is universal, so you don't have to worry about local language variations (people in Guangzhou and Hong Kong speak Cantonese rather than Mandarin.)

Leaving Your Children At Home

Many families have other children at home and leave them with family members or friends while they are overseas. You should provide the caretaker with a power of attorney to cover ordinary things as well as a specific medical power to allow for medical treatment of your children if it becomes necessary. A local hospital should be able to show you the form they use.

You should also give the caretaker your pediatrician's name and phone number, any medical conditions, medications, or allergies of your children, and the name, policy number, and phone number of your health insurance company. The caretaker should be given the health insurance card showing coverage for your children. The caretaker should be given a list of phone numbers of friends and relatives they can call if they have questions.

A map showing where the doctor's office is located and the nearest hospital should also be given to the caretaker. Phone numbers of your local car dealer, plumber, electrician, and heating and air person should also be given. Another authorization is one to allow the caretaker to drive your car and to have it repaired.

In a real emergency the hospital will treat your child, but it makes things go more smoothly if your caretaker can show them all of this information and it is critical for non-emergency situations.

A sample form is as follows:

To whom it may concern:

As the parents of _____, we hereby authorize _____
to approve any and all necessary medical treatment for our child.

Our child is covered by _____Insurance Company, policy number
_____, phone number _____. This is a
PPO (HMO). The employee member is _____.

Our child's date of birth is_____. She is allergic to
_____. Her pediatrician is _____,
at_____, phone number_____. Our child's blood
type is _____. Her last hospitalization was on
_____for _____.

Our home address is_____. Our home phone number is
_____.

Signed (<u>both parents</u>)

Notary

A problem is explaining the trip to young children who may not fully comprehend why you are leaving, but just know Mommy and Daddy will be gone. You might buy a book called *Seeds of Love* and read it to them. Other things you can do include making a map and calendar showing when you plan to leave and when you will return. Give them stars to put on the calendar to mark out the days until you will be home.

Some parents make several audiotapes and videotapes reading stories to the kids, singing favorite poems, songs, and rhymes, and telling funny stories. They also take brown lunch bags, and for each day away they write a note on each one for each child. Inside they place a small toy, treat, or craft activity. Here is an interesting web site on the issue of leaving your child behind: *http://www.adoptiontravel.com/articles/art2.htm.*

Employer Benefits

You may wish to use this time to investigate what adoption benefit programs your employer may offer and how they fit in with the adoption tax credit. One of the best benefits is derived from the federal Family Medical Leave Act (FMLA). As always, consult with your employer's human resources department or an attorney for specifics. However, the law is generally as follows. The FMLA applies to all:

1) Public agencies, including state, local and federal employers, schools, and

2) Private-sector employers who employ 50 or more employees in 20 or more workweeks in the current or preceding calendar year.

To be eligible for FMLA benefits, an employee must:

(1) work for a covered employer;

(2) have worked for the employer for a total of 12 months;

(3) have worked at least 1,250 hours over the previous 12 months.

The 12 months need not be consecutive. The 12 months include any time off spent on workers' compensation, military leave, or court leave. The 1,250 hours must be actual work hours, not including any type of leave.

A covered employer must grant an eligible employee up to a total of 12 workweeks of unpaid leave during any 12-month period for placement with the employee of a son or daughter for adoption or foster care. Leave for placement for adoption must conclude within 12 months of the placement.

Under some circumstances, employees may take FMLA leave intermittently for placement of adoption—which means taking leave in blocks of time or reducing their normal weekly or daily work schedule. This is at the discretion of the employer.

Before (or after) an adopted child is placed, the employee may take FMLA leave for making required arrangements for the placement—to attend counseling

sessions, appear in court, consult with an attorney, or submit to a physical examination. A father or mother may take FMLA leave for these reasons.

Whether the child arrives by birth or by placement, a mother or father is
entitled to FMLA leave to care for the child during the first year. No medical
justification is needed—the FMLA leave is guaranteed simply to care for the
new child. This particular right to FMLA leave terminates on the first anniversary of the child's birth or placement.

Title IV-E

Adoptions are not inexpensive. In addition to sources of funds such as
employers and state and federal adoption tax credits, the federal government
also provides a reimbursement program called Title IV-E in all 50 states. This
program was established to encourage the adoption of children who are otherwise considered hard to adopt. The federal government pays 60% and the state
the remainder. The state controls the program for the most part, subject to certain federal requirements.

The program was originally established for domestic adoptions. The states
have applied the program unevenly to foreign adoptions. Some do and some
do not. The program has two types of funds. One type of program gives recur-
ring funds, which is means-tested. More importantly, for foreign adoptions it
also gives non-recurring funds up to $2,000 for expense reimbursement. Many
people have obtained these funds for their foreign adoptions. This part of the
program is not means-tested. Check with your accountant, but the $2,000
should not be taxable, as it is a welfare benefit.

First check with your state's adoption services unit to see if they apply Title
IV to foreign adoptions. At this time it appears that Georgia, South Carolina,
Alaska, and Ohio do apply the program to international adoptions, but that
New York, Michigan and Texas may not. Maryland will also apply it to foreign
adoptions, but they throw obstacles at you. Be persistent and file before you
adopt. In Maryland call Mrs. Kirby and ask for an adoption reimbursement
packet. Her number is 410-767-7625. Don't leave a message, but talk to her in
person. The County Human Services Department or County Children's
Services Board administers Ohio's program. The initial application must be
filed prior to the adoption being finalized and the $2,000 reimbursement is

issued after the finalization. In Ohio the application should be made in advance of traveling to China, but after the child to be adopted is identified. In Georgia, the county DFACS office intakes the application, but the state DFACS office makes the decision. It should also be filed prior to travel. In Alaska, the filing can be made after travel but before any re-adoption decree. If you miss the deadline of filing before traveling, then try the Alaska method of filing before the re-adoption decree and argue that that decree is the final decree.

With a Korean adoption it may be hard to argue that the child fits under the developmentally delayed or other category. The reason is that the children are usually in good health to begin with and by the time you file you probably have had the child in your home and cured any delays.

Remember that you are the only advocate your child has. The state adoption units normally have no idea what an international adoption is or what you have had to go through. If they reject your application, do not give up, but appeal and continue to push using all of your resources.

Assuming your state does allow Title IV-E to apply to foreign adoptions, in most states it is necessary to file the application prior to adopting. There should be no filing fee involved and the application should not be difficult. Your state will require some documentation after you return from China explaining your child's health condition and the background of the adoption. This documentation may include a letter from your child's pediatrician, a summary from your agency regarding the adoption, and a copy of the adoption decree. Your agency's letter should include information on how your child was hard to place. This is the purpose of the Title IV program, so include how long your child had to wait before being adopted.

Generally the process for applying for the non-recurring funds is as follows: Step 1 is to file the application before leaving for China.

Step 2 is for your pediatrician to write up a post-adoption medical report (or you can do it and have your pediatrician print it on his letterhead and sign it). Your goal is for the state to recognize that your child has medical or special needs relating to developmental delays, medical issues, nutritional, and failure to thrive issues.

You may need to give the county copies of a few receipts showing that costs greatly exceeded the $2,000 non-recurring reimbursement.

Step 3 is that your county sends all of this information to the state's department that is in charge of the Title IV program. This department will evaluate the information and decide if you have proven your case. You should have administrative appeal rights.

Most counties also have an early intervention/baby's first program that provides a free evaluation of your child. Sometimes using this evaluation to substantiate your application can be helpful.

Here is a website with a list of each state and how much money they will reimburse for adoptions. *http://www.calib.com/naic/pubs/reim_tab.htm.*

Here are some other websites that may be useful:
http://www.fpsol.com/adoption/checklist.html#four-e
http://www.acf.dhhs.gov/programs/cb/laws/fed_reg/fr012500.pdf.

Airfares

Travel arrangements fall into two sections, travel to China and domestic travel inside China. Some agencies make all the arrangements including tickets and some require you to make all arrangements outside of China. Travel inside of China may be arranged by one of the official travel services or the agency may employ their own guides. The guides are usually quite good and may even specialize in working with adoptive parents. These guides often know the adoption process in China better than anyone else and can generally be relied upon to get the job done.

One thing you can do while you are waiting for a court date is to check on airfares and airlines. These are just some of the airlines that fly to China from the U.S.: Air China, Cathay Pacific, China Airlines, China Eastern, China Southern, Continental, EVA Airways, Korean Airlines, Northwest Airlines, Singapore Air, Thai Airways, and United Air. They fly into Hong Kong, Beijing, Shanghai, or Guangzhou.

Some parents fly to Tokyo first, then change planes for Beijing. The flight to Tokyo takes 14 hours. Others go through Hong Kong first. The flight is about 15 hours from Chicago and 13 from the West Coast. Hong Kong has a relatively new airport. It is a bit spartan, but spacious. Make sure you call your airline to confirm your reservations 72 hours before departure. If you fail to do this, you run the risk of having your reservation canceled. You will need to confirm your reservations both in the U.S. and in China.

It is difficult to get the best deal to China without using a travel agent. You can research the fares yourself, but a travel agent can sometimes get you special adoption rates and have the ticket-changing charge waived. There are also some travel agencies that specialize in adoption travel to China such as Lotus Travel at *http://www.lotustours.net/adopttravel.htm.*

If you have confidence in an airline consolidator, you can try booking through them. Some people have used Airfare Busters at 713-961-5109 or 407-391-9560. Just remember that if you use discount tickets or "buddy passes" you may have a difficult time flying out the day you want or getting your ticket changed. The National Council for Adoption sometimes has information about special fares and can be reached at (202) 328-1200.

Visas

In order to go to China you need a visa. Some agencies will arrange for the visa and others leave it up to the families to obtain them. There are also companies that specialize in obtaining such visas and for a small fee will assist families. These are very helpful when you have only a short notice before traveling. If you obtain your visa yourself, check the Chinese Consulate's web site for any recent changes to the procedure. Usually you send your application, passport, fee, and passport pictures by FedEx or certified mail to the Chinese Consulate that services your state. You will need to keep the visa in your carry-on to show Chinese immigration when you land. You will also need to show it when you leave. Therefore, do not pack the visa document in your checked luggage.

Calling from Overseas

You should also investigate how to call from China or Korea, as you are likely to want to tell someone back home your good news as well as the exact time you will be returning home. You should be able to use all of your major phone company calling cards if you are in the larger cities. Always check with your carrier prior to leaving on rates and access. In some provinces it is difficult and expensive to call the U.S. The major hotels really charge you. Some of the hotels have business centers where you can buy a prepaid card and call at a much less expensive rate. The actual calling process is not very difficult.

A cheaper method to call is to buy a prepaid international calling card. These are available at most stores such as Wal-Mart or Sam's Club. Your international minutes are less than the minutes on the card. Call for access instructions before leaving the U.S. By using one of these cards, you know ahead of time what the cost will be, and you won't discover hidden charges on your phone bill when you return to the states. Check with the carrier in case you need to activate it before you go.

Some carriers like AT&T and MCI also have special international plans that you can sign up for before you go. They cost $3 a month, but allow you to call your home for around $.70 a minute. However, if you call some place other than your home very high rates apply. After you return from overseas, you can always cancel the plan and the $3 monthly charge. If your parents live within your same local calling area, you can set your home phone to call forwarding and this way dial your parents at the low rate.

When calling with your calling card it may be possible to save the connect fee by pushing # to end a call instead of hanging up. Then you can dial another number. Check with your carrier about this before you leave. Since rates and programs change frequently, you should always verify the method you will use and the rate you will pay prior to leaving. You don't want any surprises on your phone bill when you return.

Internet Access

If you want to access the Internet overseas from your laptop, you will need a phone jack adapter as well as an electrical adapter. Most new hotels and refurbished hotels have business centers where you can access the Internet. If you will be using email, it is suggested that you set up a web email account at Yahoo or Hotmail rather than risk revealing your password to your regular account on AOL, Earthlink, or MSN.

Money in China

The Chinese currency is called the renminbi, and is issued by the People's Bank of China. The unit of renminbi is the yuan and the smaller units are the jiao and fen (10 fen=1 jiao, 10 jiao=1 yuan). Yuan, jiao, and fen are issued as paper banknotes but there are also yuan, five jiao, and fen coins. Denominations of yuan banknotes are 1 yuan, 2 yuan, 5 yuan, 10 yuan, 20 yuan, 50 yuan and 100 yuan. Jiao banknotes are 1 jiao, 2 jiao, and 5 jiao, and fen banknotes are 1 fen, 2 fen, and 5 fen. The abbreviation for Chinese currency is RMB. The Chinese have artificially pegged the yuan/dollar conversion rate at a low figure. At some point the Chinese will either let it float or raise the conversion rate to a more realistic figure. When they do, expect the cost of an adoption to increase.

The Bank of China will cash travelers' checks. Travelers' checks and credit cards are accepted at major hotels, banks, and Friendship Stores. Be careful to review the receipt before you sign in case they add something to it. You also might want to check on the card company's exchange rate before you go. Many times a card company rate will be more or less than the official rate. You can also obtain cash advances from hotel money exchange places using a credit card with your PIN number. You have to be careful that the exchange rate used by the stores and foreign currency exchange places is one with which you agree, but nevertheless it is a relatively painless way of obtaining additional funds. Do not use a direct debit card. You do not want to give anyone access to your checking account. Just use a regular credit card. You need to notify your credit card company that you might use your card in China before leaving. They will get suspicious if you use the card in Chicago and suddenly the next charge is from Beijing.

Shots for Travel

Usually it is recommended to get the hepatitis A and B shots plus a tetanus/diphtheria shot and a polio booster. The hepatitis vaccine is not cheap, and you should check with your insurance company regarding coverage. Insurance companies may reimburse for the vaccines if your doctor codes them for contact risk/exposure. If they deny coverage, appeal their decision and emphasize that you are adopting a child of unknown risks from a country with a high prevalence of hepatitis and that this is a small preventive cost compared with them paying to cure you. Also, tell them that the CDC recommends these shots. Push them on this. Your regular doctor or the foreign travel office of a hospital should be able to give these shots. Your local health department may also give them. Most health departments have these vaccines available at reduced cost. Shop around in order to get the lowest price.

The hepatitis A vaccine is two shots and the hepatitis B is three, although you obtain the majority of the hepatitis B benefits with the first two shots. You should talk with your doctor before receiving these shots.

Hepatitis A is much more contagious than is hepatitis B, and is spread through contaminated water, contaminated food, or the oral or fecal excretions of a person/baby/toddler infected with this virus. Thus, it can be communicated by sharing food, drinking unsafe water (ice in drinks, as well as water that is not boiled or bottled), eating food washed in unsafe water (including lettuce, uncooked vegetables and unpeeled fruits), and even by changing the diaper of an infected infant without washing hands thoroughly afterward. This vaccine is effective for a short term if given one month prior to travel abroad. If multiple trips are planned, it is suggested that an individual have a booster 6 to 12 months after the initial dose, as this will avoid the need for a repeat booster prior to all future trips. This vaccine should not be given to children less than two years of age. The hepatitis A vaccine has replaced the need for the gamma globulin shot, which was formerly given to most adults prior to international travel.

The hepatitis B vaccine is given three times; the second one at one month after the first dose, and the third shot four to six months after the first dose. Although the risk of exposure for families while traveling is probably low, this is an important vaccine that should be given for your protection in situations of accidental exposure to an adult or child with hepatitis B, especially if that child becomes a member of your family (since it may take more than four months for an adult to become immune from the vaccine). At the very least, the primary caregiver should receive these shots.

Although wild polio has been eradicated in North America (some vaccine-acquired polio has been seen in individuals with compromised immune systems who develop it from the polio vaccine that is given by mouth), polio is still seen in developing nations. It is recommended that all adults traveling to a developing nation receive an inactivated polio vaccine (IPV) to lessen the risk of acquiring polio abroad. This should be done even if the polio vaccine was given during childhood, as it will serve as a booster dose. The oral polio vaccine (OPV) should not be given to adults because of the risk of acquiring polio from the vaccine itself in individuals whose immunity may have waned. If children are traveling abroad for the adoption, they should also receive an additional dose of the polio vaccine, preferably as IPV. This means that they should have a total of five doses of polio vaccine by age 4 rather than the recommended four doses. Adults who receive a booster before travel do not routinely need a dose before each trip.

Diphtheria and tetanus are still seen in other countries. Adults should have a Td booster every ten years to give continuing protection against these diseases. Since none of us can predict what injuries may occur while we are abroad, it is recommended that adults have a tetanus shot booster if it has been more than five years since the last shot. This lessens the chance that a tetanus shot may be needed while overseas.

Measles, mumps, and rubella are childhood illnesses that were once common but have lessened in frequency due to the MMR vaccine now given during childhood. All adults born in or after 1957 should have a booster shot for these illnesses unless one is absolutely sure that they had all three of these illnesses. If the history is unclear about a past history of these diseases, it is not harmful to repeat this vaccine. Most adults born prior to 1957 had these three diseases during childhood, so it is unlikely that they need the vaccine.

There is now an effective shot to protect against chicken pox, which can cause significant illness in adults. The shot, given in two doses (the second 6 weeks after the first), is thought to be fairly protective against this disease, lessening the severity of the illness if an individual does acquire chicken pox. A blood test can be done if an adult's history is unclear, although the shot is not harmful if given to someone who had the disease and did not know it. This shot, as well as the MMR, should not be given to pregnant women.

For individuals traveling during the fall and winter months, it is recommended that they are immunized with the influenza vaccine.

If you have a medical condition or are simply nervous about being sick in a foreign country, then you might investigate buying overseas medical insurance. This is available at AEA/SOS for around $55. Their phone number is 800-523-8930. They have a website at *http://www.intsos.com/*Also, for

AAA+members, there is evacuation insurance at little or no charge. Check with AAA on the specifics. The only caveat is that you have to have already been an AAA+member for 3+years to qualify for the coverage. You cannot simply purchase or upgrade to AAA+just to get the Medivac coverage. Last year, the AAA+coverage included $25,000 per person for evacuation. AAA has a special international number to call if you need that service in an emergency. You must call your regional office to get the customer service number for Medivac. Your local AAA office usually doesn't have the information. It is also VERY important to check with your own health insurance coverage company before you go to find out where in Asia your health insurance is valid.

For more information on vaccines for adoption travel, see the January 2001 issue of *Adoption Medical News*. Check with *http://www.adoptionnews. org/pub3.html* on how to order back issues. See also these helpful websites for additional information:
http://www.cdc.gov/travel/eastasia.htm
http://members.aol.com/jaronmink/immunize.htm

Packing for Adults

1. Documents

You should be able to get both parents' clothes in one suitcase and your child's in another. Any more luggage than that and you have over packed. If you have packed more than 2 bags for yourself, you have over packed. Take older luggage that is plain in color. Never take luggage that does not have wheels. Don't take the kind with the cheap portable wheels, but luggage with the wheels built in.

The very first things you should pack in your carry-on are your documents. Do not pack these in your checked suitcase. These documents are worth more than all your clothes. You should place them in a large zipper case or in individual plastic sleeves or an expandable file folder. These can be found at an office supply store. You will need to pack your I-864 if your child is getting an IR-4 Visa, and copies of your tax returns for the last three years. If your child is receiving an IR-3 Visa, then you do not need to take any tax returns or tax transcripts. However, I would suggest taking the previous year's return anyway. You will need to take your I-171-H, a copy of your home study, your confirmation that the U.S. Consulate received the cable, and any other documents your agency may think is important. Some agencies recommend carrying a duplicate of some or all of your dossier documents. Just ask your agency. A copy of your passport and visa should be taken. Of course your passports and Chinese visas need to be accessible, as you will be showing those as soon as you land.

Also, as part of your carry-on you need your airplane tickets and lots of American cash. You should also put in your carry-on your agency's phone number and the U.S. Embassy's phone number as well. Some people put all of these documents in a three ring binder, but that can be bulky.

Here are some organizational tips:

1. Print out all the phone numbers of your contacts in China such as your guide, your agency in the states, the agency office in China, the U.S. Embassy, the U.S. Consulate in Guangzhou, phone numbers and email addresses of your congressional representatives in case you run into serious BCIS/state department trouble, and anyone else you can think of. Give a copy to your spouse as well.

2. Timeline and instructions from your agency.

3. Plastic sleeve holding plane tickets and airline or travel agent phone numbers.

4. Calling card and access number or prepaid card.

5. Plastic sleeve holding passports (and copies of same), visas (and copies), and customs declaration forms.

6. Plastic sleeve holding copies of birth and marriage certificates if needed.

7. Plastic sleeve to hold expense receipts for adoption credit documentation.

8. Plastic sleeve to hold extra pictures of your home life and photo of your child.

9. Type up tip sheets on traveling, including tourist sights.

10. Plastic sleeve for I-171H plus U.S. Consulate confirmation.

11. Questions to ask at the children's home and copy of all medical information on your child to use in conjunction with the questions.

12. Plastic sleeve for blue I-600.

13. Plastic sleeve for I-864 and all supporting documents, if required.

14. Extra plastic sleeve for your child's new Chinese passport and any other documents of hers you have like the new notarial birth certificate, abandonment certificate, notarial certificate of adoption, and Unified Adoption Decree.

15. Plastic sleeve for extra dossier and supporting documents, if your agency feels it necessary.

16. Copy of map of China showing Guangzhou and the province where the children's home is located. (Not a full-size copy, just a reduced one.)

17. Same kind of map of Guangzhou and of the city you are staying in showing tourist sites and streets. These are generally available on the Internet.

18. Sheets of notebook paper to be used for notes.

19. Cheat sheet for converting RMB, centimeters, and kilograms. Temperature conversions are easy. Just double the Celsius number and add 32, then subtract 4. This is within one or two degrees of the right answer.

20. A regular diaper bag will eat at your shoulder after a while. Some parents have taken a backpack instead. You don't need a special purpose diaper bag backpack, just a lightweight, internal-frame backpack with a belt and vertical side pockets. The belt will keep it from coming apart and the side pockets are useful for bottled water and formula.

21. Phone number of your pediatrician or IA specialist back home in case you need to do an overseas consult. Set this up ahead of time and only use it if necessary. (Make sure you understand the time difference.)

Sometimes, after the adoption one parent unexpectedly must return to the United States. Thus you should take two executed notarized powers of attorney giving one another permission to represent the other in all adoption proceedings.

Before you travel you should prepare a laminated card written in Chinese characters explaining the purpose of your trip. Your card might read "This is our beautiful daughter _____. We are adopting her from the _____ Welfare

Home, and are taking her to our home in the United States. We're very happy to be here in China." When you are approached by local Chinese, and you will be approached lots of times, show them the card. You will get lots of thumbs up and "Thank you" in broken English. They may want to pat the child's head, as the child has become a "lucky child" and perhaps the luck will rub off. If you are a redhead, they will also try to pat your head for good luck.

Also, have your translator give you a piece of paper on which the name of your hotel is written. If you get lost, you can simply show someone this card or paper.

2. Clothes and Sundries

The first rule, second rule, and only rule is to pack light. You will have to carry everything, including a wiggly child, by yourself through a number of airports, train stations, and hotel lobbies, usually with no help at all. It is the ultimate planes, trains, and automobiles adventure. You will need to get luggage and child in and out of taxis, buses, and vans along the way. Make sure that everything is on wheels or can easily be attached to something wheeled. Think carefully about each item and try to figure out if you can do without it or do double duty with something else.

Some suggest using hard-sided luggage with good locks. Luggage takes quite a beating on a trip like this. Cloth bags will work and are lighter, so it is a tradeoff. Start your packing plan early. You'll be astonished how time disappears once you get your referral. Set aside a place at home to collect stuff for the trip—shampoo and toothpaste samples, power converters, Ziplocs, etc. Put your packing list in there, and make a note every time you think of something.

It is much simpler to plan to do laundry once or twice in China instead of carrying additional clothes. The hotels all have a laundry service. You can have it done cheaply and well at the hotel in the baby's town, and expensively and well at the White Swan in Guangzhou. You usually have to have it in by a certain time in the morning in order to get it back the same day. At the White Swan, some parents have taken their laundry directly to the laundry service and saved some money. It is located next to the White Swan on the end as you would walk past on your way to Lucy's. And don't use the laundry order form they give you in the room, as you will have to fill out a slightly different form they use for dropped off laundry. Maybe pick up the drop-off form in advance.

Be aware that all laundry in China is done in *very hot* water so make sure that the fabrics of the clothes that you pack will tolerate these conditions. The quality of the laundry services is usually excellent, and the clothes will be returned clean, ironed, and folded. So pack light and let the Chinese laundry do the rest. You can also wash clothes in the sink. Finally, some parents avoid laundry altogether by abandoning their smelly clothing as they go. This frees up amazing amounts of space in their luggage for souvenirs!

Dress casually and wear comfortable shoes. Suits, ties, and polished shoes are not needed at any point. The officials in China will not be dressed up and do not expect it of you. Your child also doesn't expect it either, and will just view you as a giant napkin on legs. Do not take anything that needs to be dry-cleaned. Take cotton, not linen. Linen takes forever to dry and is hot. Leave your vanity behind. Forget lugging the hairdryers, makeup, and jewelry. Get a short, easy care, run-a-comb-through-it-and-you're-done haircut.

Each airline has its own baggage policies and these are undergoing changes all the time. You need to check with your airline for its specific rules. For example, United Airlines allows each adult to check two bags, one of which may not exceed 62 inches in length, width, and height, and the total of the two may not exceed 107 inches. Each bag may weigh up to 70 pounds. If your bag weighs any amount between 70 and 110 pounds you will be charged a fee. The carry-on limit is 1 bag plus a personal bag like a pocketbook, purse, camera case or computer case. Many travelers wear a coat on to the plane and stuff the pockets with books, water bottles, candy bars, a '56 Chevy, etc. A carry-on bag must fit under your seat or in the overhead bin and cannot weigh more than 50 pounds. Some parents have taken two hard sided suitcases with wheels and two carry-on backpacks, which fit under the seat, along with a large diaper bag and camera bag. If you don't do anything to attract attention to your luggage in the states or in China, the airline and customs officials seem to employ a, "Don't tell me, I don't want to know" policy.

Within China, the total of the two items may only be 40 pounds. If you take a stroller to China it will count against your luggage allowance. However, on the return trip the stroller may be counted as part of the child's luggage. This is why you might simply buy one when you are over there. A child under two is also allowed to have a piece of luggage that does not exceed 45 inches and 22 pounds.

You should try to use one suitcase for both adults and one for the child's stuff. You can have another, but it is a luxury. One person will be carrying the baby in a Snuggli, so the other person will be doing most of the lifting and toting over cracked sidewalks and through planes, trains, and automobiles. It's not fun. Whatever you do, don't buy new luggage! Since most luggage looks the same, get some colored tape (like electrical tape) and put color stripes along the length of each piece so that they are easily identified. Bumper stickers work too.

The key is to pack light. Let me repeat that: *pack light.* You will not need a lot of outfits. One sweater, two pairs of pants—that sort of thing. Everything should be of the "no iron" variety. Since there is always the possibility that your luggage will get lost, pack some clothes in your carry-on. Some people have used a vacuum cleaner to remove the air from the suitcase. This will reduce the size and weight of the bag. Remember that you can always purchase an extra suitcase or duffel bag in Guangzhou for souvenirs. The luggage shop is right across from the White Swan.

Assume for the moment you are planning to adopt from Nanchang in Jiangxi Province, 300 miles south of Beijing, in late July. It's hot—very, very hot. You might want to take 3 pairs of slacks and 5 or more T-shirts and golf shirts. You do not really need a dress or blouse, but if you must, just take one of each. It's so hot you might want a few shorts. There is no need for a nightgown, you'll sleep in your skivvies. Forget the nice shoes and go for 2 pairs of sneakers. Take a half dozen socks and a full dozen underwear and you are all set.

If you are traveling in the winter, think about layers. Beijing and Nanjing can easily be in the 20s. Take a parka with a hood, knit hats and scarves, gloves, blue jeans, long johns, sweaters with long sleeves and turtleneck knit shirts. Take extra large T-shirts for nightshirts and for doubling as an extra layer of clothes if needed. In the winter, jeans are the ticket. You can wear them for 2 or 3 days and they won't show dirt. Bring 2 pairs of sneakers or comfortable shoes.

Do not take any jewelry with you; just a simple watch. This isn't a cruise. Why tempt fate? Pack snacks like breakfast bars—your days may be long and meals delayed. Carry something to munch on.

The boiled water in the hotel really is boiled and safe. Bring two graduated quart bottles in which to cool it and to mix formula. The hotel will also supply you with a large thermos of hot boiled water and another of cool boiled water. You can get these replenished as needed by asking the attendant on the floor any time of the day. Additionally, bottled water is sold everywhere. It comes in plastic bottles of various sizes and is cheap. Carry a bottle or two with you in the diaper bag for your own drinking needs as you go about.

Pack lots of small packages of tissues to be used in the bathrooms. Also pack small rolls of toilet paper for the same reason. One tip is to use a roll at home until it's about 2/3 used, then remove the cardboard center and collapse it. You easily can store these mini rolls in a small Ziploc bag. Baby wipes work as well. You will encounter Western-style toilet paper in the tourist hotels in Beijing and Guangzhou, but you might get the local stuff in your baby's town, or in public toilets. Chinese toilet paper looks like crepe paper, comes in tiny rolls, and is treated like gold by the hotel staffs.

Take a half dozen paper or Styrofoam cups in case you don't trust the rural hotel glasses. The big city hotel glasses are fine.

You might take a small bag of powdered Gatorade to replace electrolytes in case you get diarrhea. Just mix it in bottled water.

It is impossible to take too many pictures or too much video. You will always wish you had taken more. There is conflicting advice on what to do with your film now that the airports have machines that could radiate a ham sandwich on Mars. Some say put all film in a leaded bag and others say put your film and camera in a clear bag and hand it to the machine guy. The only safe thing to do is ask parents who have just returned how their film survived going through U.S., Hong Kong, and mainland airports.

Here are some other items that are nice to have along:
Waterless hand cleaner
Lots of plastic bags, both the Ziploc and garbage kind
Washing soap packets
Asian converter for your electronics
Small Ziplocs of powdered detergent (Tide) to wash clothes in sink
Large gallon-size Ziplocs
Shout wipes for fast cleanup of stains, burp spots, etc.
Paper towels. If you take these, remove the middle roll for easy packing
Small roll of duct tape
Some coffee singles
Travel alarm
Small dual-voltage travel hair dryer

Adult vitamins—you will get stressed and you will get tired
Travel Smith clothesline (if you pack light, you might need to do a little laundry)
Plastic shoes to wear in the shower, as the floors can be wet and grungy
Comfortable shoes to walk around in

Also take a few disposable cameras. If for any reason yours quits you can still take some pictures. Take a spare battery for your camera. Also, take an Asian converter for your recharger. If you use a video camera, replace the film cassette prior to using it all up in case one of the cassettes turns out to be defective. Tape your first meeting with your new child (be sure everyone practices with all the equipment *before* you leave). Then tape the morning after your first night with your new child. That footage will be priceless. Do not skimp on videotaping or film. There is no such thing as too much. This event will only happen once with this child.

Keep a journal or make recordings on a small tape player so you can remember all the things that happen. Take some pens to write with and maybe a crossword book to pass the time. Do not take a lot of books or books on tape. You simply will not have the time to use them. Take items you can leave behind.

A hot pot can be nice. Some plugs in the hotels are loose and you will have to fiddle around to get things to connect or charge. Bathroom plugs are special culprits and sometimes don't work at all. Some hotels have a special plug in the bathroom for razors. It works for razors, but can kill a hot pot.

Take a list of your medical allergies. If you are at risk for a medical emergency you may wish to consider purchasing medical insurance and investigating what sort of medical arrangements would be available to you in China. See the AAA+program. If you have a tendency to get carsick, take some Dramamine. Car rides over China's roads can be very bouncy. Also, take the airplane sickness bags with you when you get off the plane. They may come in handy for you or your child.

Pack KaoPectate and KaoLectrolyte Rehydration Solution that comes in dry packets that you mix as needed. This saves trying to take Pedialyte, as it would be too much liquid volume and weight.

You might take Pepto Bismol chewables to eat with each meal to coat the stomach and help prevent traveler's diarrhea, and carry artificially sweetened Kool-Aid mix to use as a rehydration fluid that can be mixed with electrolyte solutions to improve the taste.

If you are taking prescription medications with you, you may want to take a letter from your doctor describing why you need them. You will probably get away without needing it, but sometimes the customs personnel can get picky. Most of the time all you have to do really is carry them in their containers. This is also true with over-the-counter medicines.

Take a few bottles of water for the plane as well as a few for traveling in China. Be careful that you don't take too many, as the weight can be heavy. Bottled water is available in all urban cities.

Take a list of useful Chinese words and phrases or even a Chinese/English dictionary, and you will have half a chance of understanding the words. There is even an electronic Chinese/English translator, but it is a little pricey.

Consider taking jet lag medicine such as melatonin. Take Imodium for diarrhea, Cipro for anything that comes along (including diarrhea), and Bactrim or Septra (trimethoprim-sulfa) for urinary tract infections. Consult with your doctor in advance regarding all of these medicines.

If you will be traveling in the summer, take some bug spray. You should also take some hydrocortisone for bites and a spritzer fan to keep cool.

Take 400 ASA film, and you'll miss fewer shots due to low light. Watch your film, particularly if you're going through Hong Kong. The security post-9/11 X-ray equipment will zap your film. You might want to take a lead-lined bag for your 35mm and camcorder film. Here is a good article on taking film through airports and the problems people have: *http://www.magellans.com/content/art_t.jsp?ruleID=86&itemID=64&itemType=ICArticle.*

Take the usual toiletries, such as a small bar of soap, toothbrushes with paste, brush/comb, shaving cream, a razor, shampoo, deodorant, hair spray/gel, alcohol wipes, antibiotic ointment, small scissors, contact lens stuff, extra pair of glasses allergy/sinus, headache stuff, prescriptions, if any, Imodium, bottle opener, Swiss Army Knife etc, etc.

You may decide that you will listen to a portable tape or CD player on the plane. Quite frankly, you should be sleeping during the plane trip over and you won't have time to do any listening on the way back.

Take a few books, preferably about China. Leave these with your translator after you finish. They will enjoy them. News or fashion magazines also are good items to take and leave behind. Also take some playing cards and maybe a Game Boy or something small with games on it. You will only have time to read one book. Once you have your child, there is no such thing as personal time for the next 18 years.

A list of clinics and hospitals in China where traveling parents might find medical services including doctor's or staff who speak English can be found at *http://catalog.com/fwcfc/ChinaMedDirectory.htm*. Print out a copy just in case.

Scotch tape works wonders for tucking in too-large diapers on a too-small bottom. Duct tape is always handy. Also, take large freezer Ziplocs or some other poopy diaper container. A fanny pack can be very useful. Also, consider taking a small alarm clock and small flashlight. The flashlight comes in handy on the plane. Pack an empty film canister so you can put a little dirt in it from your child's home.

Since you might eat a little in your room, you might take a few paper plates and plastic knives and forks.

Some people take a saline nasal spray for the airplane. The air on a plane is desert dry. If your nasal passages get too dried out, you can more easily get a cold. A water bottle is also a must.

It doesn't really matter if you lock your suitcase or not. If someone at LAX or Hong Kong wants in, it is easy to pop.

If you take a long distance calling card, make sure you bring the access number with you. (I recommend a prepaid card.)Take the number of your adoption medical specialist in America. Also take the phone numbers of your agency. Your agency will be notified by the facilitator that you have arrived in China. Arrange for the agency to then phone or email your family to that effect as well.

3. Money

Your agency should not just give you a lump sum figure of how much money you should bring with you for in-country expenses. Rather, they should give you an itemized list of the estimated cost of traveling, such as room and board, escort fees, interpreter, document translation fees, drivers, domestic air, donation to the orphanage, gifts to officials, and hotel cost. This list will still be an estimate, however, it will give you some feel for where the money will be spent. Make sure the money is in crisp, new bills. Most should be in $100s.

Take money belts for you and your spouse. Some go around the neck, others the waist, or you can even get the leg passport/money holder. Take whatever is most comfortable and easily accessible. If you take a purse, take the kind that goes over your head and hangs across your chest. It is square and flat.

You will want to divide the money between you. Have the correct amount for the orphanage donation segregated in an envelope in your money belt. Some like the belts that go around the neck and others the ones around the waist. When you change money, be careful that you do not just open up your money belt for the world to see. There are many eyes in China.

China primarily works in cash. Crime is uncommon in China so theft is not a concern. Just use common sense and don't flash large sums around. The larger hotels will accept credit cards and exchange traveler's checks, but most other places will only accept cash. Usually you will need to take $3,000 to $3,500 for the mandatory donation to the orphanage. The provincial registration fee is $100–$200. The notary/adoption fee is $400–$700. The child's passport fee is $50–$100, and her U.S. visa fee is $335.

If you plan on using a credit card in China, call your credit card company beforehand. Many banks find the use of a credit card in China suspicious and will put a hold on your card. Ask them if they have a currency conversion charge. When you do use the card, check the exchange rate used on the card. Sometimes you get a better rate and sometimes you can get a nasty surprise when you return home. You will use the local currency (RMB) for restaurants and any items you buy for the baby or yourself.

4. Electrical Adapters/Converters

China uses Asian style electrical outlets with 220-volt/50 hertz service. Korea has both 110 and 220 outlets. Assuming your equipment is 220 capable (and most modern electronics are, but check) all you will need is an adapter plug. If you have a 110-volt only item (the U.S. is on a 110 volt/60 hertz system), you will need a converter. Note that there are two options: inverters and transformers. Inverters can handle high power devices (hair dryers, etc.) but should not be used more than short periods of time (NEVER overnight). These are in the $20 range and can be found at your local Radio Shack or Brookstone. Transformers are more expensive ($50+) and heavier, but can be used continuously, and transformers are for lower power devices (<100 watts typically). You can purchase a "Foreign Voltage Adapter" kit from Radio Shack. Inside, there is a large dual wattage converter with 5 color-coded plugs plus a chart indicating which plugs to use in various countries. All of this is further explained at *http://www.magellans.com/content/art_t.jsp? ruleID=86&itemID =95&itemType=ICArticle.*

Tips for Packing for Your Child

Generally your child's size will be smaller than her age. This is possibly due to her being raised in an institution and the associated nutritional issues. The rule of thumb is to deduct a month of development for every 3 months a child has been in an orphanage. Thus, if your child is 18 months old she will probably fit into 12-month-old-clothes. She will be larger if she is raised by a foster family. Every child is different so you should take a range of sizes. Be aware that as soon as your child begins to get proper food and medical attention at your house she will likely begin sprouting like a weed. So assume that she will fit the initial size clothes for only a short time. Take clothes that you won't grieve over if they get lost, soiled, or are so nasty after a week in China that you just throw them away. Sometimes after being with a child in close quarters with food spills, vomit, and the usual diaper action, it just isn't worth bringing the clothes back, as they now qualify as a Superfund site.

You may have heard that old rule of thumb that when buying clothes for infants and toddlers you take their age and double that for their size. For example, if your child is 12 months old double that to 24 months and that is the size you should look for. This rule applies to American-born children.

This "doubling" rule does not apply to children in Asia, especially those in institutional settings. These children usually are of a smaller stature anyway, and then add in the lack of nutrition and/or stimulation and they are just not as large as American children. One idea for Asian children that seems to work is that for every month the child is in age that is what they will weigh. For example, if the child is 16 months old, buy clothes for a 16-pound child.

If you are in Beijing, Guangzhou, or another large city and you run out of items you will be able to find replacements. Such items like diapers can be found in most large towns. However, it is not like going down to the corner store and they will be an effort to get. Thus, try to bring most of what you will need. Pack the ultra-thin types since these will take less space in your suitcase. If you want to save room, take enough (60) to last until you get to Guangzhou and then just go buy some more.

Here is a list of what to take for a baby:
A few small blankets (3) that you don't plan to take back home.
2 rompers, no more than 1 dress (I know they look cute, but you don't need them); 2 coveralls if in cold weather, 2 shortalls if in hot; 4-8 onesies, 2-4 pj's, 10 pair socks (tubes), 2-4 T-shirts, 4 regular shirts
Depending on the weather a jacket, a hat, and gloves
6-9 outfits
If your child is not walking, you do not need shoes. If you need them, you can buy them there.
Disposable diapers (10-12 per day, thin style)
Small plastic tablecloth to use as a changing pad
Large diaper bag
Unscented baby wipes (200-300)
Cheerios (at least half a box); Goldfish crackers
Instant oatmeal in individual packets
Rice cereal
Several orthodontic pacifiers with clip attachments
Anti-bacterial soap
Baby shampoo, baby wash, Baby lotion, powder, toothbrush, toothpaste, hairbrush, comb, nail clipper, thermometer (rectal, so you'll know how to do it.)
Liquid baby decongestant (baby Dimetapp)
Liquid baby acetaminophen (baby Tylenol, Motrin)
Small plastic bowls, sippy cups, spoons (plastic coating on the scoop) and 2 plastic bibs

Toys: rattle, teething rings, small stuffed animal, small blocks, keys, stacking cups

Dirty diapers go in the regular trash in your hotel room. Therefore, bring a good supply of quart-size plastic bags that can be sealed airtight such as freezer Ziplocs or equivalent. You do not want to share your room with a loose, smelly diaper overnight. An alternative is the scented diaper disposal bags with a twist tie. And please, please wash your hands after changing your baby's diaper. Your child (like all carbon-based life forms) has bacteria in her stomach that will travel from her diaper to you quicker than you can say Genghis Khan. So please wash.

Also, take garbage bags or large freezer Ziplocs for laundry and miscellaneous needs. (Ziplocs are wonderful when you are traveling.) With Ziplocs and duct tape, man can go to Mars.

Take some infant suppositories along. Sometimes, when the babies change from the formula that they have been on to yours they really get constipated. Ask your pediatrician about a formula that will be easy on their tummies— maybe one with not so much iron in it, of course then you run into the anemia question.

Take some small bubble bottles. They pack well, and are by far the most delightful toy you can take with you. Kids love them. Take bubbles for your child and as presents for the other children in the home.

(Remember that all such toys are made in China anyway so there is plenty to buy if you need some more.)

Don't forget that to a child anything can be a toy. They love stickers.

Small towels or cloth diapers for burping or sitting on your lap while eating. Some parents just use the hotel's hand towels, but you need something for when you are in transit.

Elimite (in case of scabies); Nix shampoo (in case of lice, but ask your pediatrician as it may be too strong for small children).

Diaper rash ointment for regular diaper rash (Lotrimin, Desitin). If it is a fungal diaper rash (yeast) try Nystatin cream (a prescription).

Scented diaper sacks (box of 50 available at Wal-Mart). Great for "poopy" diapers while traveling. You can also use giant freezer Ziploc bags. 2 Pacifiers and 2 clips. Some babies love them and some won't have anything to do with them.

Take several packages of baby wipes. You will go through 400 of them without breaking a sweat. Do not take the hard containers, but rather the refill packages that you can put in a Ziploc.

A few band-aids.

Pedialyte packets, Infant Mylicon (for gas). Infants get so much gas, you could drill a well.

Cornstarch baby powder for baby and mommy, especially if it is hot where you are going. Take one 4 oz. container.

Skin lotion, as your child's skin may be dry, especially after a bath. Good for you too.

Changing pads should be taken, as it is a challenge to change your child in anything like a clean environment when you are traveling. Some parents take a cheap vinyl picnic tablecloth, which they then leave in China.

Since it is very common for your child to have an ear infection or other respiratory problem, take some infant Motrin or infant Tylenol to bring the fever down and some pain drops for the ears. It is rare indeed that a child does not have such an infection, particularly during the fall and winter months. Ask your doctor if you can take an antibiotic that doesn't need refrigeration like Zithromax. Zithromax should be packed in powdered form when traveling and just reconstituted when needed. Doctors like it as it can work on both ear and respiratory infections. Of course, *never, ever give a young child aspirin*. You also have to be careful for allergic reactions if you use penicillin. For a discussion about what sort of medications to take see the April/May 2001 issue of *Adoption Medical News*.

For a toddler:
A hat, gloves, scarf
Cheerios, Goldfish, crackers (no hard candy or peanuts because of choking risk)
1-2 dozen small packs fruit sacks
4-6 containers applesauce
2-3 picture books
Toys: ball, toy cars, doll or stuffed animal, stacking cups, baby rattle, coloring books and a few crayons for the airplane, hand puppet
Sippy cups, bowls, spoons, forks, plastic bibs
Soothing cream for the skin if the child has a rash.

Benadryl (Great for flying with kids. Make sure it is the clear kind and not the pink colored kind. The pink dye can cause hyperactivity in some kids. Just what you need!)
Actifed syrup-acts like Benadryl. Good for colds. Watch the dye!

Toddlers may or may not be potty trained. Sometimes the so-called potty-trained child just has very well trained adults around them. Accidents will happen while traveling. Bring some pull-ups. Talk to others who have adopted from this age group.

Bring some toys, books, picture flash cards, crayons and coloring books, a stuffed animal, things to take apart and put together again, little dinosaurs, etc. Try to avoid stuff that will fall on the floor and roll away under the airline seats. Don't spring the toys all at once. Keep some in reserve for those boring moments while traveling or waiting for the next thing to happen. Bring a little photo album of your home, siblings, other family members, pets, your town, and talk about them.

You might also take an antibiotic ointment like Neosporin for cuts, scrapes, and infected mosquito bites. Most children's homes do not have screens on their windows so during the summer mosquitoes are prevalent.

If the child's scalp appears red or brownish-yellow in areas, cradle cap may be present. If so, take some T-Gel shampoo by Neutrogena. It helps remove the scales and oil until the scalp looks cleaner.

Make sure you have baby food for when you find yourself traveling with the baby and on the plane. You might not be able to find baby food in the store when needed. It is good to have food with you in case of a delay at mealtime. Respect your child's feeding time and don't trust that you can get baby food when you need it.

Take some lollipops, raisins, or M&Ms. Healthy bonding can begin with bribery. Jelly beans, Lifesavers, and suckers are treats the children have never had. Children also like raisins, crackers, butter or animal cookies, granola bars, and instant oatmeal. You can really start the bonding process with these sorts of treats!

If adopting an older child, remember that the child might be developmentally younger than her age and therefore you should plan on taking toys that are for a younger child. Remember also that you are not trying to bring America to your child, but rather just bring enough to tide you all over until you can get your child back to the states.

International Adoptive Families of Texas used to sell a great pediatric medical kit designed for use during trips to China. They may have discontinued selling the kit. The kit, which costs $75, contains a variety of drugs (some prescription), ointments, information and other things that experience has indicated could be useful during trips to China to pick up infants. Proceeds from the kits are used for educational programs for adoptive families and to improve conditions in orphanages. For additional information, contact 972-434-3434.

Here is another web site resource: *http://members.aol.com/jaronmink/prep.htm.*

Stroller or Snuggli

The discussion regarding whether it is better to take an inexpensive umbrella stroller or a Snuggli is one in which there is no right answer. However, here are some thoughts:

If your child weighs 15 or more pounds, a Snuggli just will not cut it. A stroller also gives a calming ride to the child. They get to sit and watch the world go by! If you are in China for a while, you may find that a Snuggli gets to be a little tiresome as you travel around to tourist spots. If you take a stroller, also pack a clear plastic rain shield for the stroller. It will not only keep out the rain but also cut down on the wind blowing on the baby.

A Snuggli really starts the bonding process. The baby is next to your heart and your smell. It's good for both of you. If you are adopting a mobile toddler and decide against a stroller, remember that a tired toddler will just quit walking and collapse where they are. When you try to pick them up, you will find they have turned into cute little lumps of unhappy lead. Bricks are lighter than a tired toddler. Umbrella strollers are readily available in China. You can delay your decision and buy one there after you get your child.

If your child was kept on her back, she may not be used to the upright position of the Snuggli. However, using a Snuggli does give you two free hands and a stroller can be awkward to carry. There are other alternatives such as the Over The Shoulder Baby Holder or Hip Hammock.

Remember that if you find you really do need a stroller you can certainly buy a cheap one in China (that's where they are made anyway) and just leave it before you get on the plane.

Gifts

Small gifts for the people who help you are an expected part of the adoption protocol. These are small gifts for the officials of civil affairs and notary offices as well as staff of the orphanage such as the director, vice director, and nannies. If your child has been in foster care, you may also wish to have gifts for the foster parents. Do not sweat too much about the selection as there is not much importance attached to the actual gift. You will simply be told to "put them over there." They do not have to be expensive, just of good quality. American-made is preferred. Do not give gifts made in China such as umbrellas, fans, clocks, or mirrors. It is thought that it is customary in China to open gifts in private. This could explain the rather impersonal nature of the gift giving and why the gifts do not seem to be appreciated in your presence.

Here are some gift ideas:

Pen and pencil sets (although they may have seen lots of these)
Leather wallets
Note cards with American scenes
Soaps
Cologne
Books in English for your translator
Postcards of your city
American magazines like *People*, *Vogue*, *Glamour*, or *Redbook*
T-shirts with American logos (especially Disney)
Marlboro cigarettes for the men

Adoption Checklist

1. Expect some bumps in the road. Everyone runs into a few and you *will* get over them. Remember that your agency and the Chinese do want the adoption to succeed. (Notice I left out the BCIS.) If something goes wrong, try to concentrate on how to move forward and solve the problem. Let go of trying to figure out who is to blame and who will pay for the mistake. Don't waste energy on anything except getting and keeping your baby happy, healthy, and safe.

2. Expect to feel out of control. In a sense you are the director of a play and the BCIS, your agency, and China are all players set in motion by you. You control the really big decisions like whether or not to adopt this child, but the little ones are out of your hands. What you cannot control you must let go. (At least this is what Helga the Hun, a time management consultant, once told me!)

3. Stay calm. You'd be surprised what a warm bath, a glass of wine, and a piece of chocolate can accomplish.

4. Treat your hosts with respect and appreciation. You are an ambassador for the next couple.

5. Do not get mad at the Chinese officials. Chew on your agency instead. Their job is to be flak catchers. Do not expect your American adoption agency or guide to meet all your needs or to tell you everything, yet do not be afraid of requesting the information and help you need.

6. Do not expect to meet your child in a calm and quiet environment. It will most likely be in a loud, public place like a hotel lobby. It will be a disjointed meeting.

7. Try to ask all the questions you have about your child's history, but do not expect a whole lot of answers. In Korea you may get quite a lot of information.

8. You may bond with your child immediately or you may not bond with your child for days or weeks, but you WILL bond with your child.

9. Do not worry if you wonder if this baby is the right baby. The idea that bells ring and angels sing when you meet your child is just a myth. Be calm, follow your instincts, and do not condemn yourself for any doubts you may have.

10. Vent your fears and frustrations to your partner or close friend. Let it out.

11. The Chinese tend to swarm around you when you go out with your baby. Don't be afraid of letting them see the baby and don't be afraid of withdrawing her from view when you feel you must. It's your decision. You are her parents now.

12. If you have never been to Asia, expect it to be completely different from anyplace you have ever been. Dorothy, you're not in Kansas!

13. Keep your paperwork in one organized packet. Put all new documents and photos in this packet. Take the packet with you whenever you must accomplish any official function. Keep this packet with you as much as possible. Always keep all passports on your person. Make sure you have extra copies of your passport pages.

14. Don't lose your sense of humor.

15. Ask other parents of children from China about their experiences. Be sure to speak to families who traveled to the same city as you and/or who have traveled during the same season.

16. Expect this experience to be one of the most exciting of your life. The trip will change your life, not just that bundle of joy.

17. If you are single, <u>seriously </u>consider having someone accompany you. Anyone traveling with you, however, should understand that this is not a sightseeing trip. You and your baby will be the central focus and concern at all times.

18. Expect to be exhausted even before you receive your child. The physical, emotional, and psychological strains on this trip are enormous. Expect to be even more exhausted once your receive your child.

19. Expect to play with your child and begin to establish your own routines with her from the very first minute you are together. Eating some meals in your hotel room makes life easier. Through trial and error make sure that the holes in your bottle nipples are large enough for a baby who is used to getting her formula rather quickly.

20. The home recipe for pedialyte (used to counteract dehydration) is one level teaspoon of sugar and one pinch of salt in eight ounces of water. Pack a few ounces of sugar and salt, and carry a teaspoon and cup measure. This is very important. If the baby becomes dehydrated, this mixture will save the day.

CHAPTER XI

Over the Wild Blue Yonder

Actually Traveling

You've gotten the great "traveling phone call," and are headed overseas. First thing is to research the city to which you will be traveling. If you are traveling to China, you can find out a lot about your city and province at *http://www.travelchinaguide.com/attraction/city_index.htm* and see many virtual tours of Chinese sites at *www.chinavista.com/travel/virtualtours.html*. You can check out your hotel at *www.cbw.com/hotel/city.htm*.

For Chinese adoptions, almost all agencies bunch families together so they travel together as a group. Having another family to "buddy" with can make the experience much more enjoyable. You share information, resources, equipment (clocks, food, diapers), and help with each other's kids. If you have to pass the time for a few days before an appointment or going home, having another family can really help to fill the hours. It can also feel safer. The best advice is to just "go with the flow." Since you are not in control of your schedule or anything else, just flow along and don't let the little things bother you.

Remember that this trip is *not* a vacation. An international adoption journey is physically tiring, emotional, and exhausting work. You will be dealing with major jet lag while running from city to city and office to office. Meeting your child for the first time is very emotionally draining. You will be changing your sleep and eating patterns. Prepare for the trip as if it were a competition, because it is. It's you against your body.

When your plane takes off for Asia, look for 3 empty middle seats before the airplane takes off so you can claim them as soon as the plane levels off. Take some warm socks for the over-the-ocean flights. As soon as you get to your seat take your shoes off and put these socks on (put them on over the ones you're wearing, if your feet tend to get cold easily). No matter what kind of feet you have they will very likely get cold before the flight is over. Also, carry a bottle of water on the plane. You will get dehydrated. As you board the plane try to locate an extra blanket in an overhead bin to take with you to your seat. It gets cold on these flights, especially if you sit next to the window. The blankets tend to be small so it's good to use one on your legs and one to wrap around your torso. Wear warm, loose, comfortable clothes on the plane. Outside it's 50 below zero at 35,000 feet, even in the summer.

A generic schedule for China might look something like this:
Day 1-Leave U.S. for China.
Day 2-Arrive in Beijing or Hong Kong.
Day 3-If in Beijing you will sightsee.
Day 4-Leave for your Province and meet your child.
Day-5-Go to civil affairs and do notary paperwork.
Days 6 and 7-Sightsee in the province.
Day 8-Pick up child's Chinese passport and notary certificate.
Day 9-Fly to Guangzhou.
Day 10-Child's pre-visa physical. Sightsee in Guangzhou.
Day 11-Visa trip to U.S. Consulate. More sightseeing.
Day 12-Return to United States.
While each trip is different, 10 to 12 days is the usual time frame.

U.S. Consulates

The United States' Chinese Embassy is in Beijing. It is located at 3 Xiu Shui Bei Jie, Chaoyang District; Tel. [86] [10] 6532-3431. The U.S. has consulates in Guangzhou, Hong Kong, Shanghai, Chengdu, and Shenyang. Most parents obtain their child's immigrant visa from the Guangzhou Consulate. You can reach the Adoption Visa Unit at the U.S. Consulate in Guangzhou at No. 1

Shamian South Street, Guangzhou, PRC 510133; Tel: 011-86-20-8121-8000; Fax: 011-86-20-8121-7000; EMAIL: *GuangzhouA@state.gov*. The web site has a very good summary of the adoption process at *http://www.usembassy-china. org.cn/guangzhou/acivu/*.

Beijing

If you fly into Beijing your plane will likely park on the tarmac and you may have to climb down the stairs to a waiting bus. You then must elbow your way through the baggage carousel crowd to get your bags. One thing you'll notice about Beijing is the bad pollution. That isn't fog you are seeing.

Beijing is the capital of the People's Republic of China. It is not only the nation's political center, but also its cultural, scientific, and educational heart. It is a key transportation hub. Beijing is famous for its ancient architecture and historic scenery.

You might stay at the Poly Plaza Hotel or the Tianlun Dynasty Hotel. Both are western style hotels. The Poly Plaza is just an average hotel. It has some age on it. The rooms are of an adequate size, but the carpets are soiled. The rooms have hair dryers and 110-volt outlets in the bathroom. In the main area of the room, there is a safe and small refrigerator. A large thermos of boiled drinking water is available. Information on the Tianlun is at: *http://www.chinatour.com/tdh/a.htm*.

If your agency sends you through Beijing, read one of the many books published on Beijing and its history before you go. In addition to the Lonely Planet and Fodor guides, there is also a pretty good travel guide by Frommer. One hour to the northwest of the city is the Badaling section of the Great Wall. In the middle of the city is the former Imperial Palace, known as the Forbidden City, the largest and best-preserved ancient architectural complex in the world. The emperors of the Ming (1368-1644) and Qing (1644-1911) Dynasties lived their lives there. On the western edge of the city is the Summer Palace with gardens, beautiful hills, and winding corridors crowned with high pavilions. Further north are the Ming Tombs, the magnificent mausoleums of 13 Ming Dynasty emperors.

Safety Concerns

During the adoptive process there is bound to be something going on in China that will give you pause. Just remember that your agency will not send you to China if there is a real safety concern. When the U.S. blew up the Chinese Embassy in Belgrade, the effect on the adoption process was minor. The U.S. Consulate in Guangzhou was closed for two business days, but they still managed to conduct most of their adoption-related business off-site, minimizing any delays. U.S. citizens did feel some discomfort in the face of the orchestrated anti-American demonstrations, but all this did is make them spend more time in their hotel rooms and less being tourists.

Next year and the year after that there will be something else. Just keep your head, and when the time comes to travel take your cue from your agency. After all, they should be in almost daily contact with the facilitator in China whose job it is to keep you safe. As to personal safety, there isn't really any issue. You almost have to tape $100 bills to the outside of your clothes for someone to steal them. There is plenty of corruption in China, but crime does not extend down to the personal level.

Chinese Culture

Americans wear black at a funeral, Chinese wear white. We think dragons are monsters, Chinese see them as symbols of a deity. Americans believe Bud is the national bird, while the Chinese drink less due to many having alcohol intolerance as they lack an alcohol-metabolizing enzyme.

In China little old ladies will love to come up to you on the street. They are curious about your child. They will pull back the blanket and peer at her face. They will zip up zippers, rewrap scarves, pull up socks, pull down pants legs, and generally cluck and fuss about. They will want you to put socks, shoes and a hat on your child even if it is 100 degrees. They are the "clothing police." Just smile as they say "Lucky baby!" and "Happy mother!" and you reply "Shay shay" (thank you).

Shopping

It may be that you find yourself with a little time to kill. The answer is to go shopping! All over China are Friendship Stores, which are government owned. Russia used to have the same sort of thing. They are used to sell goods to foreigners for hard currency. Usually there is a restaurant inside. Lunch is served family-style, and the meals are good. You can buy cold beer, bottled water, and Coca Cola. The stores are stocked with good quality souvenir-type items. You might find quality cloisonné, jade, clothing, and assorted merchandise. You can find traditional Chinese outfits and kimonos for your child.

Some people buy an alcoholic drink called Mao Tai. It is one serious kind of booze and will grow hair on parts of your body where you don't want any. Buy it, but do not drink it on the trip. Many parents buy jasmine and oolong tea and silk outfits for their child.

If you have never bargained overseas, ask a friend for the unwritten rules before you travel. Generally, you should not show the clerk that you are very interested in the item. Be prepared to walk away. Ask the price but don't look too anxious. Have a price in your head at which you are willing to buy. Don't be embarrassed to make a lowball offer. If you don't like the price quoted by the clerk, start walking away. Keep walking if the vendor does not reduce the price. If you want to buy several dolls or other items, demand a discount for a bulk purchase (think of presents for friends). Ask questions regarding any discounts. Be friendly throughout the process. Remember that if they say "no," that doesn't really mean "no". Be flexible on buying a less popular color or model. Check to see if there is even a slight scratch or other damage as you might be able to use that to get a slight discount at the higher-end stores. Make sure the salesperson knows you have adopted, as they might give you a sympathy discount. Finally, you can always practice the famous "crunch, whereby you ask for an extra after you have made the deal but before paying the money.

Be sure to practice the phrase, "*Boo yow!*" Say it firmly. It means, "Do not want" You will need to say it often at the tourist attractions. Of course, if you see something you like, buy it because you will not see it again on your trip, you won't find it any cheaper in the U.S., and you will not be able to go back again and get it later.

Provinces and Cities

One web site with a lot of maps of the major cities is at *http://www.china-tour.com/map/a.htm*. It has maps of Nanchang and Guangzhou and every other large place. Once you know your province you can then contact one of the directories or lists where families that have adopted from there communicate. They can give you specific information about adopting in your city and even from the particular children's home. You can find a long list at *http://www.chinaconnectiononline.com/dirslist.htm*. A really great web site for learning about your province and city is at *http://www.magma.ca/~mtooker/cities/index.htm*. Here is some information about one of the more popular provinces:

JIANGXI

Jiangxi Province lies to the south of the Yangzi River, about 400 km (250 miles) southwest of Shanghai and 300 miles from Beijing. The province has 36 million people. Most of Jiangxi consists of mountains and hills. One of the best web sites on adopting from Jiangxi is at *http://www.gurrad.com/china/*. This web site has links to the weather in Nanchang, hotels, and lots of pictures of Nanchang. It gives a brief description of each hotel and of various orphanages in the province. One family's story of their adoption trip to Jiangxi can be found at *http://www.geocities.com/Heartland/Garden/9457/*. They have pictures of Beijing and Nanchang including the Lakeview Hotel. There is also an email group for those that have adopted from Nanchang at *http://groups.yahoo.com/group/NanchangFamilies*.

If you are headed from Beijing to the city of Nanchang in Jiangxi Province, then you might fly on a China Xinjia Airlines airplane. These are smaller commuter-type airplanes. At the airport in Nanchang you will deplane on the tarmac, just like we used to do in the 1960s. You will walk into a small, decrepit terminal building. It used to be a military facility and it has constantly leaking water. In the summer the humidity and heat are quite high so be prepared for a very muggy visit. You then wait for your agency's bus to show up.

Nanchang has a population of 2 1/2 million. It has department stores with all of the usual child necessities like diapers, formula and clothes. So if you forget something or decide to save the weight, you can find these items in Nanchang. Nanchang is a rather poor city and the poverty will surprise you.

Many families stay at the Lakeview Hotel in Nanchang, which overlooks a lake (what a surprise!). It is a top hotel. Everything is well kept and clean. It has cribs for the babies. There are no hair dryers in the rooms. There are a refrigerator and two thermoses with boiled drinking water. There is a 110-volt switch in the bathroom and a U.S. switch (220 volt) at the desk. All the rooms in the hotel overlook the 4th floor lounge, so the hallways are open. The Lakeview is not within walking distance of any shopping areas and if you go in the summer you won't really feel up to walking around. Some parents do take in the sights while in Jiangxi such as the Teng Wang Pavilion, Jiangxi Arts & Crafts Center, and People's Park. This province is known for its porcelain. The Teng Wang Pavilion is 1,300 years old and six stories high.

In the summer Jiangxi is very hot. You should pack lightweight cottons and dress for comfort. The flight to Guangzhou is only about 70 minutes. Your child will probably come from the Nanchang Municipal Social Welfare Institute or Gao An, although there are many others. The Director of the Nanchang Institute is Chen Ling Ling. The Nanchang Municipal Social Welfare Institute houses about 500 children, many of them from outlying areas. You can find some pictures at: *http://my.execpc.com/~microop/orphan.html*, *http://www.gurrad.com/china/nanchang03.htm*, and *http://www.gurrad.com/china/nanchang04.htm*.

General Procedure in the Province

After meeting your child in the hotel, you will gather your paperwork and go to the Office of Civil Affairs to complete the adoption. You can also go to the provincial Notary. The director of the Civil Affairs Office may ask you the usual questions, to wit:

1) Why do you wish to adopt a baby from China?

2) What plans do you have for her education?

3) Are you in good health?

4) What are your occupation and income?

5) Verify other information such as age, address, etc.

Your thumbprint (in red ink) will be placed on top of your signature on each document. You will need some extra passport photos. If you forget, the Civil Affairs Office has a camera and will take photos for a fee. This is where you also make your $3,000 orphanage "donation." The fee for the Civil Affairs Office is $100 and for the notary it is $200-$300. Later you will receive the child's Chinese passport, orphanage documents, adoption certificate, medical records, child's birth certificate, and abandonment certificate. Proofread the notary's documents for errors in spelling your name, child's name, address, etc. Now is the time to fix any typographical errors, not in Guangzhou and not in the United States. Some think that it is important that the child's American name be correctly spelled on the Chinese passport. What is more important is that the name be spelled correctly on the adoption certificate. This will prevent any silly problems at the Social Security office back in the United States. If you thought the BCIS was ridiculous, wait until you have a problem with Social Security.

The adoption certificate from the notary will say something to the effect that, "This is to certify that consulting with [child's] guardian [parent's name] is willing to adopt [child] as their daughter. Their adoptive relationship will be established as of the issuing date of this certificate. [Parents' name] are [child's name] adoptive mother and father. [Child's name] English name is [so and so]."

The birth certificate will say…"This is to certify that [child's name] (female) was born on [date], her natural parents and her birth place are unknown."

The abandonment certificate will say "This is to certify that, through investigation, [child's name] (female, born on [date]) was abandoned on the side of a street in [whatever] County. She was found and sent to our institute by Civil Affairs Bureau of [whatever] County on [date] and later settled in our institute. Though we went around and made inquiries for two months, we could not find her natural parents. She really is an abandoned child."

Again, before you leave the province make sure you proofread your documents for typographical errors and other inaccuracies in the English translations. It is a lot easier to have the translation re-done if you still have access to the orphanage, local civil affairs, or notary officials.

Medical Issues

In Chinese adoptions it is very common for the children to have respiratory infections. You should travel with some children's antibiotics as these are unavailable in the provinces. Take some sterile tongue depressors. The Swan Hotel in Guangzhou has a decent clinic and can help, but you may find yourself having to play doctor before you get there.

Just to illustrate the level of available medical care, the Children's Hospital of Nanchang has no English-speaking doctor, nor does the word "antibiotic" translate well. Chinese medicine typically is very different from Western medicine, focusing much more on herbal remedies rather than prepared drugs. The doctor sits on a wooden stool at a tiny table. Lying on top of the table is a pile of used tongue depressors. His instruments are a little rubber tomahawk for testing reflexes, a stethoscope, and a few other items. The hospital has no instrument to check for ear infections. There is no otoscope, and the doctor may or may not wear a headlamp. You feel like you've entered the Twilight Zone and returned to the 1950s. It's time again for poodle skirts and saddle oxfords. Payment can be in cigarettes.

The doctor might give a prescription of penicillin shots and send you to the "pharmacy." The "pharmacy" has rows of blue chairs with overflowing potty basins every tenth chair. Held up by their parents, the diaper-less dandies do their thing. The flies swarm and the smell is overwhelming.

You go to the "pharmacy" window where you are given a black, bitter-smelling cough medicine in a six-inch-long test tube-type vial with a cap. Now for the shot counter. This is a bank of sliding windows (like an old-fashioned bank) with Nurse Kratchit stationed at the windows. In front is a shelf, waist high, about two feet deep, with a vinyl pad on it. The parent is supposed to pull the child's pants down, the child is backed up to the window and sits or stands on the pad, and then the shot is given in the child's backside.

They will test for penicillin reaction, but Massachusetts General it's not. It's not even the Peace Corps clinic in Zamboango. Since all antibiotics can do a number on little kids' stomach systems, you should always take some Pedialyte with you.

If you bring your own drugs, you might study a cheat sheet of when to use them. For example, antibiotics may be in order (but ask your pediatrician) if your child has had three days of a fever of less than 103 degrees, or irritability with fever, pulling ears, thick rhino rhea, or other symptoms. It is important that the antibiotic not need refrigeration and cover the spectrum of medical problems, including otitis media, pneumonia, and furuncles of the scalp secondary to *Staphylococcus aureus*. You should try to have the pharmacist give you dry powder with the correct amount of liquid in a separate bottle for reconstitution.

Bottles and Formula

Take several travel bottles and 6 to 8 nipples of assorted sizes and shapes. Your child will experiment until she chooses the size nipple that works best for her. You can also take a lot of nipples already sterilized in a Ziploc bag and just kept using clean ones.

Do take a tri-cut "toddler" nipple, as a common problem is that the American small baby nipples simply do not provide nourishment fast enough for these kids. The holes in the Chinese bottles are much larger and the children will get frustrated with the smaller holes in the American nipples. Many parents use scissors or a small knife to make the holes larger and then transition back to a medium flow when they return home. Take about 8 bottles split between 8 ounce and 4 ounce bottles.

If you take the Playtex kind with the disposable liners, also take a few regular Gerber bottles. Some children just will not drink out of the disposable liner type. The Avent brand works well. About 100 liners of the 8 ounce and 4 ounce each are more than enough. When you are in transit, you can fill bottles with plain, boiled water to carry. Then portion out the proper amount of powdered formula in empty 4 ounce liners. Close the liner up with a rubber band or scotch tape and it is ready to mix with the water when you need it. Be sure to leave a little room in the bottle for mixing. There is no need to worry about spoilage if you do this on a daily basis. Do not stockpile them days in advance. Take about 4 bottle holders.

Many pediatricians recommend taking a milk-based formula such as Similac with Iron or Enfamil with Iron. Others recommend Lactofree (a milk with no lactose sugar, but also no soy protein), as many people of Asian descent have a lactose intolerance (sometimes it is a milk protein allergy, which is slightly different). This intolerance often does not manifest itself until the children are older, however. Lactofree seems to be the closest in taste to the Chinese formulas used in most orphanages. Soy formula can sometimes constipate the children, but some agencies recommend it as about 10% of Chinese are lactose intolerant. Formula powder packs well, and for a two-week trip 4 to5 cans will be more than enough. Liquid formula is too heavy and bulky to pack.

You can safely use the water provided in the thermos supplied in your hotel room. Take your own thermos with a narrow spout or lid for easier pouring while in dining rooms, on buses, or on planes. A funnel is also helpful for transferring hot water into the thermos without burning yourself.

To ease the transition to U.S. baby formulas, some people mix the formula in a lesser strength for a few days. This avoids some problems with constipation and stomachaches. Usually powdered formula in the U.S. is mixed at a ratio of one scoop to 2 ounces of water. You may wish to mix it for a day at a ratio of one scoop to 4 ounces of water, then one scoop to 3 ounces of water for a day. If your child refuses the change in formula, Chinese baby formula (actually made by American companies) is readily available from Friendship Stores. The same is true in many other countries. One scoop of Chinese formula to one ounce of water (1 ounce is about 30 cc of fluid) seems to be the correct ratio, but double-check this. After one or two days of using the Chinese formula, start gradually mixing in the American formula.

Do not repack the powdered formula in plastic bags to save space in the luggage. The tins do not take up that much space and are hermetically sealed. You open them only as you need them. If you repack the formula, you will never achieve a totally sterile transfer from tin to bag. Some mold, fungi spores, and bacteria will get in, as well as moisture, for a bag just can't be sealed as well as that tin.

Babies under about 6 months will have typically just been on Chinese baby formula, which is sweeter than American formula, but has little protein and fewer calories than American formula. In some orphanages, only formula is used up to about 8 months of age. Eventually they add rice powder to thicken the formula and add food value. The Chinese baby bottles are simple "straight" bottles, usually with very large holes cut in the nipples so that the baby just swallows rather than actually doing much sucking. If your baby objects to switching to American formula add one teaspoon of sugar per 6 ounces of formula for a few days and then wean her off of the sugar in a week or two. Most babies are eating well by day two or three and you can start to see some weight gain. Don't be surprised if they gain 3 or 4 pounds by the end of the first month. This is why you shouldn't get too attached to those initial baby clothes. Your child will blow right through those sizes.

You can take some rice cereal to offer a 5-6 month old baby, but it is not necessary. You've already substantially boosted the calories by the formula change and you can start up the cereal once you get home. You might pack a Ziploc of prunes in case your child has a slight case of constipation from the travel and diet change. You can puree them with hot water.

Meeting Your Child

There are two ways to meet your child: in your hotel or in the welfare center. The problem with the process established by the agencies is that they rush you into meeting your child as soon as you arrive in your province. Unless you have stopped over to sightsee in Hong Kong or Beijing, you are exhausted and the trip has barely begun. If you discover that your trip will not include a day or two of sightseeing and recuperation before meeting your child, then you must plan the trip like an adventure race. Make sure the primary caregiver gets the most rest.

If you meet your child at the welfare center, this might be the scenario: You arrive in the province and are taken to a hotel where you meet the welfare center director. Your group gets in little taxicabs or perhaps a bus and you are driven as if hellhounds were on your trail through areas of extreme poverty on roads that resemble no road you have ever seen. You are numb to it all. In the middle of nowhere, in the middle of the night, with no introduction, you arrive at the welfare center and meet your child. Your mind and body feel disconnected from what your eyes are showing you. The staff places the group in a stark room, wakes up the babies one by one, and simply hands them out.

They give you an unbelievably small baby: This one is yours, they say. And with that you become parent and daughter. The years of waiting are over.

One of the neat things that will occur is that the husband will become the center of the child's attention. A lot of these children, particularly the infants, have never seen a man or heard a man's voice before. They have been surrounded by women caretakers and doctors. It is unusual for a man to have much to do with childrearing in China. This new creature with the whiskers will be brand new to them. They will learn quickly that they can get him to do practically anything they want by simply smiling. It's in the DNA.

Start the cameras!

Do not be surprised if your child appears scared and is quiet. This is normal. After all, she has never met you before and there are all these people surrounding her. This may last for a few days while your child gets used to you and then suddenly she will blossom! They really do change once you get them home. Don't put expectations on yourself about how you or your child should react at that "first meeting." Let nature take its course.

On the other hand, if the child was in a foster home then she might be very distraught at leaving the only home and person she has known. She might cry "Aiya! Aiya!" (Auntie! Auntie!) and pound on your hotel room door. This is actually a good sign, as it means she has bonded with a human being and can do so again. At the same time, it is distressing for both of you. Just take it slow, bribe her with Cheerios and toys, and it will pass. It might take a few hours or a few days, but it does get better.

At some point, you will be told that you can now discuss your child with the children's home doctor. This is when you pull out your written questions and start to check them off. You would have been given only the bare amount of information and, quite frankly, you won't get a whole lot more. It is not a very open exchange of information. That is one of the few negatives with adopting from China. Yet it does no harm in asking the questions. It is particularly important that one of you not get so caught up in the moment that you forget to really look at the child and ask questions relating to her current condition. Ask if she has recently been sick, and if she has had any shots that morning or that week. Look for little red dots that would indicate shots. If she is fussy, check her temperature and make sure she is passing liquids. Of course, it could just be that she is overwhelmed by the whole experience of leaving her auntie and the only environment she has ever known.

Some meetings are emotional and some are not. There is no right or wrong. Bonding doesn't have to happen in a nanosecond. Fireworks and bells don't have to go off. Nowhere is it written that the earth must move under your feet. Everyone is different. Just know that there are plenty of parents who have reacted just like you, whatever your reaction may be. You may feel a great amount of pressure to conform to the expected reaction. Be true to yourself. Parents have bonded instantly, in a week, or at the end of a month or so after returning home from the trip. It is common for that certain feeling to grow as the days and weeks go by and suddenly you look back and, like a flower in full bloom, you can't imagine ever living without this child. You have to give both yourself and your child time. Remember that the family being created doesn't just start with you adopting this child, but also with this child adopting you.

In this society of ours the burden has grown on parents to become instant child development experts. The Denver Developmental Screening Test is one place to start. You should be able to get a copy from your pediatrician. It covers all the developmental activities that children should be able to do at various ages 0-6 years old. You can order it from Denver Developmental Materials, Inc., P.O. Box 371075, Denver, CO 80237-5075; 303-355-4729; 800-419-4729.

Here are some things to check if you are able to see the infant unclothed. Look for deformities and birthmarks. Look for malformed genitals. Boys will not be circumcised, so be aware of that. Put the baby on her tummy and look at the back of the legs for creases where the knees bend and at the buttocks. The creases should be the same on both legs. If they are not, the baby might have a hip problem, which tends to make her favor one side. While the baby is on her tummy, run your thumbs up the spine checking for unusual curvature. Turn the baby over and see if she has a painless full range of motion with arms and legs. Check the hands to see if she clenches and unclenches her fists. You want both. Give the child a rattle to hold and see how she grabs it. While she has one toy, give her another and watch how she figures out this dilemma. Does she reach equally with both hands? Can she pass the toy from one hand to the other? Can she find the toy if she drops it? It is normal for the toys to go into the mouth, and it would be abnormal if toys did not go into the mouth sometime. If you have a flashlight, shine it into one eye and watch the pupil constrict; then do the other eye. The speed at which the pupil constricts and dilates should be the same for each eye. The baby should show some realization at having had a light shined in her eyes. Hold the light about 18 inches away from the baby and slowly move it across from left to right and back. The baby's eyes should track the light together without crossing or drifting relative to each other. While you're doing all this, listen for vocalizations and watch for smiling. Both are good. Have your spouse stand on one side of the baby and clap hands one time. The baby should turn eyes and face toward the direction of the clapping. If not, try again and try doing it on the other side. If the child cannot find the source of the sound, she might have a hearing problem. Look closely at the face and head. The head should be perfectly symmetrical left to right.

The hair, if there is any, will normally lack luster and body. After changing to an American diet the hair will completely change texture, body, and appearance. The eyes should be on the same level and same depth. The distance between the eyes across the nose should be about the same as the opening of the eye itself. If this distance is unusually wide between the eyes it could indicate Fetal Alcohol Syndrome, although Asians tend to naturally have a wide distance. The white part of the eyes should be white, not red, pink, gray, or yellowish. The iris, the colored part of the eye, should be flecked with multiple colors if you look very closely, but there should not be a brown or yellow ring around the outside of the iris. The ears should be at the same height on the head and look the same left to right. The lobes might be attached or detached, but both should be the same. The lobes may be very small due to a lack of sucking because the nipple holes are so large. Make sure both ear canals are properly located inside the ear and they are unobstructed. You won't have the tools to examine the eardrums, so don't worry about that. The nose should look normal with two separate and distinct nostrils. Look for the ridge on the upper lip between the center part of the nose and top lip. This is the philtrum. Lack of a ridge is another indication of FAS, yet in infants ridges can be difficult to detect. See if the baby will crawl or even stand up. Some stand even before coordinating the crawling motion. Can she do the push-up needed to get into crawling position? Do both legs cooperate equally? Does she turn her neck painlessly? Can she sit up? Can she go from a crawling position to sitting and back again? Pick the baby up and hold her in your arms. She should show curiosity about your face, jewelry, glasses, or watch.

One last thought to consider. Your child is not adopted. Instead, your daughter "was" adopted on this date but afterwards she is simply your daughter. "Adoption" and "birth" are terms that describe the ways that children enter families. They are not descriptive terms about children or families.

Questions for the Director

After meeting with your child, you will then be allowed to meet with the children's welfare center director and ask questions. Prepare your questions ahead of time, as you will be so distracted by your child and the whole emotional experience that you will forget what to ask. Generally you want to find out as much about the child's living patterns as possible. This will make it easier to transition her to your home.

Being in a foreign place is intimidating. You have the added stress of having just met your child, and you probably feel like you should not cause waves. You don't want to be the ugly American. However, in a way, by asking these questions at this time you are fighting for your child's personal history. It is your first advocate fight for your child. No one has as much interest in these questions and answers as you and your child. A lack of assertiveness will cost you the only chance you will ever have to have these many questions answered. The truth is that your gut instinct will tell you a lot when you first see a child and you should trust your instincts, however, you should still ask questions and obtain as much information as you can.

Ask about your child's nap schedule and sleeping habits. How long and when does she sleep? What is her typical schedule for a 24-hour period? What type of bed does she sleep in? By herself?

What kind of foods does she like? What do you feed her? How much? When? Does she drink milk? How is the food prepared? Does she have a favorite food? Does she have a food she dislikes or reacts badly to? What is the feeding schedule?

When and how does she go to the bathroom? Does she have a cribmate? Does she have a favorite friend? What does she spend most of her time doing? What is she good at? What is hard for her? Has she had any prior illnesses, accidents, or injuries? How does she act when sick?

How does she bathe? Alone? With other children? In the tub? In the shower? Is the water hot, cold, or warm? How long is the bath?

What makes her happy? What toys, games or songs does she like? What does she like to do most when playing outside? What makes her angry? Upset? How does she react when she has done something wrong, or when she is tired?

What is her story? Are there any baby pictures of her that I can have or get? Where and how was she brought to the children's home? Who named her? Does she have a pet name or nickname? What do you know about her biological parents? You might try to get the director off to the side to answer these and other questions about your child's family history. She might know, but it might not be written down anywhere.

You may also want to ask if the child has (or previously had) any siblings or half-siblings anywhere in the orphanage system. Have they been adopted? By Americans? It can be difficult and expensive to attempt to acquire this information later, and your agency probably will not be interested in helping you, as it creates work and expense for them without generating revenue.

Are there any mementos of her life that I can keep? A favorite toy? A favorite shirt? You will be surprised at how much a young child will later want something of her past just to hold. Conversely, an older child may wish to forget.

Ask all about the time your child has spent in the children's home, how she arrived, with whom, and what she did on different milestone dates. You might try to fill in the gaps in her baby history, as these items become important to kids as they grow older.

Take pictures of the caretakers/foster parents and have them write their names, and if possible a small greeting to your child to be remembered by or something they remember special about your child. One nice touch is to take some pretty writing paper and have the caregivers write a letter to your child. You can then give it to her when she is old enough. Give any leftover paper to the caregivers as a gift.

Ask to have the complete medical record on your child explained, even if you already have heard much of this when you accepted the referral. You may obtain more information regarding the child's medical conditions, which you can then pass on to your pediatrician when you return home. Ask about the medical history of the parents and any siblings. Ask why they applied that diagnosis and what was the medical evidence. Look for how the child is similar/different from others in the age group. Ask about the routine the child is used to. Take measurements yourself. Ask the primary caregiver for her impressions of the child and the personality. If the child is fussy, look for reasons why—hungry, tired, gas, shoes too tight (shoes rarely fit), etc. These things will help you evaluate the child.

If you are allowed to see the children's home, ask to see the child's play area and sleeping quarters and take pictures. This may not be allowed as they are protective of the other children, but some baby homes will give you a complete tour!

You might gather some background information that may be of interest to your child later such as age of the facility, number of children there (average and right now), number of caregivers, and number of kids in their group or in their room. Ask where the birth parents were from if from another city. Does your child have a favorite caregiver, playmate, or toy? What treatments or tests would the orphanage doctor recommend for the child after you return home? Has the child been baptized? If so, are there any mementos? Some homes maintain photo histories on children and will allow you to purchase or give you photos of your child when they were younger. This can be important to your child when she is older.

If you adopt an older child, make sure you ask the children's home what information they have told the child about you. You should ask if the child remembers her birth parents. Also, with older children you might want to know more about their mental state. Some of these questions can tip you off to attachment issues, therefore, you might ask:

Has the child ever bonded with a caregiver in the children's home?

How does your child treat the other children in her age group? This could be important if you have other children at home.

Does she receive and give affection easily? Does she have good eye contact?

What are her temperament and personality like? Is she easily disciplined?

How is her attention span?

Is she equal in language and physical development with the other children in her home age group? Just remember they will likely all be delayed somewhat.

Some developmental red flags might be poor eye contact, being socially withdrawn, engaging in self-stimulating behavior or self-injurious behavior, aggression, and hyperactivity.

Here are some other possible questions. You may not want all of this information. Also, it is not likely the Chinese will know all the answers. They may even roll their eyes when you start asking the questions on the "American list." But if you don't ask, you don't get. (This is an old Maclean family proverb.)

Birth Mother Information

In general, the majority of abandoned children in China are from married households having older sisters. Ask about the birth mother's date of birth, the city where she currently lives or used to live, and the city of her birth. Ask about her appearance and personality, her general health, her education, and specific schools. Try to get information on her career/work specifics, and any other information that would help to fill in your child's story—information about the birth mother's personal struggles, a description of reasons for her decision, her situation in life, health, and family health history. Try to get information about the specific timing of entry into the registry and relinquishment papers signed (or parental rights terminated).

Ask about her relationship with the birth father, the circumstances of pregnancy and birth, the condition of her health during pregnancy, if the pregnancy was full term, and if the pregnancy or delivery involved complications. Seek information regarding the birth mother's parents, siblings, etc. Ask if there are any children living with the birth mother, i.e., ask about those children. Is the father of the siblings also the father of your child? Inquire about the talents and interests of the birthmother.

Birth Father Information

Ask for such information as his first name, his last name, his general appearance, his personality, his general health, his date of birth, the city in which he currently lives, and any cities in which he used to live. Also ask about his education, specific schools he attended, his career/work specifics, and seek any other information that would help to fill in your child's story. Try to get specifics about the birth father's personal struggles, a description of reasons for his decision, his situation in life, his military background, his education, his health, and his family's health history. See what you can learn about his relationship with the birth mother, and seek information regarding the birth father's parents, sibling's talents, and interests. All of this information will become very important to your child as she grows up.

Actual Birth History

See what kind of health information or general information regarding the circumstances of pregnancy and birth they will give you. What about the birth mother's health during pregnancy? Try to get prenatal care information, prenatal records, the original birth certificate, and other medical records. Ask for records about immunizations, any drugs given to the birth mother during childbirth, or to your child afterwards. Ask about any allergies or reactions to such drugs, and any hospital records.

Orphanage Caregivers, Director, and Doctor

Describe my child, her favorite likes and dislikes…toys, food, games, sleeping, and eating patterns, special relationship with any caregiver(s), personality, how she relates to other children and adults, any favorite stories or friends? Developmental milestones: roll over, crawl, smile, sit up, first tooth, solid food. Special events, celebrations, or memories? Any other visitors who inquired or visited my child? Original relinquishment papers or other documents?

Health Care at Orphanage

Health when arrived at orphanage and while at orphanage? Discuss specific diagnosis from referral medical and treatment—-what, when, severity, when recovered? Names of doctors or nurses while in orphanage? Approximate ages in year of adoption? Health information or medical records while in orphanage? Original birth certificate or other records? Immunizations? Any drugs used? Any allergies or reactions? Growth records, weight records? Milestone records or memories? Ever in isolation or in hospital? Did she go directly from hospital to orphanage? When? Any medical records I can take with me? Other people special to my child?

Baptism

Has the child been baptized? If so, when, what is the priest's name and his church affiliation (Christian, Muslim for some families), what is the location of the church, is there a certificate of baptism, cross or other memento of the baptism? If possible, meet and thank the priest and get a photo of him. Ask if it is possible to see your child's baptismal records and to photograph them. Ask them to describe their baptisms. Is there a full immersion? Who performed it? Do you remember when? Get the church address(es) and priest's name(s)

Ask caregivers to write a letter to your child about what she was like as a baby/young child and include a message from you. Go to see her birth mother/parents' neighborhood and home and take photos. See some of the city where your child was born. Immediately write a description in your journal.

You may want to take a tape measure and measure the child's head circumference yourself. Try to use a paper tape rather than an elastic one. As far as height goes, infants and young toddlers are usually measured lying down. Standing measurements are typically started at about two years old. If you can, observe how your child interacts with other children. Does she play quietly by herself or join in noisily with the others? Is she a chatterbox with her friends? Is she outgoing or withdrawn?

If you are planning to send information back to an IA doctor in the states before making your decision, find out from your agency or the guide where the best place is to fax or email that information. There have been instances where parents have decided not to continue with the adoption. It is rare, but it has happened. There have also been instances where a child was so seriously sick that the Chinese offered another child. It is like they are embarrassed if things do not go well. You can imagine the roller coaster of emotions when a couple is asked if they want a different child.

CHAPTER XII

Homeward Bound

From Ugly Duckling to White Swan

After you leave your province you will need to travel to Guangzhou. The Guangzhou Airport is bigger and more modern than the one you left. It is not quite up to U.S. standards, but you no longer care. You have your child. Avoid the gray market exchangers prowling the Guangzhou Airport. You never know if the money they give you is real or not. Just use official exchangers.

Guangzhou is a small village of 7 million people. It is a more modern city than others in China. The high-rise residential buildings are less decrepit and signs of urban revival and investment are all around. The traffic is very heavy, but not chaotic. The United States has established its immigrant visa office for adoptees at the consulate in Guangzhou. Your stay will be at least 3 days and probably 5. On the first day you will take the baby's photos for her visa and complete her medical exam. On the next day you will go to the U.S. Consulate for the visa interview. On the third day you visit the consulate and pick up the child's visa. After that you can make a 40-minute flight on China Southern to Hong Kong, lay over for a day, then fly out the next.

Most agencies try to place their clients in the White Swan Hotel (five stars), which overlooks the Pearl River. After your stay in the province it is like a piece of heaven. The only time it is difficult to find a room is during the large trade festival in October. The White Swan is on Shaiman Island. This used to be a sandbar, but when Canton became the trading center for the west it was diked and filled in and the western trade missions were built on it. The Chinese wanted to wall off the bad influence of the west and the west wanted to wall off the Chinese. At night all Chinese had to leave the island by crossing over the canal.

The White Swan is very popular with families since it is about 100 yards from the U.S. Consulate. The White Swan's web site is at *http://www.white-swan-hotel.com/eng/Public/index.asp.* Other hotels that some parents stay in are the Dong Fang and Victory Hotels, but the White Swan is the cool place to be. It has an incredible lobby with a neat waterfall and cage of parakeets, a pool, and lots of shops. The rooms are somewhat small. There are cribs, but no 110-volt plug-ins, although housekeeping can set you up with whatever you might need. There's a refrigerator, but no hair dryer. Just remember that on the elevator buttons the first floor is below the lobby.

It is quite normal for you to want some quiet time with your child in your hotel room. There are snack foods readily available in any of the hotels. There is also room service. It's not that expensive and you can refrigerate what you don't use. Some hotel meals are part of your package. You can fill a bottle with juice for use later at the hotel's breakfast buffets. You can take bananas, Cheerios, and Rice Krispies for snacking later. There is no rule that says you must get out and tour the countryside everyday. If you are worried that your child is becoming dehydrated, try the fruit milk—a coconut children's drink that no child can resist.

Some parents are lucky enough to adopt from Qujiang Welfare Home, which is almost 5 hours north of Guangzhou. They are lucky in that they do not have to travel to some far-off province first. Local laws do require you to pick up your child's passport there, but that is a minor inconvenience. The Welfare Home is actually very interesting in that the orphanage is very small, housing only about 20-30 children and the same number of older people. The children and the older residents have an opportunity to interact, which is a great thing.

There are many sights to see in Guangzhou and you will have the time. There is the Qingping Market that has food unlike any you have ever seen or smelled. Don't go if you're weak in the stomach or if you don't like to eat your pets. Also, wear old shoes when you go.

Many parents kill the time by visiting the Chen Family Temple and the Six Banyan Temple. They also go to Yuexiu Park. The Six Banyan contains three golden Buddhas, each about 20 feet tall. You can take your baby up to them and receive a blessing. This Buddhist temple dates back to 537 A.D.. It features large, old (1663 A.D..) cast bronze Buddhas. You can light incense and offer prayers for your daughter, her first family, and her new family. The Chen family was headed by a wealthy industrialist who had this private estate built to house the family temple and a school for boys. Now it is a museum of Chinese folk art and houses the Guangdong Folk Handicrafts Gallery. Its ornate architecture is exceedingly beautiful. The buildings are decorated with numerous carvings of wood, brick, stone, and clay. Beautiful pottery moldings decorate the roofs. Inside are a courtyard and many exhibits of the local folk arts. You can have a chop carved here for your child. It only takes a few minutes. There is also the Guangzhou Zoo with animal areas designed to re-create a natural habitat. The grounds are like gardens.

At some point you will do a little shopping. One of the first things parents do after getting their bearings is to order a chop made for their daughter. Most souvenir shops in the White Swan are reasonably priced. One of the most talked about is the Shop on the Stairs near the White Swan. Two doors down is Sherry's Place. Here parents buy chops, bookmarks, straw art cards, coloring books, jade necklaces, silver bell bracelets, hand embroidered blankets, red embroidered shoes, and Mao buttons.

Guangzhou also has the usual Friendship Store. Each major city's Friendship Store specializes in one or two types of gifts: In Beijing they are cloisonné and freshwater pearls; Nanchang has porcelain, and Guangzhou has jade and painted glass objects.

If you want to eat some Americana, check out Lucy's Bar & Grill just down the street from the White Swan, about a block away. All the waitresses wear ball caps and blue jeans, and the decor is American. There is a good selection of American and Asian foods, and the prices are quite reasonable. Guangzhou also has a Hard Rock Café with burgers and fries, oh my! It's about a 10-minute taxi ride from the

White Swan. There is also a McDonald's and a 7-11 with cold American sodas. You can eat Thai at the Cow and Bridge restaurant.

If your child is heavier than you thought (congratulations!) you may want to rent a stroller or even buy one. This can easily be done in Guangzhou.

Medical Exam in Guangzhou

Before your child can receive a visa she must have a medical clearance. The form is known as the "pink form" although it is white, not pink. The exam is not thorough but rather a general look at the child. The evaluation is done for the purpose of preventing immigrants with infectious diseases from entering the country. They look for things like leprosy. They do not do a full medical screen. That is not the purpose. The evaluation should last about 30 minutes. If you know your child has some illness, point that out to the doctor and obtain medicine. Review with the doctor the list of medical conditions you were given when you first received the referral. It might shed some additional light, which you can then pass on to your pediatrician. The examination requirements can be found at *http://www.foia.state.gov/masterdocs/09fam/0940011N.pdf.*

The medical examination can be performed in Beijing, Shanghai, Guangzhou, or Taishan. The most convenient site for medical examinations in Guangzhou is the Guangzhou Health and Quarantine Service, which is a short 3-block walk from the consulate and the White Swan at 33 Shamian North Road, telephone: 020-8188-9513. The cost is about $30.00. You basically make three stops for 1) weight; 2) eyes, ears, mouth; and 3) heartbeat. The doctor will listen to your child's heart, check muscle tone and range of motion in her limbs, and count fingers and toes. The doctor will shake a rattle to see if the child can hear and move it from side to side to see if your child's eyes can track it. You might spend all of 3 minutes having your child evaluated.

You should submit the expense to your insurance company when you return to the states. The medical clearance form is given to the U.S. Embassy. Ask the doctor to make you a copy so you can keep it for the child's medical records. This is particularly important if you are adopting an older child and she had to have vaccinations. You will need proof once you are back in the states. Make a copy for your pediatrician as well.

The United States also requires certain vaccinations prior to the issuance of an immigrant visa for an adopted child. This is not a requirement for any child under 10 years of age as long as you promise to have them vaccinated when you return to the states. Since you were planning to do this anyway, this is not a problem. The affidavit form can be found at *http://www.foia.state.gov/masterdocs /09fam/0940011X2.pdf.* For older children, bringing the child's record from the home so that the panel physician can certify it may satisfy the vaccination requirement. Of course, even for these children you may want to reimmunize once you are back in the states.

U.S. Consulate in Guangzhou

By the time your consulate visit arrives, you are in countdown mode. You are making the big push for the finish, knowing that the Flight From Hell is coming. You are checking things off. You've registered the contract, received your child's Chinese passport, gotten the child, created a family, traveled to Guangzhou, done the medical visit, and are headed for home. Emotionally you are wearing down. Physically, you and the child are likely a little sick. Just hang in there it will soon be over. The consulate's address is U.S. Consulate General Guangzhou, Adoption Unit Adoption Unit,1 South Shamian Street PSC 461, Box 100, Shamian Island FPO AP 96521-0002,Guangzhou 510133, PRC; tel: (86)(20) 8188-8911 fax: (86)(20) 8186-2341. The Adoption Unit is on the second floor.

The consulate visit is no big deal. You need to check the holiday and office closing schedule on their website. There is no need to dress up for the interview. The consulate personnel are very happy for you. The purpose of the consulate visit is to obtain an immigrant visa for your child to enter the United States. Without such a visa, your child cannot enter the U.S. Just because you have completed a valid Chinese adoption, which is recognized by the United States government, it does not automatically confer upon your child the right to enter the United States.

The U.S. Consulate strongly advises adoption agencies to set an appointment for the immigrant visa interview before departing the U.S. and not to make final travel plans until the appointment has been confirmed in writing. Appointments are scheduled on a first-come, first-served basis, Monday through Thursday beginning at 9:00 am. Visas are generally available the day after the interview. After you file your paperwork there will be a brief inter-view. They ask you questions such as if you saw the child and if you under-stand her medical condition. Since the Chinese process is completely controlled by the Chinese government, there are rarely any big problems. At the end of the brief interview you will be asked (along with dozens of other parents) to raise your right hand and swear that whatever you said was true and correct. Most of the consulate staff is American. They may look ethnically Chinese, but they are as American as you. You should never assume that some-one at the consulate is not an American nor should you treat them any differ-ently because they are not Caucasian. For some reason parents seem to treat this consulate staff differently than parents do in almost any other country. This is wrong.

You will need to submit the following documents:

American Documents

1. Both adoptive parents' passports with a photocopy of the information page of each passport.

2. Power of Attorney, if applicable. If one parent is not present at the interview, the remaining parent should provide photographic proof that they have met the child and sign an I-600. You only need such a power of attorney if one spouse has returned to the states and will not be present for the interview. If you traveled to China without your spouse, you must have a notarized, certified, and authenticated Power of Attorney dated no earlier than six months prior to the time of travel, with two copes. Also, you must have a notarized letter from your spouse indicating his/her awareness of any special needs, desire to pro-ceed with the adoption, intention to re-adopt in the U.S., and reason spouse is unable to travel. In addition, make sure the non-traveling spouse signs the I-600 before you leave for China.

3. Form I-600-Petition to Classify Orphan as an Immediate Relative (the "blue" form) completed, signed, and dated by both parents. The visa unit will now accept a downloaded copy of this form on white paper.

4. Form DS-230-Application for Immigrant Visa (the "white" form). This form should be completed from the perspective of the adopted child. You will fill out this form, but only sign the application in front of the consular officer.

5. You will need to pay the visa fee of $335 per child when you submit the application. Payment may be made in cash (dollars or RMB) or travelers' checks. They do not take credit cards or personal checks. The $335 visa fee is unrelated to the $460 you may have paid when you filed your I-600A. Keep the receipt. You will need to show it when you return the next afternoon to pick up the visa. If you are adopting children from different birth mothers, you will also have to pay an additional $460 for each unrelated child. For example, if you adopt 2 unrelated children, and paid $460 when you filed your I-600A back home, then you will pay $335 for each child's visa application and another $460 for the second child for a total of $1,130. If the children are siblings (birth mother is the same), then a second $460 is not paid.

6. Form I-604-Request for and Report on Overseas Orphan Investigation. This form should be completed by you. This form contains information about the child before adoption. This form used to be filled out by the consular officer, but they now want you to do it. Since it speeds up the process, it is an efficient change.

7. I-864-Affidavit of Support. This is only required if one of the parents did not see the child before the court hearing or if parents reside outside the U.S. The result will be that your child will receive an IR-4 Visa. See the chapter on the I-864 for further information. If you are required to file it, you need to attach photocopies of your last 3 years' tax returns and proof of current employment. The tax returns do not have to be notarized, but you have to provide complete sets (all the schedules and forms you submit to the IRS). If you are adopting more than one child, you must submit a separate I-864 and set of financial documents for each child. If your child is receiving an IR-3 visa, then you do not need to bring any tax returns with you. Even so, many parents bring the most recent.

8. A copy of your home study and I-171H.

9. You will need two passport photos of your child. There is a small photo place within walking distance of the White Swan about ¾ of a mile away.

10. The email or fax confirmation of your cable (Visa 37 cable), if you have one. You should email or fax the Visa Unit prior to traveling asking them if they have received the BCIS cable regarding your I-171H approval. Take this confirmation with you when you go to the con-

sulate and give them a copy. It proves they have your file somewhere in the building.

11. Federal tax returns for 3 years (See I-864 discussion). If your child is receiving an IR-3 Visa, you do not have to show any tax returns. Nevertheless, I would still take a copy of last year's return.

12. Pre-visa medical report. This is the "Pink sheet," that is actually white. It is given to you in a sealed envelope. Do not open it. Give it to the consulate, still sealed. Usually you can obtain a copy from the clinic at the time of the physical.

13. You may be asked to sign a waiver of immunizations. This form is just a promise by you that when you are back home your child will be given all of the age appropriate immunization shots. Since this is what you plan to do anyway, it is an easy promise. If you adopt a child 10 or older, you cannot ask for a waiver except under certain circumstances. If you are adopting a child 10 or over, look into the exceptions to see if you can get this requirement waived.

Here are some web sites that are helpful in preparing for the embassy visit. For the current forms and fees of some of the BCIS necessary forms see: *http://www.immigration.gov/graphics/formsfee/forms/index.htm*.

For Department of State form (they begin with "DS") DS-230-Immigrant Visa Application; see *http://www.state.gov/documents/organization/7988.pdf*.

Chinese Documents

14. The child's original birth certificate. Make sure you have a *certified* copy.

15. Information on the resolution of the birth parents' rights: This could be in the form of death certificates of the parents, or some other official document regarding the birth parents' absence.

16. The registration of the adoption and notary's document.

17. The adoption certificate.

18. The amended birth certificate showing you as the parents.

19. The child's Chinese passport and a photocopy of the information page.

Each official Chinese document must be presented in the following way: the original document or a copy *certified* by the custodian of the document and an English translation, one photocopy of the original, and a second translation.

The copies and translations will become part of the child's immigrant visa. All originals presented to the consulate are returned to you immediately following the interview with the consular officer. Make sure you remind the officer before you leave regarding the return of the originals.

If the paperwork is all in order, you will be asked to swear that all the information you have given is true and correct. If you have changed addresses before traveling, you may be asked to produce the home study addendum to that effect. The reason the visa interview is a non-issue is because the adoption process is completely controlled by the Chinese Government. Therefore, there are none of the problems with whether the child is really an orphan and available for adoption that sometimes arise in other countries.

When the visa is approved, the consular officer (perhaps Mary Quistorff) will sign the appropriate forms and hand the entire visa package to an Immigrant Visa Unit employee who will complete the processing of the visa. You will receive the sealed immigrant visa envelope the next day. If there is a problem with the documents, the consular officer will discuss with you what the remaining issues are and suggestions as to how they might be resolved.

After you receive the visa, and unless you are just too tired, you will have a huge grin on your face, as you will have finished with all official paperwork to adopt your child. (There is some follow-up paperwork back in the states, but why ruin the moment?) Do NOT open this package and do NOT pack it in your luggage. It goes in your carry-on that is with you at all times to be delivered to immigration once you have landed in the United States.

Your child's immigrant visa is valid for six months, beginning with the date of issuance. Any visa issued to a child lawfully adopted by a U.S. citizen and spouse while such citizen is serving abroad in the U.S. Armed Forces, or is employed abroad by the U.S. Government, or is temporarily abroad on business is valid until the adoptive parent returns to the United States. In such cases the visa is valid for up to 3 years.

Almost all U.S. visas for adopted children from China are IR-3s. If the child will receive an IR-3 Visa, you do not have to file an Affidavit of Support, Form

I-864. If your child will be receiving an IR-4 Visa, then you do. The difference is that an IR-3 means that both parents saw the child. Usually an IR-4 is reserved for those adoptions in countries where the child was escorted to the United States or where only one married parent saw the child.

If you are approved for more children on your I-171H, but are not adopting them all at one time, tell the officer to keep your file open. This may allow you to use your same I-171H the next year to adopt additional children.

Leaving China for Home

You will likely need to confirm your international reservation a day or so before your flight. You should think about whether you want to buy a seat for your child. Some parents recommend a seat even for an infant, as otherwise you will likely have to hold your child for the entire flight. Also, if you ask for a bassinet, remember that there are not many of those and you might not receive one. Talk to parents about which airlines have empty seats on the return. Make sure you have your child's visa document package in your carry-on. You will need to give this to U.S. immigration when you land.

Get to the airport no later than 2 hours before your flight, and even earlier if you want a bulkhead seat. These seats are wonderful if you have adopted a young child and are reserved on a first-come basis. Some airlines have a bassinet that attaches in bulkhead seating. It is really a plus. You will have much to do. First, go to the airline counter and pay the change of flight penalty if applicable. Do not use a credit card but pay in cash. Then go to your airline. They will want to see everyone's passports and tickets. Then go through customs and give them your customs declaration form. Then get in line to go through passport control. They will review your passport, exit visa, and anything else they want. They may wish to look at your child's sealed U.S. visa package, but you will get instructions from the consulate that they should not.

For a child under two, you do not have to pay full price. Usually it is 10% of the adult fare. This does not provide your child with a seat, just breathing room on your lap. Of course, if there is an empty seat next to you then you are in luck. Once the plane is in the air, consider moving to a seat that has a vacant one next to it. You should try to get a bassinet. Bassinets are handed out on a first-come, first-serve basis at check-in. Consider buying a full fare seat. The argument against buying a seat is the cost. The argument in favor of it is that your child will be much more comfortable and happy in his seat. He will be able to sit up and play with his toys on the fold down tray and sleep in it also. You can change him there rather than in the tiny bathroom or on your fold down tray.

Now for the Flight From Hell!

Flight From Hell

Imagine being taken from the only home you know, surrounded by people you don't know who are speaking a language you don't know, and then being placed in a flying machine, which you may never have seen. Add to this mix that you are hungry, sleepy, not feeling well, and generally cranky. This is your child. It might also be you. This is why the return flight to the United States is called the Flight From Hell. It can be very noisy.

You will not sleep on the plane. Therefore, it is critical that you get a very good night's sleep the night before. It may be 20 hours or so before you are able to sleep again. Through it all just keep clicking your ruby slippers and repeating, "Home, home, there's no place like home…."

You might take something to soothe your child on the flight like Benadryl or Dramamine. Ask your pediatrician regarding the correct dosage based on the child's weight. Test its effect in China before flying, as the pink kind may have the opposite effect because of the dye involved. Many children are affected by Red Dye 40 and will act like they have just had ten cups of coffee. I highly recommend the clear kind. Also, a child might have an ear infection or be congested, which flying would aggravate. If you know that your child has an ear problem, ask your pediatrician what you can give her to make the flight better. You can also ask the doctor at the clinic. Pack some Dimetapp just in case. You might give an infant something to drink while the plane takes off and lands. An older child should chew gum or also drink something to keep the ears open. Entertain them with toys like a set of stacking cups, small cars, rattles, plastic keys, or small stuffed animals. Crayola makes markers that only write on the paper that comes with the markers. These are great. Also, take some snacks, as the little creatures do quiet down at feeding time! Do not give your child a peanut butter or egg product until you get home, as you do not want him to have an allergic reaction while overseas. Also, be careful about too much fruit juice since their bodies may not be used to it and you may end up dealing with toddler diarrhea.

The trip itself will be something you will file purge once you get home. On a flight with 20 babies, you will see little heads popping up and down over the tops of seats like prairie dogs. You can relax in the full knowledge that whenever your child is shrieking or throwing food, there is no doubt another child on board screaming even louder and chucking whole grocery stores down the aisle. You will want to change your child's diaper out on the wing, but they have a rule against that. Instead, you are allowed to use the changing table in the bathroom, which is the perfect size for your child, but only if he's a hamster. I would say it all passes like a bad dream, but it doesn't, since no dreaming is allowed. You will be wide awake for every excruciating 43,000 seconds of the trip.

Some families have spent the night in Los Angeles before continuing home the next day. They appreciate the break and the chance to re-energize. Other parents, though, are just as eager to get home no matter what they look or feel like. When you land in the U.S., just follow the rest of your fellow passengers to the line for U.S. citizens at immigration. You do not have to go through the non-citizen line. If you return on a foreign carrier, this means the line will be very short as many are Chinese citizens. If you return on a U.S. carrier, the line may be longer. If you plan to land in Hawaii, research the BCIS office. They used to expedite citizenship certificates so you could pick one up for your child before taking the next leg.

Immigration is usually not very difficult. After they check your passports you will be directed to an immigration's office where they will check your child's visa. Do not take any pictures of the BCIS personnel or office. This is a bad idea and they do not like it. At immigration they will take that sealed package you received at the U.S. Consulate in Guangzhou. (Remember, do not pack it in checked luggage or open it.) Your whole customs and immigration experience will likely be 25 minutes tops. BCIS will stamp your child's Chinese passport with "IR-3" and give her a number. Double-check your child's passport that this is what they did. You will then be free to pick up your luggage, run it through customs, and recheck it. If you are making a connecting flight, do not hesitate but go directly to the connecting gate. Getting to the other gate can take longer than you think. You do not want to spend any more time than necessary in an airport with your very tired family. You just want to get home as quickly as possible.

If you are lucky, your child's green card (which is not really green) showing her to be a Resident Alien (even though she is automatically a citizen) will show up within 6 weeks to a year later with the same number as written in her passport. It really is an irrelevant document, as you do not need it to file for your child's citizenship if your child has an IR-3 Visa.

When you arrive home, you will be exhausted and probably a little sick. If you can have a relative or family friend stay with you for a week while you and the child adjust, it would be better for all. You may even have a meltdown yourself. Just know that this does happen and that it in no way reflects on your ability to parent. You are just running on empty and need to get home and recharge.

CHAPTER XIII

Home Sweet Home

Insurance

The Health Insurance Portability and Accountability Act of 1996 helped remedy problems with health care coverage for adopted children. The act mandates that all employers who provide *group* health coverage for their employees must extend the same coverage to adopted children as they do other dependents. Coverage may not be restricted because of "pre-existing conditions" and must take effect at the time of a child's placement. There are some exceptions and you should check with your plan administrator.

You have a period of 30 days in which to notify your insurance company/plan administrator of the adoption. If you do not notify them within 30 days, it is as if you are adding an existing family member to the policy and there will be pre-existing conditions limitations as per your policy's description. To be on the safe side as far as when that 30 days begins to run, notify your insurance company as soon as you return to the states. You may wish to send the notification by certified mail in addition to sending it through your company.

For persons with *individual* policies, coverage depends on the terms of the policy, which can vary based on your state's regulations.

Bathing

Bathing adoptive toddlers from a children's home can be a problem when you first try it. Sometimes it is because they were only bathed in cold water, or simply hosed down, were washed with a brush, or treated roughly. The soap may also have been very harsh and painful to their eyes. If your child shows anxiety regarding bathing, it will be a short-term problem. Here are some techniques to reduce the anxiety:

1.   Make the water warm before placing the child in the tub and then get into the bath with her. Just put in a little water at first. There is no need to fill up the tub.

2.   Put a few familiar toys in the tub. Not a lot, just a few. You can let her play with them from the outside first.

3.   Reduce the light in the bathroom so that it is not too bright.

4.   Talk or sing softly to your child in a calming voice during the entire bathing experience.

5.   Hold your child during the entire bath.

6.   Do little actual washing the first couple of times to try to get the child used to the environment. You might even do sponge baths for a while.

7.   Dry her very gently in a warm towel.

8.   Let the child set the pace of acclimation. She needs to learn to trust you and the tub.

Go through this experience a couple of times and the child should lose her anxiety.

Sleeping

After such a long flight, children's biological clocks change at a rate of approximately one hour per day. China is twelve hours ahead of Eastern Standard Time. Therefore, nearly all children should be adjusted to U.S. time within two weeks of returning home. Getting the child outside in daylight will help the adjustment process. However, you need to be careful about exposing the child to the outside world too fast. Your child's immune system may not be too used to her new environment and your pediatrician may recommend that your child stay inside most of the time for the first two weeks.

Sometimes nighttime brings out fears that are not present during the day when you are around. You have to appreciate that you may be this child's fourth placement. There was her birth mother, an institution, possible foster parent, then you. This is a lot of transition in a child's first year of life. Some children are afraid to go to sleep and cry even when sleeping. Realize the stress this child has undergone from the sudden transition of leaving a long-time foster parent, going to a strange hotel, taking a long flight to the U.S., then ending up in a place where sounds and smells are completely unfamiliar. It may take a few months before trust and familiarity bring comfort.

Some children may never have been rocked in a chair or made eye contact with a caregiver. Activities that are normal for an infant-mother relationship may actually be new to the child. Allow the child to find her own comfort zone. Give her room to explore and let her open emotional doors at her own pace. Create an open structure and just sit on the floor and see which toys and games catch her interest. Eventually she will get comfortable with the sounds, sights, and smells and learn to trust that you will always be there and she will become more relaxed at night. Some parents have experimented with the amount of sleepwear or covers in case the child just naturally runs hot or cold. White noise like a fan is also an option.

There is another sleeping phenomenon that is not necessarily more prevalent in adoptive children and that is a night terror. This is not a nightmare and has nothing to do with nightmares. Nightmares occur during the end of the night when REM is most intense. Night terrors occur during the first few hours after your child has fallen asleep when non-REM is deepest—very deep non-dreaming sleep, usually 1-4 hours after falling asleep. A child having a night terror will scream and cry without opening her eyes. They do not want you to touch them and will arch and scream more if you attempt to hold them or soothe them. They are sensitive to touch. This is terrifying for a parent, but the event pretty much has to run its course. The child will have no memory of the event. There is not much you can do although some parents will try to gently distract the child and wake her up. This has limited success. Upon waking up, the child will not have a fear of going back to sleep like a nightmare. The child might even be relaxed, as the agitation has disappeared.

Do not try to wake him by holding him strongly or shaking him. Do not pester him with questions about what he was dreaming or what caused him to fear. He truly doesn't know and there is no answer. He may even make up a story for you. Do not remind him that he was acting strange. That's the last thing a child wants to hear, that he is strange or something is wrong with him. If you become upset, then he will become upset. Try not to have an extended waking period afterwards like watching TV or playing games. The child will go right back to sleep quickly.

For some children night terrors are related to stress or being overtired from the day. Children can have them because of a change in schools or another stress-related event. Each child has a different stress-triggering mechanism. In one child it might be having to go to the bathroom and being afraid to wet the bed. This subconscious conflict then triggers the night terror event. On rare occasions night terrors also occur in adoptive children and will stop a few weeks after returning home when their sleep pattern stabilizes. Children usually outgrow them after 3 years of age, but they can also go on for quite a while and in rare instances into the teenage years. It may be an inherited trait from the birthmother, but that is not certain.

Circumcision

There is no medical reason to circumcise a child, therefore most health insurance plans will not pay for it unless your doctor recommends it as medically necessary (hint, hint). Instead, it is a cultural decision. You do have to be sure to teach your son to clean the area more thoroughly during a bath. You will also need to teach your son to pull back on the foreskin during tinkle time as otherwise the penis may get infected. The cost is roughly $600 to the surgeon, $1,400, to the hospital and then something for the anesthesia bill.

Most European men are not circumcised, and in the states it currently runs about 60/40 in favor. Contrary to what women may think, men do not check out each other's personal equipment in the locker room. One consideration is that the child will be under general anesthesia and will experience about 5 days of discomfort. Sometimes there is a problem with changing the diaper and then dealing with a bloody scab. If you're going to have a circumcision performed, do it in a hospital with a reputable pediatric urologist. Some places do not give anesthesia to a baby.

The way it usually works is that a bell like thing is placed over the foreskin to protect the head, and then WHACK! Ok, may be it's a little more scientific than that. Some children are given Tylenol with codeine for pain. Others are fine with regular Tylenol. You be the judge. Apply Neosporin or Vaseline to the area so the diaper or underwear does not stick. Give the bandage plenty of time to fall off on its own. Don't pull it off! There is a very informative policy statement on the American Academy of Pediatrics website. The web address is: *http://www.aap.org/policy/re9850.html.*

Some parents wait to circumcise little Johnny until he has to have his tonsils or adenoids taken out or PE tubes put in. The theory is that there is no sense having him undergo two operations when one will do. Boys have been circumcised at 4 1/2 years and even as late as nine years of age. You do not have to decide the minute you get back. One consideration is to wait and see if your son develops repetitive infections under the foreskin. If you have to treat several infections, you may want to circumcise.

There are some studies that conclude that circumcision reduces the risk of cancer, AIDS, sexually transmitted diseases, urinary tract infections, and probably hairy palms. These studies are subject to a great deal of debate as evidenced by the Academy of Pediatrics' article cited above. The issue is not with circumcision itself, but with the fact that the foreskin needs to be kept clean. If you don't have a foreskin, then it isn't a problem. If you do have a foreskin, then it is another place for dirt, infection, or a virus to find a foothold. Thus, sons need to be taught to give the area a little more attention at bath time.

Rocking

Many children raised in a children's home rock themselves to sleep or when they are stressed or tired. It may even appear to be quite violent. If you do nothing, this behavior will most likely disappear after six months or so. The rocking is a symptom of a deep need for comfort through tactile stimulation. Your child had no one to hold or hug her, so she learned to hug herself. You may want to practice some techniques that will fill this void and give her the comfort she so much desires during these times.

You should not try to stop a child from rocking. You should just let her rock and pick her up and rock with her, or try to get her attention focused on something else. Some parents gently rub their child's head or back when she goes down for her nap. They sometimes lie down next to their child so she feels their body against hers. In one of Caroline Archer's books she suggests sitting down next to the child and rocking in rhythm together with her. This transforms the rocking from a self-contained, self-stimulating activity into a joint activity with the parent, and the child is drawn out of her isolated world. You may end up laughing together as it slowly becomes a game. By the way, it comes as no surprise that "rockers" love swings.

These babies need a soothing routine at night. They need to build confidence in you as a parent that you will take care of their needs (hunger, calm, tender care, and development needs) and they need to have their own rhythms respected (which is not the case in the orphanage). They have developed ways to tell you they are not comfortable with something.

Try singing or a music box. Rocking is about rhythm. Some parents place a loud ticking clock in the child's room on the theory that if the child focuses on the rhythmic ticking he might lie still. Sometimes babies who do some rhythm exercises before bedtime quit rocking sooner. Also check for ear infections, as they are more painful when lying on the back.

Pediatrician Visit

As soon as possible after you return home, your child should be given a thorough medical screening. It is best if both spouses are present to help with questioning the doctor. You may find that your child is the first Asian adoptee the doctor has seen. If so, you will need to educate the doctor on the necessary tests and immunizations. You may have to be insistent. If the doctor resists, change doctors. A pediatrician may hear you talk about your child's history in a children's home, but they may not really "understand" how that institutional experience MAY affect your child. It simply is not covered in medical school. The pediatrician just sees a very healthy child. You want someone who sees and understands the bigger picture or is willing to learn.

Go to the appointment with copies of medical articles on adopted children and their medical issues. Leave these with him so that the next family can have an informed doctor. You might give him a copy of the American Academy of Pediatrics' article on the initial medical evaluation of an adopted child. See *http://www.aap.org/policy/04037.html*, and also an article from *American Family Physician* at *http://www.aafp.org/afp/981200ap/981200a.html* and one from Dr. Aronson at *http://www.adoptvietnam.org/adoption/infectious-disease.htm*. Suggest that she consult the 1997 Red Book, *Report of the Committee on Infectious Diseases*, American Academy of Pediatrics.

Dr. Gordina has developed a medical testing chart. While the chart is directed at Eastern European children, it has broad applicability. EEAC has created a special autoresponder that will send you the MS Word document. You can send a blank email message to *MedTests@eeadopt.org* and it will be sent to you as an attachment in a reply message.

You might remind the doctor that Chinese babies are bundled up in the winter, which can lead to developmental delays, and that it happens to every Chinese child, orphaned or not. As soon as they spend a few weeks in light clothing they can move around just fine. So don't let the pediatrician scare you when he sees your baby just lying there. Give it a few weeks. Physicians unaware of this cultural difference have scared more than one parent half to death by telling them their wonderful new child has any number of severe problems. They need to be aware of this social difference so they can properly examine the baby.

Have the child checked for strabismus (eyes), giardiasis, anemia (both iron and B12 kind), rickets, salmonella, and scabies. The child should have vision and hearing tests by pediatric specialists. These tests are very important. as vision and hearing problems can hinder language acquisition. This can cause your child to be frustrated and lead to behavior issues. Correctable hearing problems are not uncommon in infants as they have had untreated respiratory and ear infections. Indeed, it is not uncommon for an American pediatrician to remedy the usual ear infection with the short 10-day program of treatment. The problem is that he is facing a child who may have had untreated ear/respiratory/bronchial/sinus illnesses, which can cause the bugs to be more numerous and hidden in unusual places (like the Eustachian tube where medicine doesn't reach) and just generally be of a tougher variety than your average middle-class kid's ear infection bugs. Just be aware that your child might need a longer regimen, PE tubes, or stronger drugs like Augmentin ES.

HIV-1 and HIV-2 should be tested by ELISA (Western Blot), or if your child is under 18 months of age by PCR or culture. Syphilis, like HIV, is not usually found in Chinese infants. Nevertheless, the VDRL for syphilis should be given and is another required test. You might go ahead and have your child's lead levels checked just in case. You might find higher levels in school-age children than in infants. Some studies indicate that Chinese adopted children have higher lead levels than children from other countries, but that all children have much lower levels after several weeks of being in the United States.

Ask your pediatrician if your child can be given EMLA cream prior to having blood drawn. This cream deadens the skin area if applied an hour before and reduces the pain of the needle considerably.

Also, test for hepatitis A and C, and include a hepatitis B profile with HbsAG, anti-HBs and anti-HBc. A second hepatitis B profile screening is recommended after the maximum incubation period of 12 weeks passes. Most IA doctors recommend that a child be retested for hepatitis B and C and HIV 6 months later, in order to cover any incubation period.

Do not be surprised if your child has rickets. The children typically have a severe vitamin D deficiency that may or may not be evident in the child's bone development and overall skin complexion. After about 2 months of being home and drinking good American milk, you will see a marked improvement in your child's overall health (complexion, strength, etc). Remember hearing about "fortified" milk on TV commercials? That means we add a lot of good vitamins (primarily vitamin D) to our milk. The Chinese do not. The light from the sun activates vitamin D. This is another reason the children are pale and often look sickly. When you get them home, expose them to natural sunlight as much as possible (make it a daily routine) and your child's health will benefit greatly.

There are 2 types of rickets: vitamin D deficient and vitamin D resistant. If deficient it can be treated with sunlight, calcium, and vitamin D. If resistant, there is a more concentrated vitamin D approach. One effect of rickets can be bowed legs. With proper treatment, the legs should straighten out within a year.

If your child has a serious rickets problem, you might want to discuss with your pediatrician or pediatric orthopedic whether your child should have a baseline X-ray of her legs. That way they can compare the growth one year later and determine if any orthopedic intervention is warranted. A discussion on rickets in Chinese children can be found at *http://www.orphandoctor.com/medical/4_2_5_4.html.*

A stool examination should be conducted for ova and parasites. Giardiasis is usually treated using an awful-tasting medicine called Flagyl or with Furoxone. If your child has Giardiasis, there is a strong possibility that it has been passed on to you and you should be checked as well. Make sure your pediatrician and his lab know how to properly test for Giardiasis. Query him on the specifics. The stool samples should be taken over three days and from different areas of the stool. Just taking one day's sample is not enough.

Also, have your child checked for head lice. Lice are not uncommon in any institutional setting. The way they work is they feed on scalp and the by-products cause intense itching. The louse deposits its eggs (nits) on the base of the hair shaft. Nits are sometimes mistaken for dandruff, but are very different. Dandruff is flat and flaky and will easily slide off the hair with your fingers. Nits are tiny, oval, white shells that stick to the base of the hair shaft near the scalp. Lice do not travel through the air or jump from one head to another. They are caught only from direct contact. One cure is Nix. Be aware that Nix is not recommended for small children as it is a toxin and there are lice that are immune to Nix. It shouldn't be used to treat anyone more than 2 times and you should wash all clothing and bedding. Mayonnaise and Vaseline are home remedies that also work. Some over-the-counter medications do not really work. Also, fingernails are better than little combs at getting out the nits. Another home remedy is olive oil. You put it in the hair, top off with a shower cap, and wash out the next morning. The lice suffocate and the oil is easier to wash out than mayonnaise. A diluted solution of white vinegar (one part vinegar to one part water) can also help loosen resistant nits. Remove the dead nits in bright sunlight, with hair wet, and look at each strand of hair. This is quite tedious and time-consuming, but well worth the effort. Even if you think you got them all, check every day for at least 2 weeks. Wash everything in hot water that has had contact with the infected person. Boil hairbrushes, combs, headbands, etc. If live lice are found, repeat the olive oil (you must have missed a nit that hatched). The good news is that lice can only survive a day or two away from a warm body.

There are also some rare parasites called *Entamoeba Coli Cystus* and *Blastocytus Homoflous* for which you could test if your child is not gaining weight, and eating poorly, but has no giardiasis-type symptoms (diarrhea, very smelly stools, blood in the stool). You can also test for *Helicobacter pylori*, which is a bacteria that lives in the thin layer of mucous membrane that lines the stomach. The symptoms are similar to that of giardiasis. If your child is not growing, I would rule out the other more obvious problems before testing for this. You can also test for hypothyroidism, which can retard growth.

Your child may have what is called a Mongolian spot on the lower back. It looks like a bruise, but it is not. It is completely benign and fades over time. You may wish to point it out to your doctor and take a picture of it so that you can explain to whomever that your child was born with it. The name is actually a misnomer, as all children have such a spot but it just shows up more prominently in non-Caucasian children. A good description is at *http://catalog.com/fwcfc/mongolianspot.htm*.

Immunizations given to children in foster homes in Korea are thought to be reliable, and may not need to be repeated. As an alternative to re-immunizing your child (which is highly recommended), you can also have a blood titer test, which will show for which childhood diseases your child has been immunized. This test may reduce the number of shots that need to be given. However, the blood titer is not inexpensive and you need to check if your insurance will cover it. Also, quite a bit of blood needs to be withdrawn which may be a problem in a child suffering from anemia. For all of these reasons, most people opt for simply re-immunizing. Be sure to avoid immunizing on a day your child is running a fever. If your child is sick, choose another day. For the recommended schedule of shots, see the CDC's web site at *www.cdc.gov/nip/publications/ACIP-list.htm*.

With Chinese children, some have received immunizations but there is no way to guarantee that the vaccines have been stored or administered properly. Therefore, for these children re-immunization is the better course.

Balding on the back of the head probably indicates that the infant was lying on her back a lot. It's not necessarily a sign of neglect and is now commonly found in U.S. babies due to infants sleeping on their backs to prevent Sudden Infant Death Syndrome (SIDS). Never place a child on her stomach to sleep.

Some children are unfamiliar with milk and may not like the taste. This does not necessarily indicate lactose intolerance, simply unfamiliarity. However, with Asian children lactose intolerance is very common. Some families spike the milk with loads of cocoa, which usually never fails to entice a drink. Others have to resort to Pediasure. An alternative to Pediasure is Carnation Instant Breakfast with a little canola oil in the bottle. Ask your pediatrician about these and other ways to increase your child's weight and overcome her malnutrition. Of course, if your child has chronic diarrhea but no parasites, lactose intolerance should certainly be tested.

There has been some discussion regarding testing internationally adopted children between six and twelve months of age with the full metabolic screen that is done on all newborns in your state. This test screens for some very rare conditions that need immediate treatment. Ask your pediatrician about whether this screen is recommended.

You should see a dramatic improvement in your child within the first six months. Malnourished children generally catch up with their weight first then height. If your child is not responding appropriately to her new healthy environment after a few months, you may wish to have her screened at an international adoption health clinic. Ask your pediatrician or local children's hospital for the one nearest you. Other resources can be found at: *http://www.adoption-research.org/favorite.html.*

Scabies

Have your pediatrician check for scabies. Skin mites cause scabies. They look like small red bumps that are very itchy. The bumps typically occur on the face, head, belly button, hands, or feet. The incubation period for scabies is about 2 weeks. It is extremely contagious and very hard to identify in a small and/or malnourished child. If the child's scabies were treated with corticosteroids, especially with fluorinated corticosteroids, the scabies may be resistant to treatment.

The usual cure is Elimite Cream 5% (brand name). The Elimite Cream is applied from head to toe and left on for 8 to 12 hours, then washed off. All bedding and clothing, including your clothes that have come in contact with the child, should be washed thoroughly. If applying Elimite Cream to an infant, apply it to yourself at the same time and leave it on for the night. Some infants should not use Elimite, as it is a poison. You need to check with your pediatrician first. One suggestion is to have a dermatologist make a salve from a Vaseline base with sulfur in it and then "grease" up the child for a few days. Some children will seem to have scabies but in reality have infant actopustulosis. This is a condition that is an aftereffect of scabies where the scabie mites are completely gone. It is not contagious. It is an allergic reaction to the dead scabies mites that are still under the skin. Once the dead mites have disappeared, the bumps will also disappear. The usual prescription is a strong hydrocortizone cream or Benadryl and anti-itch lotions such as Aveeno anti-itch lotion, Sarna lotion, or Calamine lotion. Do not use Caladryl due to its connection with Benedryl. Be careful if using these on an infant, as their skin is sensitive. Secondary bacterial infection is common in prolonged scabies and if this is a case it should be treated with topical antibiotics. In severe cases such an infection should be treated with oral antibiotics. Definitely see a doctor if your child has a serious case.

If you are able to treat your child for scabies as soon as she leaves the children's home, apply Elimite Cream all over her body from head to toe, not leaving any area uncovered. The usual rule of thumb is a 60-gram tube is for one application for an average adult, 2 applications for school-age children, and 3 applications for infants. Give your child a bath in the morning. Throw away all clothes she was in on the way from the children's home to the hotel/guest house (plastic garbage bags will come in handy). Change bedding and wash it in very hot water (boiling linens is usually sufficient). Think about what to do with clothing you were wearing to visit her in the home—those are contaminated too.

Do not reapply Elimite until 2 weeks after the initial treatment, and try not to use steroid creams, especially those containing fluorinated hormones ("Ftorocort", for example). When you will return home you will have to re-treat everybody who traveled, including disinfecting the luggage (washing in hot water or dry-cleaning is sufficient). Ask your family doctor to check you several times if any itching lesion appears.

Here are two good links on the topic: *http://www.aad.org/pamphlets/ Scabies.html* and *http://www.orphandoctor.com/medical/4_2_1_5.html*.

Tuberculosis

Tuberculosis is an ancient disease that was even mentioned by Hippocrates in 460 B.C. TB is not normally found in internationally adoptive children, but all should be tested nevertheless.

Your child may have had a BCG vaccination for TB. BCG is made from the *Calmette-Guerin* bacillus. Look for the small scar on the left shoulder. You will need to have your child tested using the Mantoux/PPD with Candida control regardless. One consideration is that if the BCG was given recently the reaction might very well make your child sick. Also, since the BCG may cause a reaction, your doctor must be competent to recognize when the reaction is from the BCG and when it is from an underlying TB problem. Another problem is that your normal pediatrician will not know that he can test for TB where BCG was given. You will have to educate him. A skin reaction of <10 mm is usually due to the BCG. A result >10 mm should be interpreted as positive for exposure. Russian children are at a high risk for exposure. It doesn't mean they have the disease, but they were exposed to it at some time. BCG wanes, so never assume that a positive reaction is because of the vaccine.

If other children from the same home have tested positive but your child has not, you may want to have your child retested in a year to cover any incubation period that may have been missed with the first test. If your child has a positive TB skin test (Mantoux) and a negative chest X-ray, the protocol is to treat with a daily dose of INH (isoniazid) as a prophylaxis for 9 months. The INH pills do have side affects such as diarrhea. An ingredient added for taste called sorbitol causes this diarrhea. If you can get your pediatrician to agree, have your pharmacist crush the pills and mix them in jam. That should stop the diarrhea. Some pediatricians may not want to mix it with food, as the INH tends to bond with the food and not be completely absorbed. Some parents have switched to liquid INH and mixed it with a little water and then given it as a nighttime bottle. Some pharmacies will make the INH without sorbitol. In New York City, a pharmacy called Apthorp on the Upper West Side will make it and send it all over the country. If your doctor prescribes a two-month regimen of rifampin and pyrazinamide rather than the INH, be sure to check the CDC web site and get a second opinion. These drugs have been linked to severe liver damage.

Before starting this protocol when there is a positive skin test but negative X-ray, consult with a pediatric specialist. He may say that it is normal for her to show some reaction to the skin test due to her anemia and mild malnourished state. He may then suggest that the TB test be repeated in 1 year when she should be more nourished, anemia corrected, and a stronger immune system developed, which would result in a negative skin test.

The only children who probably should not be tested immediately are those who have a *fresh, still-healing* BCG scar. Those children should be tested 6 months to a year after the scar has healed, sooner if they develop any suspicious illness.

Here are websites with helpful information on TB:
http://catalog.com/fwcfc/TB_BCG.htm
http://members.aol.com/jaronmink/tb2.htm.

Children's Dental Care

If you adopt an older child, you may face dental issues as soon as you return. One of your first stops should be to a dentist. Be aware that some of the children:

1. Have never had fluoridated water
2. Have rarely had milk
3. Have never taken vitamins
4. Were weaned from milk to sweetened tea
5. Drank sugary tea several times a day
6. Never saw a dentist
7. Never brushed their teeth before arriving in the children's home

The consequence is that the children may suffer from porous teeth, as they do not have enough calcium in the diet to support good bone growth. They may also have weak tooth enamel and lots of cavities or even gum disease. They may have had delayed development of adult teeth. Once the immediate work is completed, the good news is that after fluoride treatments, the establishment of good teeth brushing habits, vitamins, good diets, lots of calcium, and regular checkups, their teeth are remarkably improved. If a lot of dental work is needed, yet your insurance will not cover it, consider having your child seen at a school of dentistry. They sometimes will provide free dental care as a teaching tool.

Not all children will have these problems. In some of the homes they do brush their teeth, but the problem is common enough with older children that a dentist visit should be on your list.

Hepatitis

When you return from the United States it is recommended that your child be screened for hepatitis A, B, and C. Until recently there were only limited treatments for hepatitis B and C. At this time most treatments for chronic hepatitis involve the patient taking Interferon, which is rather expensive at $300 every 10 days. There are new drugs in the pipeline such as Pegintron and for hepatitis B one called adefovir dipivoxil, which is made by Gilead Sciences. If your child does test positive, he should see a hepatologist as soon as possible. If you have not been vaccinated, you should be tested as well.

Hepatitis A is usually transmitted by drinking water or eating food that has been contaminated with fecal matter containing the virus. Symptoms only develop after the time when you are most infectious. It may cause flu-like symptoms such as fatigue, fever, poor appetite, or nausea. Hepatitis A usually resolves itself in a few weeks and does not cause permanent liver damage.

There is a theory that the Chinese do not allow known infected children to be available for adoption. Thus, the rate of hepatitis B may be lower than in the native Chinese population. Regardless, hepatitis B is a widespread population problem in China and sometimes occurs in adoptees. Because the incubation period for hepatitis is up to 6 months, a child's hepatitis status is usually not clear until she has had two screening tests 6 months apart, or at least one test 6 months after leaving China. Apparent health is the normal condition of hepatitis B chronically infected children. Thus, every child must be fully evaluated. Chinese doctors usually use a killed virus vaccine rather than the more expensive recombinant DNA vaccine used in the west. The killed virus vaccine can result in a false positive test for hepatitis B.

Anyone who has either acute or chronic hepatitis B is infectious. It is acquired mainly by bodily fluid contact and particularly blood-to-blood transmission, which is why you should always ask if your child has had transfusions and if her medical records show a hospital visit. Hepatitis B is very contagious. If your child has hepatitis B, all family members should have the vaccine and all caregivers should use "universal precautions" (latex gloves and a cleaning solution of 1 part bleach to 9 parts water for example) for diaper changes and blood spills (i.e. bleeding nose, cuts, etc.). A person who converts to hepatitis B antibodies will not be contagious. Basically they have the disease and develop natural immunity. Most children who actually have the disease do not convert, but remain chronic carriers. However, it's not uncommon when the birth mother has hepatitis B for her hepatitis B antibodies to circulate in the newborn child's bloodstream. They may not clear for 18 months. In that case, when and if they do clear the child may then test negative for hepatitis B antibodies and be free of hepatitis (actually never had it, just the antibodies). Double-check with your pediatrician regarding the type of test performed, since some are falsely told they have tested positive for hepatitis B when what is actually detected are the hepatitis B antibodies from a vaccine or from their birth mother's antibodies. It is a positive detection of hepatitis B surface antigens that indicates the presence of an infection.

In a study by Dr. Aronson of 153 adopted Russian and 346 adopted Chinese adopted children, only 14, or 2.8%, tested positive for the hepatitis B surface antigen. She also studied 495 children for hepatitis C, and of those, 4 tested positive. Of the four children, one was from China, one from Moldova, and 2 from Russia. Two of these four children were under a year old and the antibodies disappeared by the time of re-testing. In summary, these studies are confirmation that foreign adopted children are not generally carriers of hepatitis B and C.

If your child tests positive for hepatitis C there is a chance that the child will die from liver cancer in 20–30 years. But nevertheless there are treatments. Sometimes the disease never actually becomes "active," which means your child might never get sick from hepatitis C at all. The medical world should be more advanced in treating hepatitis C in the coming years. New treatments for chronic hepatitis C are two peginterferon products: Pegintron and Pegasys. Pegasys has been approved by the European Union. Ribavarin is also sometimes prescribed. Pegasys has been tested against another standard drug, Roferon-A, with a greater improvement in patients. The FDA recently cleared a more effective and longer-acting form of Rebetron for hepatitis C that has proven very popular. In 2002 an NIH panel said that the most effective treatment for chronic hepatitis C was combination therapy with pegylated interferon and ribavirin for a period of up to 48 weeks. The panel's conclusion was that combination therapy resulted in better treatment responses than monotherapy. See the NIH's statement at *http:// www.consensus.nih.gov/cons/116/116cdc_intro.htm.*

Two very good articles can be found at *http://catalog.com/fwcfc/hepatitisb.html* and *http://catalog.com/fwcfc/livingwithhepb.html*. A good website is *www.pkids.org* (click on the child, then look for the links for hepatitis). The Hepatitis Foundation and CDC are also good resources.

Parasites

Giardiasis is a disease caused by the intestinal parasite, *Giardia lamblia*. It is very common worldwide. You can get even get it from hiking in the backwoods in America where it is found in streams contaminated with animal feces. It is also common in children from institutions. Symptoms include those you would associate with gastrointestinal discomfort: diarrhea; cramps, bloating and gas; smelly stools; weakness, and weight loss. These are similar for *Helicobacter pylori*. Sometimes the disease exists even though no symptoms appear. Testing is usually done by detecting antigens in the stool samples (preferably 3 samples, collected on 3 separate days). Antigens are the immunological "signature" of the parasite. Relapses are common, especially in an immunocompromised host and newly adopted children are considered temporarily immunocompromised. Dr. Aronson has reported a study of 461 adopted children from various countries and 94 or 20.4% were positive. Out of the 94 children, 35 were from China, 38 from Russia, and 21 from other countries.

As a result of the disease, your child's development will be delayed. She is also at risk of passing it on to other children and family members. It is very important that your pediatrician test for giardiasis. Symptoms range from diarrhea to weight loss to abdominal cramping. Giardiasis can block the absorption of major nutrients in the smaller intestines, including all fat-soluble vitamins, so a child may develop vitamin A and E deficiency.

The most common medicine given by doctors is called Flagyl (Metronidazole). The liquid version tastes just awful. Most adults hate it. Your dog will hate it. Your cat will sue you if you bring it into the house. But it is necessary in order to get rid of the disease. The trick to getting children to take liquid Flagyl is to find a compounding pharmacy. These are few, but well worth a long drive to get to one. Any pharmacy can mix the medicine with a flavored, sugary syrup, but only a compounding pharmacy can truly mask the bitterness of the medicine. If Flagyl is mixed properly, your child may even ask for more! Some doctors prescribe Furoxone (furazolidone), which is easier to take. You may want to suggest this to your doctor. One problem with compounding the Flagyl is that some insurance companies have no clue as to why you have to and will refuse to pay for it. They insist on an NDC number of which none exists when mixing this type solution. If this is a problem try submitting the NDC of the tablets used to make the compound or ask if a universal claim form will be accepted. Another idea is to take Flagyl in pill form rather than as a liquid. This is better tolerated. You could ask for small sugar coated pills.

Finally, there are other drugs just as effective as Flagyl. I would suggest recommending some of these to your doctor and see if he bites. Remember that your child may be the only child your pediatrician has ever treated for giardiasis, so it may be you that educates him and treats your child rather than the other way around. Retesting is necessary after the cure has run its course.

There is another parasite called *Dientamoeba fragillis*. If your child is having chronic diarrhea and it is not giardiasis, have a test for this one as well as. You will also find that although a whole range of parasites were tested for the first time, a second set of stool samples may reveal the little buggers. It is not unusual for parasites to be overlooked in a stool sample. If the stool sample is taken from a diaper, try to place cellophane inside so the stool does not come in contact with the diaper.

Dealing with giardiasis-type symptoms that do not respond to the usual treatments can be very frustrating. You do not know if you should continue with further Flagyl or Furoxone treatments, have a biopsy done of the gastrointestinal tract for other pathogens (like *Helicobacter pylori*), look for the presence of secondary infection, or test for lactose intolerance. All of these things can cause the same symptoms as giardiasis, thereby masking the results of Flagyl treatment (since results of stool samples are often unreliable). It can be hard to tell sometimes if the Flagyl treatment was successful in eradicating giardiasis if loose stools remain, as these might be caused by other pathogens or the result of antibiotic treatment or food allergies.

Even after the infection is cleared you should be on the lookout for consequences of the disease. For example, a child may suffer post-giardiasis from malabsorption and may need to be treated with an enzyme preparation (Ku-Zime, etc). Fat free diets, especially milk-free diets, can sometimes only add to the problem. Lack of fat—the building material for the intestinal wall—can predispose the child to delayed healing of the intestinal covering.

Subsequent to giardiasis treatment, the child may suffer from disbacteriosis, which is an imbalance of the intestinal bacteriathat help to digest food in the colon and discourage overgrowth of pathological flora secondary to either intestinal disease or antibacterial treatment or both. If the child is taking an antibiotic you may want to ask your doctor about bacterial preparations together with any course of antibiotics. You can buy acidophilus or lactobacilli in any health food store and probably pharmacies. To a lesser degree, yogurt and other sour milk products such as buttermilk, cheese, and sour cream can also help.

Interestingly, it has been seen that in recently adopted children overeating can cause diarrhea. Their bodies cannot digest the larger amounts of food. That condition is very common among adopted toddlers. Be sure not to limit their access to food, but provide them with easily digestible, high fiber, healthy snacks such as bananas, applesauce, and bread.

There is also toddler's diarrhea, which is caused by many factors but typically by apple juice. Sugars in apple juice are known to cause abnormal fermentation in the intestines and to predispose to diarrhea even in the absence of conditions. Toddler's diarrhea is frequently "treated" simply by normalizing their diet, especially their fat intake. One of the most frequent causes of constipation in children is excessive consumption of milk.

Useful web sites: *http://members.aol.com/jaronmink/giardias.htm* and *http://www.mc.vanderbilt.edu/peds/pidl/gi/giardia.htm.*

Helicobacter Pylori

This is another parasite that can cause gastritis (i.e. giardiasis-like symptoms). If giardiasis is not found, ask your pediatric gastroenterologist to look for this bug. This bacterium is also associated with gastric antral inflammation, and the infection is strongly associated with duodenal ulcers. Nevertheless, the bug causes a different reaction in different people and these disease outcomes are not always certain. Transmission seems to be the usual saliva and fecal route, so be careful changing those diapers.

The cure is easier than the diagnosis and a lot less painful. The usual method of diagnosis is to have an endoscopic biopsy test. This is not something most children enjoy. Almost as reliable, but not quite, is to test for the antigen. This can be done through a breath, blood, or stool test. The cure is usually a treatment consisting of 3 medications: an acid suppression agent (i.e., proton pump inhibitor) and 2 antibiotics, given twice daily for 1 to 2 weeks. The antibiotics are usually a combination of amoxycillin, tetracycline, or clarithromycin. Metronidazole resistance occurs often enough so that this is not the optimum antibiotic (although doctors seem to prescribe it for giardiasis). Infected children who are asymptomatic are not thought to need treatment. Pediatric infection has not been studied as well as adult infection. More than you wanted to know can be found at: *http://www.bioscience.org/2001/v6/e/lake/list.htm.*

Rare Food Absorption Problems

Note that the title above includes the word "Rare," so only read this if all else fails. If you think your child is eating enough but doesn't seem to be absorbing the nutrients, you should consult a pediatric gastroenterologist. This doctor will need to do a food absorption test (stool sample). There are some rare problems that children sometimes inherit. One is celiac disorder and another is called Alpha 1 anti-trypsin deficiency. Alpha 1 is an enzyme produced in the liver. When you have the deficiency your liver is unable to allow the enzyme into your bloodstream to do its work. One of the symptoms of the disease is malabsorption of vitamins A, D, E, and K and also fat. Your child can eat and eat yet always be skinny. There is more to it, but for the short story ask your doctor to check for it. It is just a blood test. It is not well known in the medical community and many doctors would not even think to check for it. Most people who have it never know they do until they are in their twenties or thirties. It is genetic and passed on by both birth parents being carriers. With Alpha 1, their stools are frequent, loose, and a grayish color with a foul odor.

Sometimes they even test for cystic fibrosis, since there is a very close correlation between the liver and the lungs. The Alpha 1 enzyme is what protects the lungs from harmful stuff, and when you are deficient you have trouble with respiratory infections that can damage the lungs.

Sensory Integration Disorder (Dysfunction)

Sensory Integration Disorder is a form of behavior by a child that is the logical reactive response to a lack of early stimulation and which manifests itself as inappropriate or peculiar behavior. In general, early sensory stimulation enhances development of the central nervous system. If you consider that everything an infant touches, tastes, or feels sends an information flow to her brain, imagine what happens when there is no such information flow. Notice that infants are interested in unusual textures like a bumpy ball, grit of a nail file, or soft ears on a stuffed bunny. Your child may not have had any of these sensory experiences if raised in a children's home.

A child with Sensory Integration Disorder has problems with tactile and auditory senses, as these have failed to develop properly because of this lack of sensory information flow. The child may exhibit difficulty with hearing, touching, sound or sight. A child may be overly sensitive to noise (hypersensitive) or not react normally to things that should hurt (hyposensitive). The child may be clumsy or give hugs that are too strong. The cause is not well understood. Some doctors believe that when children lack essential nutrients or human contact, or both, the links between different clusters of the brain do not work efficiently or are not formed at all. There is also a certain hierarchy in which these links are formed, so if you are trying to teach such a child you need to return to basics and rebuild weak or missing links Otherwise there will be nothing but frustration. That frustration manifests itself in behavioral problems related to the sensory integration disorder. Luckily, occupational therapy (OT) has had very good success in re-integrating the senses. OT will use and train you to use such techniques as brushing, compressing, swinging, and playing "wheelbarrow."

Another form of therapy that has had mixed reviews is Auditory Integration Training (AIT). Another is the Tomatis Listening Method. In rare cases some children may even have problems accepting solid foods, as the issue might be a severe oral aversion, which means they do not like food in the mouth. The book *The Out of Sync Child* is excellent on this subject and is highly recommended.

Some behaviors may manifest themselves as a child having a very difficult time going to sleep, being very sensitive to smells and loud sounds, preferring to eat with his fingers, having a hard time sitting still during meals, or when sleepy or nervous walking only on his tiptoes. A proper diagnosis leads to a proper method of therapy.

More resources can be found at *http://www.mindspring.com/~mariep/si/toc.html* and also at *http://www.sinetwork.org/*.

Post-Adoption Education Issues

If you adopt an older child, one of your first questions upon returning to the United States, in addition to a medical evaluation, may be about education. Some of the children will pick up English at an incredible rate and within months be practically fluent. Others may have difficulties due to developmental delays and need help. There is a debate on whether it is better to put an adoptee immediately in school or hold him out until he is more culturally integrated. It all depends on the child. Some children respond very well to the stimulation of being in a school. Others may feel overwhelmed if they are not acquiring English fast enough.

Some basic questions to ask yourself are:
How quickly should I put him in school after coming home?
Should I place him in his age-appropriate grade or his appropriate developmental one?
Should I keep him out and just do home tutoring for a few months?
How do I handle ESL (English as a second language)?
How should I handle objections of school officials?

A consideration in starting an older child in school is that they will likely make new friends quickly. These friends help in social and language development in a way no one else can. It helps them feel like they do belong here. Don't be surprised if they have a slight accent. It will be part of their exotic charm.

By law school districts must provide ESL/LEP classes. LEP stands for "limited English proficiency," although some call it ELD (English Learning Development). The school districts don't want to provide LEP classes, but they must. These may meet from one to two times a week. Many ESL classes will have bilingual children where the home language is different than English. Their progress may be different than your child's although the ESL teacher may not recognize the reasons. Your child has a lot more on his plate than other children in these classes. He is trying to integrate into a new family where he must learn the family routine, family customs, how to handle new siblings and parents, trust and attachment issues, etc. The other children are not juggling all of these other issues, and therefore your child's progress should not be compared to theirs. Another issue with ESL classes is that they are usually focused on Spanish or Asian speakers. This may mean that your child is better off with a private tutor or just learning at home.

You may find that your child progresses faster than the usual ESL/LEP child. The reason is that your child's native language is not being spoken at home, so he is undergoing total immersion. It is tougher for him at first, but eventually it will pay off in better English comprehension. Also, there can be a problem with the pullout ESL type of classes in that they focus on language alone while in mainstream classes they are learning actual subjects. You may have to supplement their learning by teaching them at night and on weekends until they are caught up in their subject matter knowledge.

One warning about your child becoming fluent in English is that this sometimes fools the teachers into thinking that comprehension and social language acquisition are at the same level. Indeed, they may not even know they are separate pieces. Social language skills are obtained much more easily than academic comprehension. So your child's teachers may say that your child understands, but just doesn't get it. This is incorrect. Your child may take 2 or 3 years before he fully comprehends, in a real sense, everything being said and its context, even though he was fluent in six months. Just be sensitive to that fact that fluency can mask a problem that his teachers do not appreciate. More on this difference can be found in this article at *http://www.ncbe.gwu.edu/miscpubs/ncrcdsll/*, click epr5.

Some older children have trouble "hearing" the difference between such similar sounds as "b" and "d" and "p" for instance. They may know the letters but not fully register the sounds of each letter. This may cause you to privately tutor him in this area using one of the private programs that are available. Some older children also may need help in learning English grammar and writing. It all depends on the child and whether he had any schooling before adoption. If he did have such schooling, then learning English may be easier. Dr. Boris Gindis has a very informative article on the web entitled "Language-Related Issues for International Adoptees and Adoptive Families." I highly recommend it. You can read it at *http://www.bgcenter.com/adoptionPublication.htm.*

All parents of older children are urged to have thorough assessments done on the child in the language of the child's country of origin to pinpoint present and future learning difficulties. Testing her as soon as she comes into the country will clarify what kind of difficulty she is having, how serious it is, and what kinds of therapy will be most effective in her treatment. Testing will also show any discrepancies between IQ and performance skills. If there are any discrepancies present in her base language, the assumption will be made that these discrepancies will also exist in the same subjects in English. This prevents your future kids from falling into "ESL limbo."

"ESL limbo" occurs as soon as your child loses her base language (often within a matter of a few months). The school personnel will start the "just wait until she has more English" litany. That wait can interfere with your child's ability to obtain services for the REAL issues of actual learning disabilities. This can inhibit you from seeking speech therapy for your child long before it is actually verified that there is a problem. Testing soon after arrival is just another way to avoid possible problems in the future. It is no different from re-inoculating your kids or checking for parasites or testing for HIV, hepatitis B and C, and TB. If you're lucky, your children will never need services from the school system, and you can use the tests as a baseline and file them away in your records.

Some children may need a school's special education services. Special education falls under the acronym of IDEA (Individuals with Disabilities Education Act), which is a federal law. Each state has its own special education regulations. Each state also has some kind of parent training education center. There is an organization that has state specific information called the National Parent Network for Disabilities (NPND). One recent change in IDEA is that the use of "developmental delay" now includes ages 3-9 whereas it was previously only for 3-5.

Getting "help" for your child obviously begins with a determination by an evaluation team that your child is "delayed." The outcome of such an evaluation should be an Individualized Education Plan (IEP). Make sure that the child study team allows you to share your insights into the child's strengths, weaknesses, and overall development. Evaluations should be non-discriminatory, which includes being done in the child's native language if necessary. This is tricky because after a few months the children are between their native language and English so it's hard to know which language to choose. Also, the written evaluation should reflect the child's strengths, not just weaknesses. The most important component of the resulting IEP should be goals and objectives. Also, the IEP must show strategies to deal with behavior problems. Remember that you are your child's only advocate. He has no one else. Don't let the school put him in a class or assign him a designation that you don't feel is appropriate.

If your child is about to enter elementary school you may find that a planned introduction is a great icebreaker. With the approval and assistance of the class teacher (and your child, of course) you might introduce their new classmate and show a bit of your Chinese videotape. You can explain about China and give a brief version of your child's adoption and the obstacles she is facing such as a new country, new friends, new family, and new language. A class exercise using a map of the world and letting the students find their city then your child's, might be helpful. Then you might give out little flags or something indicating China. This exercise can be an icebreaker and the children will actually compete to help your child assimilate.

Most of the above discussion relates to adopting the older child. However, it also applies to much younger children who were adopted with some of the risk factors as outlined by Dr. Dana Johnson. These children may manifest behavioral problems in school of which you were not aware. These issues may have always been there, but because they stayed in a family setting they were more easily dealt with and not recognized as serious. Once these children are in a non-family environment where they are interacting with others all the time, their problems become more public. Part of their behavior can also be related to being challenged by their schoolwork. They do fine in kindergarten and first grade, but in the third grade or fourth is when schoolwork becomes more abstract, more challenging, and demanding of more focus. Some of these at-risk children find themselves frustrated and begin to have developmental behavioral difficulties.

Attachment

After the initial physical medical issues are taken care of, one of the most important psychological issues is "attachment." Attachment means bonding between a child and a parent. It happens very early with an infant and the more delayed the process the more difficult it can become. That being said, it is not impossible to have attachment at any age and if the child attached to caregivers at the children's home, or spent some time in a family setting, foster family, or is bonded with a sibling, then the groundwork has been laid.

Children adopted from China are in no way immune from possibly having problems with attachment or with Sensory Integration Disorder or the rest of the alphabet soup of issues. If an agency or parent tells you that Chinese children never have these issues, they are either selling you something or haven't done any research. Being adopted at a young age and from foster care does mitigate the problems, but it in no way means that a child might not need some help. Children from an institutional environment, no matter the country, are always at risk. Some parents hope that when they receive their child in the hotel, the child will give off the mother of all tantrums. This is an indication of having bonded with the caregiver (Auntie) and thus having a foundation upon which to bond again. Here is a very good web site on bonding and children from China: *http://www.attach-china.org/*.

Initial bonding by a child is not so unusual. Yet this bond can sometimes be an "insecure bond" and it may be longer before the attachment is deep and permanent. After all, you are a stranger to this child and she to you. The attachment process is something on which you should focus and work hard to nurture. Some signs of "insecure attachment" are that the child continues to be withdrawn or stiff or will show affection indiscriminately to strangers or just simply go off with anyone.

If it is possible to stay home for a while this will help the bonding process. Also, try to limit social situations so that your child and your family spend as much time together as possible without outside distractions. It is also helpful with toddlers if you can say some words in Chinese, so that your child can communicate basic needs and wants. You may also consider trying to be the sole provider of food and comfort to the child for a short time in order to establish dependence and trust. For a young toddler, you can augment bonding by holding the bottle for the child while cuddling and making lots of eye-to-eye contact and skin contact such as stroking your child's bare arms and legs during feeding. It's best not to let them hold the bottle or run around the house with a bottle like a typical toddler might. It has to do with the child giving up control to you and trusting you to provide for them.

Another idea that people have also used is to engage in deliberate holding, hugging, and touching as much as possible. Some call this Holding Time (Dr. Welch) or baby time. You should carry an infant around as much as possible. Not in a car seat, but on your hip or in a pouch holder. If they are too heavy to carry, then sit and hold them a lot. If they are rocking, pick them up and rock them. Don't let them take care of themselves, you take care of them. You should try to make eye contact—lots and lots of eye contact—and talk softly to her.. You can promote this by bending down and giving your child cookies or snacks at eye level. Let her follow you around the house or climb into your arms whenever she feels a need. Make faces, say silly words, and interact. Let him take a bath with you or spend time massaging his skin with lotion in order to promote close contact. Put the same lotion on you so you smell alike. Smells are very important to infants. Home should smell like home and Mommy should smell like Mommy. You might even wear the same color clothes once a week to promote how much you both are alike. Prominently place a picture of the whole family somewhere in the house. You have to recreate that early attachment time that was missed. You may even have to teach your child how to give hugs. Some parents have successfully used Theraplay, so this is another avenue to try.

Also, part of the normal integration process of a child into a new family is a process called "reparenting." It means that the child, no matter how old, may regress to a former developmental level in order to be "reparented" by the new family. This is an unconscious/subconscious effort to find his or her proper place in the fabric of the family. In many children, reparenting means rolling back to very young and immature levels because they have missed so many of the normal developmental milestones. For them, it's a double load to carry. For children who have spent entire lives within an institutional setting, they struggle with a lack of knowledge about normal family interactions.

You need to build trust and reciprocity. You can't break promises in the early stages. Their whole life has been a broken promise. Because of that these children view the world very concretely. They are black and white thinkers. They have no experience on which to base a proper response to the fuzziness of life. If you say, "We *might* go to the movies," they don't know what that means.

You will know you've succeeded when she loves to cuddle, seeks consolation from you when hurt, and is eager to see Mom and Dad when you return from the store or work. If she wants only you when other adults are around and her eye contact is good, then you should take this as a measure of success.

There are books on this subject and medical experts who specialize in the attachment field. One such book is *Facilitating Developmental Attachment: The Road to Emotional Recovery and Behavioral Change in Foster and Adopted Children* by Daniel A. Hughes. Try to avoid a traditional therapist or social worker. These professionals simply do not have the training to help a child with an attachment issue. It is like calling a plumber when you need an electrician. These professionals have been taught to look to the parents for fault rather than believe the parents about the child. This approach is completely counter-productive and tends to make the situation worse.

Other behaviors to prepare for that may or may not manifest themselves are anger and grieving. Many things cause anger. Your child may have anger at his birth family for giving him up or for a lousy home life. He may be angry and grieving at leaving the only life (and friends) he has known. He may have anger and frustration at initially being unable to communicate in English or his native language with anyone. The symptoms will be tantrums, hitting, and crying. If they go on too long, seek professional help.

Some early signs of serious attachment disorder can be the existence of "triangulation" after you return home. In this scenario, "Mom" bears the brunt of the disorder since she is at home with the child. The child never takes to "Mom" at all. He generally ignores her, disobeys her, and may even hit her. "Dad," on the other hand, is the good guy and his time and attention are always sought. If you see this developing, read the books but do not hesitate to call in the help of a therapist who specializes in attachment disorders. Do not wait too long if the behavior is serious or becomes dangerous. The Attachment Center at Evergreen, P.O. Box 2764, Evergreen, CO 80437 (303-674-1910) has many good articles on the subject at *http://www.attachmentexperts.com/*.

One part of attachment disorder that is counterintuitive is that children from physically abusive situations are in better shape than neglected ones. What these kids learn, even in a sick environment, is something about cause and effect. They learn they have some control over their environment, and that they are not completely powerless.

This attachment discussion should not scare you. It is the thin edge of the wedge. Many older children who do not have a background of abuse just breeze right through these stages without missing a beat. They have no attachment issues to speak of, and for them the more stimulation the better. Their point of view is "World, bring it on, cause I'm ready for you." You will know the right approach to take with your child. Some children want to go to the mall the day they come home. They want to visit people and see things and finally have some real fun. If you are aware of the possible behavioral reactions, even the negative, you can be better prepared to help your child and that is what parenting is all about.

One book that many people read is *Toddler Adoption: The Weaver's Craft* by Mary Hopkins-Best. It is a good book and a scary one. It discusses all of the negative behaviors that could possibly happen. Do not view it as a prediction of what will occur. Some of her conclusions you may even disagree with such as that single people should avoid adopting a toddler because it's so difficult. In my opinion, all good parenting is hard work and the age doesn't really matter. Her book is a good place for starting discussions and to help you identify problem behaviors. Just don't rely on it as a road map of how your adoption will go. Indeed, her study of children does not include any children from Asia. The children she bases her research on had very different beginnings than the Asian adoptees, most of who are from stable foster family settings. Some had several placements. Some were domestic adoptions and others were from South America, which has a different system than China or Korea.

Transition Issues for Wobblers, Toddlers, and Older Children

It is also perfectly normal to have other transition issues with an older child. First, and foremost, is the fear and helplessness she might feel about being transitioned from everything and everyone she knew into an entirely new and different environment. This is culture shock to an extreme degree. All her underpinnings are gone, and it will take time and lots of patience on your part to wait for her new foundation to be built and for her to become part of your family.

Second, don't underestimate the language frustration she might go through. Even if you speak perfect Chinese, she's hearing English all around her that she doesn't understand. Americans who travel to foreign countries feel the same thing. It's very disconcerting, especially if you are a verbal processor. She has all sorts of thoughts and feelings that she isn't able to express right now. The frustration of that is sometimes overwhelming. That is why an older child's transition anxiety is greatly reduced if there is someone she can speak with who knows her native language.

Additionally, when you just return from overseas you are extremely tired. You've all had a very hard trip and will need to emotionally and physically recuperate. Be sure to eat well and get plenty of sleep. Transition work is HARD work and requires more sleep than normal. You are also extremely concerned about your new child's well-being and peace of mind, but there are some rough spots she may have to work through on her own. Think about cutting down on stimulation and visits with friends and extended family for a while. Try to keep things real simple. Set a routine and stick with it. It is probably not a good idea to suddenly shower the kids with fifty new toys and then take them to Disneyland during their first week in America, or even make them the center of attention of many huge, smiling strangers' faces, however well meaning they may be. All things should happen in due time.

Some older children fit in to a new family like a hand in a glove, but many need extra work. Provide comfort, calm, and quiet as well as some space and distance for all of you when she seems overwhelmed.

The message from professionals is to go younger on toys and games. Let them figure out the Fisher Price stuff before moving on to age appropriate toys. If they want to play baby, play baby with them. Before a child learned to run she had to learn to crawl. If she missed an early stage of development, she has to go back (with your help) and pick it up. Look at it as being akin to Pac Man and having to go back and pick up the cherries you missed. What is interesting is that when she acquires a skill she will then move on quickly. Many families describe going through these catch-up stages as watching a childhood video running at fast-forward.

Transitioning an older child can take lots of time, but things do get better. The temper-tantrum/frustration stage of transition is very common for older kids. With improved English language skills this too passes. Get some posters with different facial expressions on them like "angry" or "sad" so they can point and let you know how they are feeling. Let them listen to native language cassettes with songs on them. Hearing familiar sounds may help them feel comfortable.

They will not have taken baths frequently, nor changed clothing as often as we do. Oral hygiene will not be up to American standards either. Get some cute toothbrushes and flavored toothpaste. Many children do not know how to bathe themselves and they might need a lesson. Try cute towels and washcloths or sponges. It is likely that the boys are not circumcised and they may need some instruction on keeping the area clean in order to reduce infections. If the genital area is red there is a likelihood of an infection, which you should bring to the attention of your pediatrician.

They may not be used to sleeping in pajamas. Try having them sleep in oversize T-shirts. There will be many, many little differences that you will see. A thousand little things will amaze them, from how to buckle a seat belt to how to use a single-lever faucet.

Institutionalized children have had less experience in making choices than children raised in a family. They do not know about food choices, clothing choices, activity choices, etc. Don't overwhelm them by presenting them with what to them are difficult choices. Don't send them to the closet to just "pick something." Let them choose between just two items instead. Be careful not to overdo anything. Reduce the amount of stimuli to which they are subjected. Going to the grocery store is like going to the circus for them. You also have to be very careful taking kids out in public who do not speak English and could not ask a stranger for help. You need to be sure they will stay with you and not run off. Give them structure by providing them with a schedule or a plan on what you and they will be doing that day or that week. Don't just let them do anything in an open-handed manner. They want and need guidance from you.

With a toddler you may find that he needs and wants to be treated like a baby. This can be wonderful if you thought you might have missed out on his "baby time." Even a 12-year-old will like an affectionate hug and maybe sitting next to you or on your lap during quiet time. A toddler may also want to stay in a crib longer than other children. He may consider it his private or safe place and enjoy "his crib." There is no urgency to moving a child to a bed. He'll get there before he goes off to college. The children will love being praised, as they have never had that before. They also like it when adults act silly and joke around. This will be new to them as well.

An older child will not know how to get in and out of a car and how not to ding other cars' doors, so you might consider parking away from other cars until he learns. They won't know how to cross our streets or use a seat belt. Also, be prepared for initial motion sickness. They may play with all the buttons, dials, and switches they can get their little hands on so make sure the door locks can not be opened by them *while the car is moving!* Even if your child is 8 years old, childproof your home as if he were a toddler. He will figure out the rules pretty quickly, but during that transition stage he will try every dial on the stove and microwave, every light switch, electric outlet, and gas switch. Put the cleaning fluids away.

Sometimes you may see behavior such as gorging. This is usually a reaction to suddenly having lots of food available and three times a day at that! They have to learn that you will give them another meal as good as this one and soon. You have to find a balance between letting them eat a lot and not letting them eat so much they become sick. Usually this behavior does not last longer than a few months. Other manifestations of this behavior are to count the food in the cabinets to make sure there is plenty there and to eat any crumbs that fall on the floor. Just be understanding and this too will pass.

Hoarding is another behavior sometimes seen in toddlers and older children. It is for the same reason as the gorging phenomenon. Be understanding, as you would act the same if you were in their shoes. You might find food under beds, in sock drawers, or in closets. This behavior can go on as long as six months, but eventually it slows down.

Many of these children have had nothing to call their own. What they did have they shared with their "group." You may be surprised when something you bought your child ends up with a playmate. At the other extreme, some children react to this early experience by taking little things from you and hiding them. They can also be very sensitive to other children in the house taking items from them. All of these behaviors are normal reactions to their experience, of which you need to be aware and gradually modify.

Before you leave the children's home try to find out how the kids were disciplined. In some children's homes, children are placed in time-outs by being isolated in a room with the door shut. You may find that by repeating this punishment at home you are scaring the child and that a better time-out is just to place her on a couch in view of people. You are the judge of what is appropriate; just realize that certain responses that mimic orphanage life will be frightening to her.

Older boys tend to play rough, as there wasn't anyone at the children's home to referee. It is like growing up in the *Lord of the Flies* preschool and suddenly being told you have to play nice. There is an adjustment period before the new rules sink in. While this behavior could be a sensory issue, it could also just be that you need to modify the behavior by putting him on a short leash until he learns what is appropriate play. Dads know about this.

Again, these are just general comments. Your child may have none of these issues. Children are very much like snowflakes.

Adoption Disruption

Not every adoption is a success story. Sometimes an adoption just doesn't work, no matter how much effort is put forth. When an adoption fails after the decree, the term used to describe the event is "disruption." It describes adoptive parents cutting ties with a child and handing him back to the agency for placement, or placing him in state custody if the agency refuses to help. When an adoption fails before a final decree of adoption is issued, it is described has a "dissolution." (Note that some professionals use the terms in the reverse.)

One comment you hear from adoption professionals is that the American culture of wanting everything done in a minute with a no-hassle home study and no medical reviews of the child makes families vulnerable. The attitude is "Just get it done and give me my child now so I can have that perfect family and then back to my life." I think this is a mischaracterization of most families, but it still paints a portrait of how moving too fast and wanting an instant family works against families when it comes to adoption. Adoption needs to be a carefully thought out process. It is for a lifetime, not until the next model comes out.

To my knowledge, there haven't been any studies done on the causes of disrupted international adoptions. Most do not happen with infants but rather with older children in specific family situations. There is very little disruption of Chinese or Korean infant adoptions. It just doesn't seem to be an issue. It is with older child adoptions that the risk is greater.

Most disruption studies have been of domestic adoptions, particularly those involving special needs children. Therefore, it is difficult to use the findings from domestic studies and apply them to international adoptions. One unofficial survey of agencies placed disruptions at 2 percent of all international adoptions. Again, this isn't from any official source or study.

So what we are left with is anecdotal evidence of factors that might be called "red flags." Red flags do not mean that an adoption should not proceed, but rather that parents should recognize that this adoption under these circumstances poses a greater risk to their family and marriage, and to the success of the adoption.

Some parents want to adopt two unrelated children at one time so that they can save money and only travel overseas for one adoption process. That is a red flag. They have their instant family and they saved money in the process, but there is more to making everyone feel like they are part of a family than just a decree. Neither the Chinese nor the Koreans generally allow two adoptions at the same time.

Parents who want to adopt and have an instant family with two unrelated children may be setting themselves up for a very difficult time. Often one child is more delayed that the other and needs much more attention, so that child gets the attention and the one who is doing pretty well gets less attention. These kids have never been "filled up" and they all deserve their "own" time in a family where they are the only one special. Institutionalized children come with different backgrounds and situations and need to be able to be the "new" child. This is similar to when a family gives birth to a second child. The first one still gets attention, but the second one also needs to gain "their own place" in the family.

Parents have good reasons, usually financial, for adopting two children at once. Many parents have done so and it has all worked out, but red flags are meant as warnings that in some adoptions it has not worked out and needs to be completely thought through.

Where it has not worked out is when there is a wide difference in age between the two children, for example, a 4-year-old and a 12-year-old. Also, if the couple has no other children they are suddenly thrust into the learning curve of parenting a toddler and a teenager. Add to this the extra attention one or both may need and the time involved with their medical appointments and speech therapy appointments, and you have one stressed-out mom. You can have the same stress where you adopt two and they are close in age, but the children become "Irish" or virtual twins and can play with each other. That is a benefit to adopting two close in age that can help.

If you want to adopt two at once, consider siblings. Siblings who knew each other in their family or the children's home have learned to create a family with each other. Sibling adoptions seem to do better. In a study of internationally adopted children in the Netherlands, 399 children placed with one or more siblings were followed up approximately ten years after placement. A comparison of problem behavior in this group with that of 1,749 children placed alone shows that the adoption of sibling groups was relatively successful. Attachment issues when siblings are placed are low. Just make sure that they are real siblings and not just siblings by birth. Some siblings are either too far apart in ages or live in different homes or simply never have been together to create that "family bond" that is the essence of being a real sibling. If you adopt an 8-year-old and a 2-year-old sibling pair, it is possible that you are actually adopting two children that have no bond and act unrelated.

Another red flag for adoption is a child who has been sexually abused coming into a family that has younger children. These children need to be adopted by a family that has no other child living in the house. Not only will therapy be a long process, demanding time and attention from the parents, but also the other children in the house will be at risk. One rule is that you never place your newly adopted older child by himself with your younger child until you are sure.

Some domestic studies have also concluded that older parents have fewer disruptions and that the higher the educational level of the mother the greater the risk. The explanation of the first is that older parents have more patience and more time to spend. The theory on the second is that mothers with higher education levels have higher expectations. These expectations push against the reality of an adoptive child who not only does not have the same DNA, but also did not have the best pre-natal and post-natal care. When the expectations push too hard, the adoption breaks. Without adequate studies there is no way to tell if these same findings hold true for international adoption. You can find a discussion on disruption at *http://www.calib.com/naic/pubs/s_disrup.cfm* and *http://specialchildren.about.com/library/weekly/aa103000a.htm*.

However, note that these discussions are only on domestic adoptions and focus more on special needs adoptions. Both discussions rely extensively on the work of Professor Barth at Chapel Hill, North Carolina.

A factor that does seem to hold true for both domestic and international adoptions is that the older the child the greater the risk of disruption. Again, this does not hold true for sibling adoptions and just means that with an older child adoption you must push for as much information as you can before making your decision. An older child adoption benefits the most from you traveling overseas, as you have the opportunity to spend more time with the child in his original environment.

Here is a quick checklist for red flags:

1) The parents are divided about the child or adoption process.
2) One parent becomes the target of the child's behavior, while the child presents a completely different picture to the other.
3) Parents begin to dread the inevitable call from day care or school about the child's behavior.
4) The marriage begins to resemble a negotiation session between parents and the marriage part is ignored.
5) Parents feel like psychiatric workers rather than Mom and Dad.
6) There is little joy or happiness in the house.
7) A parent begins to feel rage toward the child.

Finally, some disruptions occur through no fault of the child or children. The parents are just not able to give the child what she needs and vice versa. The adoption may have occurred because only one parent wanted it, or it occurred because the parents thought it would save the marriage. There are also those rare cases, usually with older adoptions, where a child has been so damaged by her institutionalization that she simply cannot meld normally into a family environment.

Children from disrupted international adoptions are available for adoption domestically and there are adoption agencies that assist in these placements. As an example, Tressler Lutheran Services and 1st Steps have placed disrupted children and Global Adoption in Wyoming has a small camp/ranch where the children can go to heal. Other agencies have provided services as well. There have been many cases of successful forever families being formed from these placements. Here is a helpful email group: *http://groups.yahoo.com/group/adoptfromdisruptedadoptions.*

CHAPTER XIV

Almost Done

Social Security

Applying for your child's Social Security card is the easiest thing you can do. You should try to do it as soon as you return and have a chance to settle down. You must go personally to the Social Security Office. If you are in an urban area, there will be several to choose from. Take all of your originals with you. You can fill out the form before you go or fill it out at the office while you wait. It's a short form so it won't take you but a minute to do. It is Form SS-5. You can call Social Security at 1-800-772-1213 and they might send it to you. You can also download the form from their web site at *http://www.ssa.gov/online/ss-5.html*.

Most Social Security personnel do not know that your IR-3 child is automatically a U.S. citizen, nor do they care. Do not try to argue the law to these people. It is like talking to an orange. You can try a supervisor, but the odds are against you. If they do give you any trouble about anything, an alternative is to find another office where the IQ is above room temperature or wait until the person you spoke with is not there.

If you can wait until you have received your child's U.S. Passport, then do so. Amazingly, the Social Security Office will actually honor an American Passport and allow your child to be entered on their computers as a U.S. citizen. However, if you do not have the U.S. Passport then they will want to see your child's green card. The odds of having such a card within a month or two of returning are astronomical so do not worry if you don't have it. If you do not have the U.S. Passport, show them her foreign passport with the IR-3 number stamped inside. This proves that she is an authorized resident alien. Show them her adoption documents and the English translation. They will make a copy of both and tell you that they have Chinese translators who will verify the translation. (Yeah, right!) They will give you back all originals once they have used their trusty copy machine. Show them her amended birth certificate with translation. They will also want some identification as to who you are. A passport or driver's license will suffice.

The terrific thing is that you will receive the Social Security card within 2 weeks to a month later. The Social Security Number will allow you to file your tax return and claim all child deductions and credits. You can do all that without the number, but having it just makes life easier. The first three digits on the card refer to location and are determined by the zip code of the mailing address shown on your application. Each state is assigned a series of numbers, for example 318-361 for Illinois. More than you ever wanted to know can be found at *www.ssa.gov/foia/stateweb.html*.

If you did not have her U.S. Passport when you applied, be sure to return to the Social Security Office once your child has her BCIS Certificate of Citizenship (COC) or United States Passport. The reason is that you will need to change your child's designation in their computers from "alien" to "citizen." It makes a difference as to available benefits. If they make an error on the spelling of the name or anything else, it is easy to change. Just take another trip to the Social Security Office and fill out the same form again.

Here is a Social Security Administration memo in which the agency acknowledges the existence of the Child Citizenship Act, and although it is a federal law they say they will refuse to follow it. *http://www.ssa.gov/immigration/children.htm*.

The form itself is easy. First put in the full name of your child. Ignore the part about "Full name at birth if other than above." This does not apply. At paragraph 3 mark the box for "Legal Alien Allowed to Work." If you don't believe it, just look at the IR-3 stamp in her foreign passport. If you have already received her United States Passport, you can check the citizen box instead. You can try to explain to the Social Security Office that your child is a citizen automatically and does not need a U.S. Passport to prove it, but they will not believe you. At paragraph 6, just put down whatever information is shown on the amended birth certificate. If you have changed the date and place of birth, then use those. The answer to paragraph 10 is "No."

With a Korean adoption you have a few extra things to think about. Since you have not yet adopted the child, the Social Security Number will be in the child's Korean name. The name is legally changed by the adoption petition. This will mean you will ultimately have to make two trips to the Social Security Office. You will have to file a third time when you obtain your child's U.S. passport or COC in order to change your child's status from "Alien" to citizen. There really is not a great advantage in obtaining the number before the child is legally yours. However, many parents do. Anyone lawfully admitted for permanent U.S. residence is eligible for a Social Security Number, so do not let the Social Security Administration personnel tell you otherwise. Of all federal agencies, the Social Security Administration is notorious for not knowing any law and not following what little law they do know.

Green Card
(Not Green and Not a Card)

There is a secret about the famous "Green Card." It's not green, it's sort of pink, and it's not a card, it's laminated. The BCIS will automatically send it to you after you return, even if your child is a U.S. citizen. When we talk about the government wasting money, there is no better example than the BCIS manufacturing and sending an alien registration card to someone who is already a U.S. citizen. The card will have on it your child's picture and the IR-3 number. It usually arrives at your house between two months and a year after you return. You should place it in your safety deposit box as a memento of your trip. You will need it though, if you are planning to take your child out of the country before you have received your child's U.S. Passport. In order to be able to leave and return, your child will need his Green Card and one other document from the BCIS.

Tax Considerations

This is not meant to be tax advice—you should consult your accountant for that—but here are some informational reminders. When you return you should obtain your child's Social Security Number as soon as possible. It should not take more than a month to receive it. With this number, and barring a few exceptions, you may be able to receive the following benefits: dependent deduction, child tax credit, and adoption tax credit.

The Adoption Tax Credit is a wonderful gift from your government that was extended in 2001. It is also more complicated than it looks. In general it provides a tax credit (worth far more than a deduction) up to $10,000 per international adoption. It also has provisions relating to employer-provided assistance. To take the credit you need to fill out and follow Form 8839 when you file your tax return. You should carefully read IRS Publication 968. Both of these documents can be downloaded from the IRS website at *http://www.irs.ustreas.gov* or you can call 1-800-TAX-FORM. The publication is located at *http://www.irs.gov/pub/irs-pdf/p968.pdf.*

The Economic Growth and Tax Relief Reconciliation Act of 2001 ("EGTRRA") enacted on June 7, 2001, incorporated the provisions of the Hope for Children Act previously passed by the House. These provisions extend the adoption credit for children and raise the maximum credit to $10,000 per eligible child. The beginning point of the income phase-out range is increased to $150,000 of modified adjusted gross income. This is double the previous amount. The phase out is complete at $190,000 of modified AGI. Finally, the adoption credit is exempt from the provisions of the alternative minimum tax. EGTERRA also extends the exclusion from an employee's taxable income of employer-provided adoption assistance and raises this amount to $10,000 per eligible child.

The act left several provisions alone. It did not change the carry forward section that allows you to carry the credit forward for up to five years. It also allows you to apply the credit against expenses incurred in the year prior to the adoption becoming final. You are still required to provide a tax identification number for your child in order to take the credit.

One idea to consider if you are close to your adoption is whether you want to pay for your adoption by reducing the amount of your federal withholding.

This would allow you to take advantage of the credit while the adoption is still a work-in-progress rather than having to front the expenses and wait for the refund. Obviously there is a risk that you might under-withhold, but it is something to discuss with your accountant.

Also, do not forget to check into any state credits for which you may be eligible. For example, Missouri gives a $10,000 credit for special needs adoptions, including international adoption.

The Child Citizenship Act of 2000

Children who arrive in the United States on an IR-3 Visa acquire U.S. citizenship automatically upon admission to the United States. Children with IR-4 Visas have to wait until they are adopted or re-adopted before they qualify under the Act. Re-adoption requirements may be waived by the state department, if the state of residence of the United States citizen parent(s) recognizes the foreign adoption as full and final under that state's adoption laws. Michigan appears to be one of these. The Child Citizenship Act, public law 106-395, was signed in 2000 and amends the Immigration and Nationality Act (INA) to permit foreign-born adopted children to acquire U.S. citizenship automatically if they meet certain requirements.

To be eligible, a child must meet all of the following five requirements:

1) The child has at least one United States citizen parent (by birth or naturalization).
2) The child is under 18 years of age.
3) The child is currently residing permanently in the United States in the legal and physical custody of the United States citizen parent.
4) The child is a lawful permanent resident.
5) An adopted child meets the requirements applicable to adopted children under immigration law.

The new law applies retroactively to adopted children who were under the age of 18 on February 27, 2001. It is not retroactive as to those children over the age of 18 as of that date.

Your child will not receive automatic proof of citizenship. If you want a Certificate of Citizenship, you must file the N-600 form and pay a fee of $145.00 and wait the usual long time. You will not be required to submit any evidence that is not already contained in the BCIS file, including translations of documents. (Your child's BCIS file is the material in the unopened visa envelope you give the BCIS when you reenter the U.S.) You only need to submit photographs and a check for $145.00. There will only be an interview if the BCIS has questions. In most cases BCIS will simply send you the COC and ask you to return the Alien Registration "Green" Card.

An adopted child that lives with her adoptive parents outside the United States cannot acquire citizenship under this new law, but must file an application with the regular supporting material. If a permanent U.S. address is given, and the residence abroad is actually temporary, then a child can gain automatic citizenship by simply making an airplane stop in the U.S. and getting the IR-3 number (BCIS I-551 stamp) stamped into her passport.

The BCIS has promised to work toward streamlining the process of obtaining a Certificate of Citizenship. No such streamlining exists as of this date and indeed by creating the N-600 form the BCIS has gone in just the opposite direction. The BCIS suggests that if you need proof of citizenship, you should get a passport instead and further states that you do not need a Certificate of Citizenship in order to obtain a passport. The BCIS' position is that a passport is both cheaper and quicker to obtain as a proof of citizenship.

More information on the Child Citizenship Act can be found at *http://www.immigration.gov/graphics/publicaffairs/factsheets/adopted.htm,* *http://frwebgate.access.gpo.gov/cgi-bin/getdoc.cgi?dbname=2001_register&docid=* *01-14579-filed.pdf* and *http://www.immigration.gov/graphics/publicaffairs/backgrounds/cbground.htm.*

Passport

The best and easiest piece of paper to obtain in this whole journey is your child's U.S. passport. The benefit of applying is that you will no longer have to use her original foreign passport or adoption certificate to prove she is an American citizen, but can use a derivative document like a U.S. passport. You can download the application at *http://travel.state.gov/download_applications.html.* You will need to file the forms DS-11 and DS-3053.

Once you have obtained your child's passport you can use that as proof of identity and citizenship for such things as school, job and future passports. It is also easier to replace if lost. Obtaining a passport is important, as you can then safely put away all of the other documents.

To apply for your child's passport the passport office requires you to submit:

1)   A certified copy of the final adoption decree. This will need to be translated if it is from overseas. If it is from your state, have the clerk give you a certified copy.

2)   Either the child's foreign passport with the BCIS stamp (IR-3# or 4#) or the child's resident alien card.

3)   Parent's identification.

4)   A notarized letter from the non-filing parent stating he/she wants the passport.

5)   Two photographs and a $70 fee.

If you have a state adoption decree in the case of a Korean adoption or re-adoption decree in the case of a Chinese IR-3 child, you can submit the state birth certificate and adoption decree rather than the foreign documents. Some passport offices want the translation of the foreign decree notarized. In other offices this is not a requirement. If you do not have a notarized translation, just submit it to another office or to another person in the same office.

The passport office promises to treat these documents as carefully as they used to treat the Certificate of Citizenship and return them with the passport. You can avoid being nervous about your documents if you go to one of the 13 passport offices (not a post office or probate court) where they will make copies of your documents and hand them back to you. These offices are only in the largest cities. Be aware that these offices say they will only process passports for those who will be traveling within two weeks. The list of these offices is located at *http://travel.state.gov/agencies_list.html.*

It takes about 6 weeks to receive the child's passport if you do not pay for expedited service Like the BCIS and Social Security, not every passport office has the same rules. Big surprise! Some offices will accept the foreign adoption decree as translated into English by your translator. Others will require you to have it re-translated in the states. Also, some offices require you to provide your child's amended birth certificate and others do not.

Your child does not need to have a Social Security Number in order to obtain a U.S. Passport. If you do not yet have your child's Social Security Number, you can just put a string of zeros in box #6. If some post office clerk claims that you do need a Social Security Number, first, tell him he is wrong and second, show him a copy of the federal statute at 26 U.S.C. 6039E. Once you have the passport, you can use it at the Social Security Office to have your child designated a citizen rather than an alien.

Some parents have suggested paying the passport office for expedited service and enclosing an overnight envelope. Be aware that technically you are suppose to show an immediate need to travel before you can use the expedited service. This requirement is not strictly enforced during the off-season, but it is during the busy season like the summer. It is suggested that you take a copy of the state department's fact sheet on the act, located on their website, when you apply for the passport. Also, ask for a supervisor if the entry personnel appear unaware of the act.

Here are some helpful web sites:
http://travel.state.gov/childcitfaq.html and *http://www.immigration.gov/graphics/publicaffairs/factsheets/adopted.htm.*

Re-Adoption

Re-adoption is also called domestication of adoption. The federal government and all states recognize your child's adoption if your child enters the country on an IR-3 Visa. This visa designation means that both parents saw the child prior to the adoption. Iowa used to make you file for a re-adoption before they would recognize the adoption even under an IR-3 Visa. Iowa finally changed its law in 2002 because one adoptive parent decided enough was enough. Never underestimate the power of one to make a change. About half the states make no provision at all regarding re-adoption. They simply have no law on it at all. Here is a web site containing a full review of all 50 states' requirements in regard to re-adoption: *http://www.calib.com/naic/pubs/l_abroad.cfm.*

If your child entered the United States on an IR-4 Visa, then you have to look to your state's laws to determine if you need to re-adopt. You will, in almost all cases, need to do so. The state department says that generally where a child has an IR-4 Visa because only one married parent saw the child, the child has entered the United States on a sort of "proxy" basis (even if it is final according to the sending country). The IRS calls this a "simple" adoption (although there was nothing simple about it). Whether both parents must re-adopt or just the one who did not see the child depends on your state's laws. The State Department will honor whatever your state says is a final adoption and let the Child Citizenship Act kick in and give your child a U.S. passport. Michigan doesn't seem to like re-adoptions and appears to recognize the foreign decree regardless of whether the adoption is a proxy or not.

Actually there are good reasons for filing for re-adoption even if your child enters on an IR-3 Visa. When your child has to show some school authority or employer his birth certificate it is better to use a derivative document like a state's Certificate of Foreign Birth than original Chinese documents. If you have to pull out the original amended Chinese birth certificate or decree from the safety deposit box, you will be fearful of losing it and you will have to deal with the Chinese translation issue. It is far better to be able to use the Re-adoption Decree and the state's birth certificate for this purpose. Furthermore, if you lose the original birth certificate it is practically impossible to get a replacement. Also, there will be no question whatsoever of inheritance rights, and if you ever move to another state that does not recognize the adoption you have a state adoption decree that the other state must recognize.

The downside to re-adoption is that it may cost money. In some states it is a very simple process and you can do it yourself. In others, it is so complicated that you have to hire an attorney. Check with your county's adoption clerk, court clerk, or probate clerk as to the procedure. Another problem is that some clerks will ask you for your Chinese originals. Do not give them to her, but instead insist on speaking to a supervisor. Most courts will allow you to file copies and the judge will simply compare them with the originals in the courtroom.

As an example of how some states approach re-adoption, in New Hampshire there isn't any particular international re-adoption law. Instead, you have to fit the adoption into the domestic framework. This is not unusual and in some states you just have to shake your head at their requirements. In New Hampshire you file two forms (basic information) and provide copies of birth certificates and adoption certificate, and have a criminal records check done (no charge). There is a $50 filing fee. You do not really need an attorney. There is a 6-month supervisory period before a re-adoption can be final. (Yes, the adoption is final but not the re-adoption. All you can do is shake your head and smile.) A social worker visits 3 times, at 2 weeks, 3 months, and 6 months and then writes a report that can double as a 6-months post-placement. The court hearing takes 5 minutes.

In New Jersey, you can just go to vital records with the adoption certificate, birth certificate, foreign court decree, proof of residency, and I-171H and for $6.00 you will receive a New Jersey birth certificate.

New York makes re-adoption very, very troublesome. It isn't worth it. The laws of New York are antiquated and do not work well in the international adoption field. The good news is that you can get a certificate of foreign birth easily by contacting the state office of vital records. It only costs $15 and is what you really wanted anyway, primarily because is what you will need for the schools.

In Pennsylvania, re-adoption is virtually a free service. Usually you just file copies of your adoption documents at the county courthouse and they send them on to Vital Statistics. In a month or so you receive a Pennsylvania Birth Certificate and Pennsylvania Adoption Decree. You should check with your local county for the actual procedure, but re-adoption will not cost you much in time or money.

In Tennessee and Georgia re-adoption is a matter of drawing up a petition of re-adoption and having a 5-minute session with the judge in his chambers between his regular court sessions. The filing fee is about $100.

Texas is a little different. It doesn't have any state rules governing re-adoption so each judge makes up his own. Friendly judges modify foreign re-adoption cases as best they can to fit regular old adoption law. What they wind up doing is winging it, making it up as they go along, and rubber-stamping the foreign adoption decree. Austin, San Antonio, and Fort Worth (Tarrant County) seem to be reasonable in their practice, but Fort Bend County (Houston) is a disaster. Every county and every judge has its own rules. Some of the better judges are in counties where there are large agencies so they have been educated on foreign adoption. Definitely ask other adoptive families before filing in order to find the right judge. To confuse the matter even further, there is a countervailing theory that re-adoption petitions can only be filed in the county where the child or parents reside. There are some bills that have been introduced in the Texas Legislature. One is Senate Bill 151. This bill will allow for the recognition of Foreign Adoption Decrees. Perhaps the Texas families can band together and get one of these bills passed.

In Virginia you do not need an attorney. The filing fee is about $29 and all you need is 3 post-placement reports within a year.

With Korean adoptions where there is no foreign decree, you will always have to finalize the adoption under state law. This is not re-adoption, but real adoption. State law is where you find the procedure. You may find this hard to believe, but foreign adoption only has a little to do with the BCIS or State Department; it has more to do with your state. You may be able to file the petition to adopt yourself or you may have to use an attorney.

Citizenship Application

If your child does not qualify for citizenship under the Child Citizenship Act, then your child only becomes a citizen of the United States upon the issuance of a Certificate of Citizenship. Until then she is a Resident Alien. The Certificate of Citizenship is also another way to actually gain documentary "proof" that your child is a citizen even if she does qualify under the Act.

To apply, you used to file a very straightforward form N-643, *Application for Certificate of Citizenship on behalf of an Adopted Child.* In 2003, under the guise of efficiency, the BCIS deleted this form and in its place created the N-600, *Application for Certificate of Citizenship.* The filing fee is still $145. If 4 months passes since you filed and the BCIS has not cashed your check or sent you a receipt, then that is bad sign. You will need to re-file the whole thing as the BCIS has lost the application. You may be able to find out the status of the application by calling 800-375-5283, but it won't be easy. You will need to include a copy of the full, final adoption decree and if the child immigrated as an IR-4 (orphans coming to the United States to be adopted by U.S. citizen parent(s)), evidence that the adoption is recognized by the state where the child is permanently residing. The form can be found at *http://www.immigration.gov/graphics/formsfee/forms/files/N-600.pdf.* An explanation of the difference between the N-600 and N-600K can be found at *http://www.immigration. gov/graphics/lawsregs/handbook/PolMem95Pub.pdf.*

Some offices are quick to issue the certificate, but most take 1 to 2 years. California and Texas are the two states most backlogged. Also, the offices tend to process them in alphabetical order rather than by the date when the application was filed. Usually you will receive a notice and receipt that they have received your application. About a year later you will receive an appointment notice giving you the date and time for the interview. Do not lose this notice, as you will have to show it to the BCIS as confirmation of your appointment. Other than these two pieces of paper, you will receive no other contact from the BCIS. On the date of the interview, you may take your child and meet with an overworked BCIS person. If your child is under age 14, you do not actually have to take him with you, although most do. The BCIS person will ask you a few questions and then hand you the Certificate of Citizenship to sign. He will also ask you take an oath that the answers on the application are true. Proofread the certificate carefully. It is not unusual for it to have typographical errors. It is far easier to change the certificate right then rather than afterwards. *Do not leave the room before proofreading the certificate.*

The BCIS will type your child's name exactly as your translator translated it from the official foreign document granting you parental rights. Therefore, you must make sure that your translator has done it correctly. The best time to do this is prior to your consulate visit in Guangzhou. If your translator has made a mistake, she can correct it on the decree and then sign a statement at the bottom that she made a mistake and write the correct name. If you return to the states and there is an error, the re-adoption court order will cure it. The BCIS will go by the re-adoption court order in that case and not by the court decree.

Some BCIS offices have a ceremony, but this is rare. Usually for children it is more of an administrative process. The certificate may say at the bottom that it is against the law to make copies. The law has now changed and you can and should make copies. If you get tired of waiting, call your congressman. They are good for that sort of thing.

One very neat idea is to have your congressman send you the flag that flew over the Capitol the day your child becomes a citizen. The cost is around $10. They run these flags up and down all day long every 5 minutes. You can also order a small flag set on a stand showing your child's heritage with flags of the U.S. and China or Korea. These can be obtained from Gates Flag Co. at 1-800-US-1776 and from other places.

Actually filing the N-600 can be a troublesome process. The requirements state that the three photos must be identical, unglazed, and taken within 30 days of the date of filing the citizenship application. Their regulations further state that the photos are to be in natural color and taken without a hat. The dimensions of the face should be about 1 inch from the top of the hair to the chin. The face should be a frontal view with the entire right ear visible. The photograph must be on thin paper with a light background.

Most places that take passport photos cannot accommodate these requirements because their photos are on glazed paper. If you find that you cannot get anyone to follow the requirements, then go ahead and file regular passport photos. The BCIS is fairly reasonable when it comes to filing for a child's citizenship and will likely ignore the technical defect. There are few offices that will not waive this requirement.

Do not send any originals with your application; just send copies. Bring the originals with you to the interview. Mail the application by certified or express mail so you have a record that it was received.

Since you will likely not yet have the "green" card or Alien Registration Card when you file your application, just put in the IR# number that was stamped in your child's passport. That is all they want anyway. Include a copy of the amended birth certificate and final adoption decree, both the foreign and English translations, and a copy of the photo page from your passport, and a copy of your marriage certificate. Bring all originals with you to the interview. By the time you have your interview you will likely have the "green" card. Since you will have to turn it in to the interviewer, make a copy of it for your child's lifebook.

The BCIS would like a statement from a translator that he is competent to translate and that the translations of the Amended Birth Certificate and the Final Adoption Decree are accurate. The separate statement should say something like, "My name is _____, and I am a resident of _____. I certify that I am competent to translate in both (Korean or Chinese) and English and that the English translations of the Amended Birth Certificate and Final Adoption Decree are correct and accurate." Then have him sign and date it. If your translator does not give you such a statement, just have someone in the states who is fluent in these languages sign one.

Some parents do not want their Korean children to have dual citizenship with Korea. I would review this option before taking the step to terminate the Korean citizenship. If you wish to terminate, contact your closest Korean embassy or consulate after your child is a U.S. citizen and request, in writing, that your child's name be removed from the Korean citizenship roles. There is a special form that is used and you will receive a confirmation after the removal is complete.

Post-Placement Reports

The CCAA requires a certain number of post-placement reports after you return from China. They want to see that their children are being taken care of and are in good shape. It is a very reasonable request. The CCAA requires a report 6 months after you return and another at one year. Post-placement reports must be sent in every six months after that until the child obtains U.S. citizenship. If the child enters on an IR-3 Visa, the only requirement will be the first two reports. The CCAA asks that parents send an updated family photo as well as an updated photo of their child when you send in the 6- and 12-month post-placement reports.

Your agency then translates everything and sends it on to the CCAA. If the agency does not file these reports in a timely fashion, the CCAA will not be happy with them or you. So it is important for the agency, as well as for you and future adoptive families, that they be timely filed. You do not want to harm other American families and these children by failing to complete timely post-placement reports.

A social worker must complete the report. It should contain the name of the adopted child (the original Chinese name and present given name), date of birth, recent photos (at least two), the name of the institute that placed out the child for adoption, and the health status of the child at the time of adoption. It will also contain the parents' names and address as well as the name of the adoption agency, the date the parents came to China, and the document number of the Notice of Coming to China for Adoption.

There is usually a discussion regarding the child's physical development such as growth and weight gain, any illnesses and treatment, speech, and other age-related milestones. If a child has any delays you should discuss progress and therapy. You should not sugarcoat the description of the delays. You are not a "bad" parent because your child has some. The Chinese expect that there will be some issues related to the institutionalization of these children, so it is important to let them know that you are addressing these issues. Include the results of any physical exams such as dentist and eye check-ups.

You may want to discuss the child's adjustments to life in America. This would include your child's emotional health. Speech therapy or your child's progress at speech acquisition should be mentioned. Of course, bonding and attachment progress or concerns and sibling interaction should be included. Paint a real picture. Tell them that your child attends preschool a few times a week and that he has good friends in the neighborhood, at school, and at story time, and describe some little things that have happened in your child's life since coming to America.

Rude Comments

After you return to the states you may be faced with rude comments from friends, family, and strangers about adopting a child from another country. Here are some examples and suggested replies:

Question: (if you have other children) "Which one of you is adopted?"
Answer by the child: "We were all adopted by one another."

Question: "How much did it cost?"
Response: "She's priceless." Then you look them in the eyes for several seconds and say, "Oh (long pause), why do you ask?" or "Why do you want to know?" Just look at them, not responding to their question. Of course, if they say they are interested in adopting you will probably want to actually give them information.

Comment: "What a good Samaritan you are for helping this poor orphan." or "What great people you are to take this poor little child into your home."
Response: "What a great child this is to come to our poor little home."
or
"I feel very blessed to finally be a parent. Parenthood is a lot more than a good deed. It is a lifelong commitment to love."
or
"Actually, we're the lucky ones. We have a beautiful son/daughter who has added so much more to our lives than we could ever hope to give him/her."
Avoid agreeing with the savior concept. Your child didn't want a savior, she wanted a family.

Comment: "What were her birthparents like?"
Response: "I consider that to be her personal information, so I don't discuss it." (Usually people apologize.)

Comment: "I could never adopt. I just couldn't love a child that's not my own."
Response: "Fortunately, this is our child and we love her."

Question: "Why there-why not the U.S.?"
Response: "Why do you think a child in one nation is more or less important than another? Every loving adoption is a success."

If the person is truly interested, you could explain that it is difficult to adopt in the United States. So many parents are looking to adopt that birth mothers and agencies are selective. They may disqualify single parents and people of a certain age or race or income. They may prefer couples that have no other children or request a couple with a stay-at-home mother. Depending on who is asking, you could go on to explain that you wish to parent an infant and because many young girls now keep their children, infants are not very available in the United States. In the end, it is completely your choice as to what you say and to whom. You don't owe anyone an explanation as to what is a very personal decision. Indeed, if someone is adamant that you should have adopted from the U.S., turn the tables and ask them why they have not done so.

Question: "Why are you going back for a second (or third) child?"
Response: "When I adopted my daughter, I promised that I wouldn't forget the children who were left behind."
Or

"My family is not complete and when it is, I'll call you." (A bit of sarcasm.) With transracial adoptions you will attract attention and receive comments that are beyond rude.

Comment: "I would like to adopt, but I don't think I could be comfortable with a child of a different race."
Response: "Fortunately for us, the only children available are from the human race."

Question: "I don't really care for Orientals, but she's kind of cute."
What in the world can you say to that?

Some other situations:
Question: "Is she yours?"
Response: "Yes she is."
"No, I mean is she *really* yours?"
Response: "From the very first moment I held her."
or "Why do you ask?

This last response sometimes works best as it puts the burden on them. You can determine if they have a real interest and proceed with more information, always keeping your child's personal history private. Of course, if they are just cluelessly curious just walk away.

Question: "Is her father Chinese?"
Response: "Her dad is right here, why don't you ask him?" Then just walk away leaving them to deal with your husband.
Some singles respond by saying "I don't know, I never met him." This can leave them stopped dead in their tracks.

Question:"Does she speak Chinese?" [Vietnamese, Korean, Spanish, whatever.]
Response: "Yes, she is only one year old, but she's been teaching me everything she knows." Then just leave. There are just some people who cannot walk and think at the same time.

Here is an incredible question. "Are you going to tell them they are adopted?"
The children are Chinese or Korean and this fool wants to know if the Caucasian mother just might get a wild hair one day and tell them that they were adopted.

Transracial Adoption

There is a great song from the musical *South Pacific* by Rogers and Hammerstein called "You've Got to be Carefully Taught." Its lyrics are timeless:

> You've got to be taught to be afraid
> Of people whose eyes are oddly made
> Or people whose skin is a different shade
> You've got to be carefully taught!

You can read the rest of the lyrics at *http://www.turnofftheviolence.org/Carefullytaught.htm* or, better yet, buy the soundtrack!

There are lots of books and articles on how to raise a child from a different race. If you have older biological kids, tell them that people may stare at the family. Have an open discussion of why and how you and they might react, then progress to questions that people might ask and how you might respond. Each child can think up his or her own answer and you can role play. Questions range from curious to hostile and each question can have a varied response. Emphasize family privacy rather than secrecy.

Only a handful of studies have been done on the success of transracial adoptions, but most show that the adopted children generally are well adjusted and comfortable with their families. In a recent study, the Search Institute found that a sample of 199 Korean-born adolescents scored as well as same-race adopted counterparts on 4 measures of mental health, and were more likely to be highly-attached to both adoptive parents. Sharma said 80% of Korean adoptees said they get along equally well with people of their own and different racial backgrounds, though 42% said they're occasionally ashamed of their race. Sharma noted that any family that adopts transracially, "becomes inherently a transracial family, not a white family with a child of color."

An interesting point by one family was that in their travel through China to adopt they experienced what it felt like to be a minority, and from that experience could get a sense of what their daughter might later feel. With the Korean escort program, parents do not have this experience. This doesn't mean parents have to come away with glowing feelings about the home country. Some Chinese orphanages are not very good and in these the children are not treated decently.

There is no doubt that transracial adoption introduces a layer of complexity into the child's life, but so does illness, divorce, and everything else that goes along with living. It is also possible to emphasize adoption too much, creating a sense of differentness in the child. Teach your child that everybody is different. They have different hair, size, race, height, etc. While acknowledging the difference, also treat it the same as anything else. It's just there. It would probably be the wrong approach for parents to pretend that the transracial adoptee is not different. They are different. It's a difference that makes no difference, but it is still there. Once reality is acknowledged, then the child and the family can search honestly for the answer to the questions, "Who am I?" and "Who are we?"

When a child is 3 or 4 that child is more into being 3 or 4 and not so concerned about anything else. Toys, sticks. and popsicles dominate their lives. But soon after that they begin to notice the little things like Mommy's hair isn't straight like theirs or they want to be blond like Mommy. Nevertheless, it is really during the angst of the teenage years that this question becomes more of a concern for the adoptee, as this is when children want to fit in the most. So you need to be particularly aware of the need for identity at this age. Yet, you may find that it is precisely at this age that your child really wants to "just fit in" and doesn't want any culture camps or anything dealing with China or Korea. A child can actually go into denial, not the parent. Instead, for many it is only after 18 when they go off to the "big city" that they begin to seriously approach the identity question.

This search for identity is not just an adoption issue, but also one with which many ethnic minorities in the United States grapple. Maya Lin, the American architect, once said that although she grew up in a Chinese household all of her friends were Caucasian and she thought of herself as Caucasian. When she went to Yale, she even declined to join the Asian American students group because she didn't feel a connection. It wasn't until long after she graduated did she begin to explore that aspect of herself.

A parent should acknowledge that her child is Chinese or Korean. She is still your child. It doesn't change that. The worst thing a family can do is never discuss their child's racial difference, but live in denial and allow the difference to just exist, festering and eating away at your child. Avoidance creates its own adjustment issues.

It is sort of funny, but understandable, that sometimes a parent will simply not see the child's racial makeup at all, but view the child as *Caucasian*! The main goal is to instill in children enough self-confidence to deal with any problems, and to come to parents or others if they can't. There are as many approaches and theories on how to address the issue as there are grains of sand on the beach, but you know your child best. They have to understand that if they allow the opinions of others to influence their behavior, then they are in some part accepting those opinions and allowing them to limit their life. The worst prisons are those that we create.

The real problem for parents is matching the appropriate kinds of cultural information to the appropriate age of their child. Maybe not so much is needed when they are infants, but more so as they get to be 6 or 7. The child's home culture should be introduced at the child's pace. Culture shouldn't be forced on them. They go to school in America as American children and live in an American family. At the same time, there are many benefits to "culture camps," and time spent with other adopted Asians can help the child become comfortable with herself and her background. Although some parents go overboard with the whole culture idea and forget that these children live in a non-Asian family, here are a few ideas for bringing their home culture into the home: (1) Go to Chinese or Korean cultural events or exhibits that come to your town; (2) Provide your daughter with books with Chinese or Korean children's faces; (3) include Chinese language classes in your children's playgroup activities; (4) Buy Mandarin cassettes or Mandarin children's songs and play them as background music; (5) Show English-language videos featuring China, including *Big Bird Goes to China*; (6) Have "things Chinese" around your home. You have to find the right balance. Too much emphasis on things Chinese and being Chinese is likely to create in the child feelings of exclusion or being different; too little attention to things Chinese is likely to create the impression that this aspect of the child's identity is not valued or an appropriate subject for discussion.

As parents you will have to be sensitive to racism and discuss it with your child. To some extent it will depend on where you live. There might be more instances in places where Asians are not so numerous like Minnesota, but it exists everywhere. The worst is "silent racism," such as where restaurant waiters are courteous to everyone else but rude to Asians, or teachers who put your child in the back of the classroom. The child needs to be able talk about her experience as an *Asian-American*, about the existence of racism in America, and about its effect on them. The ability and room for them to talk about their experience of being "raced" won't prevent painful experiences, but will allow them to understand and move on from those experiences. It will allow them to express the anger and pain such experiences cause and thus keep them from being mired in silence and denial.

Your child may encounter some prejudice as he goes through life, but many people do. Your family may be gawked at or may encounter awkward comments and questions, but such is life. Don't worry; through it all you will survive. You may even be better people with stronger character, better insight, and more compassion because of it.

Afterthoughts

Adopting a child is a walk into the unknown. But then, that is the way it is with all children. You never really know what their personality will be like or how they will be when they reach adulthood. In one sense though, you have a head start. Like a child who comes from a family with a history of a hereditary disease, you know that your child may be at risk for certain problems. Because you are aware of the possibility, you are more in tune to your child and more likely to get help if such a situation occurs.

You will be more sensitive to your child's development and take action if it is necessary. The action may be to hire a tutor one summer to help them with a subject, or to get medical help if that is the issue. You will be more tolerant, more accepting, and more knowledgeable. Enjoy the journey!

I once read about a beachcomber who was observed picking starfish off the sand and throwing them in the water before they dried out and died. The beach was littered with thousands of starfish so the observer told the beachcomber that his actions made no real difference. At that moment the beachcomber picked up a starfish and tossed him in the water to safety and replied, "It made a difference to him."

All children have the right to be loved, to be nurtured, and to reach for a dream. A chance is all they ask. I'll leave you with this imaginary discourse from a toddler taken from one of the toddler adoption books:

"Please learn as much as you can about me before you decide to be my mom or dad, so you won't be surprised about me. Don't think of me as a helpless infant, even though I may not yet be able to do all the things most kids my age can do. Don't treat me as if I'm older than I really am just because I act as if I don't need you to take care of me, however. When I push you away is when I need you to hold me and tell me that you will never let me go. I had to learn to do many things for myself before you came into my life, and it's hard for me to learn to depend on you as much as I should. Please recognize and help me with my special needs, but remember that I am still a lot more like other kids than I am different. See me first as your child, not as your adopted child or a child with special needs. Sometimes I feel really sad and really mad. Don't pretend that I don't have these feelings, and don't get discouraged when I take out my strong feelings on you. Most of the time I am not really mad at you, but you're the one who's here now and the one I can safely show my feelings to. I know in my heart that you didn't do anything to hurt me, but I get all mixed up. My memories of other moms and other places where I've lived are all in my mind, but they're stored in pictures, sounds, feelings, and even smells. I don't have the words to talk about these things. I can't figure out why that other mom disappeared, and I'm worried that you might go away too. I often have to test you because it's hard for me to believe that you won't leave me. In fact, it's pretty scary for me to love you and trust you, so I might have to test your love the most when you start to become important to me. Sometimes I just want to curl up in a ball and be a little baby again so someone will take care of me. Other times I want to do everything by myself and I feel like running away from you. Please be patient. We have a long time together. After all, the really worthwhile things in life usually aren't very easy and they don't happen overnight."

CHAPTER XV

Lagniappe

Chinese and
Korean Reading List

There are lots of books on China. For travel information see the Lonely Planet guides as well as their phrasebook. They cover a lot of cities in China. Laura A. Cecere has written a book called *The Children Can't Wait: China's Emerging Model for Intercountry Adoption.* For an interesting return story see *Wuhu Diary: On Taking My Adopted Daughter Back to Her Hometown in China* by Emily Prager. See also *When East Meets West* by Rick Tessler. This book was written in 1999 and is about Chinese adoptions and parents. Also, *The Lost Daughters of China: Abandoned Girls, Their Journey to America, and the Search for a Missing Past* by Karin Evans, *Kids Like Me in China* by Ying Ying Fry, and an academic, but very readable work *Intercountry Adoption from China: Examining Cultural Heritage and Other Postadoption Issues* by Jay W. Rojewski.

Some Korean adoption books are: *I Wish for You a Beautiful Life: Letters from the Korean Birth Mothers of Ae Ran Won to Their Children* by Sara Dorow (Editor); and *Seeds from a Silent Tree: An Anthology By Korean Adoptees* by Tonya Bishoff (Editor).

Adoption Reading List

For general adoption issues read *Twenty Things Adopted Kids Wish Their Adopted Parents Knew* by Sherrie Eldridge. This is a good layman's outline of adoption issues. Others include *Being Adopted: The Lifelong Search for Self* by David Brodzinsky; *Talking With Young Children About Adoption* by Susan Fisher and Mary Watkins; and *Journey of the Adopted Self: A Quest for Wholeness* by Betty Jean Lifton.

For attachment issues, read Caroline Archer's books, *First Steps in Parenting the Child Who Hurts: Tiddlers and Toddlers* and *Next Steps in Parenting the Child Who Hurts: Tykes and Teens, Toddler Adoption: The Weaver's Craft* by Mary Hopkins-Best, *Facilitating Developmental Attachment: The Road to Emotional Recovery and Behavioral Change in Foster and Adopted Children* by Daniel Hughes; *Holding Time: How to Eliminate Conflict, Temper Tantrums, and Sibling Rivalry and Raise Happy, Loving, and Successful Children* by Dr. Martha Welch; *Give them Roots, Then Let them Fly: Understanding Attachment Therapy* by The Attachment Center at Evergreen. Their web site is at *http://www.attachmentcenter.org, Attaching in Adoption* by Deborah D. Gray was published in 2002 and has had good reviews.

For sensory issues, good books are *The Out of Sync Child* and *Teaching Children to Love.* Also, see *Raising a Spirited Child,* which concerns children who have some of the behaviors, but do not actually have sensory issues and are just considered wonderfully "spirited."

For the multi-cultural family aspect of adoption, see the book *Are Those Kids Yours?* by Cheri Register; *Inside Transracial Adoption* by Gail Steinberg and Beth Hall; *Birth is More Than Once: The Inner World of Adopted Korean Children,* Hei Sook Park Wilkinson, PhD; and *Mommy Far, Mommy Near,* Carol A. Peacock, Shawn C. Brownell.

Frequently Asked Questions

Can I adopt from Hong Kong?

Although Hong Kong is now part of China, its adoption program is not part of the CCAA, but runs on a different process. The children come from the welfare system that is well run. Paperwork is simpler by far and costs are much less. Hong Kong tends to view education and income stability as primary considerations and a usual limit of four kids in the household with some consideration given for more depending on the need of the child. The available children usually have some special need. There is a high volunteer ratio per child so the care is optimal for international standards, as is medical availability. The time frame is well under a year from start to finish and they have an escort option in at least some instances though they prefer that at least one parent travel. You can find out more about adopting from Hong Kong from the Mother's Choice web site at *http://www.mchoice.org/html/1_what _is_mc/index.html.*A great story of adopting from Hong Kong can be found at *http://www.geocities.com/Heartland/Estates/7740/nathanael.html.*

What do I do if my spouse must leave early?

Your agency will know the rules. Generally, if a spouse has to leave China before the consulate visit, the departing spouse must sign a completed (no blanks or incompletes) I-600 form and give you a Power of Attorney authorizing you to act in his place. The consulate needs proof that the absent parent has met the child, such as a photo of them together. The remaining parent cannot sign the I-600 for the departing spouse; the Power of Attorney does not extend to the signing of the I-600 petition. Always call the consulate before you leave China to make sure they do not want anything else. Sometimes they have asked to see airplane tickets.

What do I do if I have no crib in China?

Most of the newer hotels will have them, but here are some ideas if you find yourself in need of a crib. You can push your twin beds together and put the child between you. Be very careful about rolling over if the child is an infant. You can place the baby in an empty suitcase with a blanket. Or you can pull an empty drawer out, put a blanket it in then the baby. What also works is to place the baby on a soft blanket on the floor and surround her with suitcases so she can't go anywhere.

How do I explain my reason for adoption to my family?

There are so many reasons people adopt that there is no one explanation. Some people adopt because they have boys and want a girl, or vice versa. Some have children that are grown and want to start another family. Then there is the fertility reason. A woman's fertility slowly begins to decline as early as 27 and falls rapidly after 35. The chance of pregnancy from in vitro fertilization (IVF) is about 17%, excluding male factor cases. The first IVF has the best chance with diminishing chances after that. Because of the adoption tax credit, the cost of an IVF is twice that of an adoption, without the certainty.

What is a "chop"?

Generally, a "chop" refers to a stamp in red ink. In China, a chop conveys the authority of a particular Chinese official, office, or agency in the same way a notary seal does for a state notary in the U.S. Your personal documents, copies, and/or signatures are notarized by a state notary, and the state certifies that the notary that you have used is properly licensed by the state. Next the Chinese consulate that is assigned to handle documents from your state confirms the documents, the notary statement, and state certification as authentic. This authentication is conveyed when the Chinese consul places his/her stamp or "chop" on the back of each set of documents.

The "double chop" usually refers to the approval granted by both Civil Affairs and Justice Ministries that is issued by the China Adoption Center in Beijing after you've accepted your referral. This document carries the chop of both ministries, hence the name. This double chop is sent to the local or provincial office of the Ministry of Civil Affairs, which usually originates the invitation to travel. Many parents have a "chop" made for their child, which is their child's name carved like a stamp.

Why doesn't the U.S. have orphanages?

It still does. The oldest orphanage in the United States, Bethesda, is still operating. John Wesley founded it in 1743 in Savannah, Georgia. Now the he residents are troubled youths rather than true orphans. The reason the U.S. doesn't use orphanages anymore is because of studies in the 1940s that found a connection between caregiver-child disruption and later psychopathology. Three responses were theorized as derived from that disruption: protest, despair, and detachment. Other studies found that institutionalism caused not just physical delays but also cognitive, emotional, social, and language delays.

These studies started the movement in the U.S. away from orphanages and toward foster care for young children.

How safe is the water?

Not even the Chinese take a chance on tap water. Only bottled or boiled water is used for drinking. Bottled water is inexpensive. A 20-ounce bottle cost about 37¢. Many like Grand Canyon Water, if for nothing else than the name. Even seltzer water is better than taking a chance with a faucet. Of course, it is hard to tell when a bottle has gas in it or not. The only way you can reliably tell is to squeeze the bottle. A bottle with gas is almost solid when you squeeze it. A bottle without gas dents in quite a bit.

You might drink bottled water but brush your teeth with seltzer. You can always boil water using a small hot plate. If you plan to stay a few weeks, take a water distiller or pump. They will cost around $165 from Magellans. Anything costing under $100 probably won't really help you get rid of the *Giardia* organisms and heavy metals, although some swear by filter bottles at www.safewater-anywhere.com. Iodine tablets also work. If you drink the public water, the odds are you will make it home without Mao's Revenge. However, pack some antibiotics just in case.

Should I take a car seat?

The Chinese do not use car seats. After you put your luggage and yourselves in the car there is simply no room. Add in another family and there really isn't any room. Normally you just hold your child on your lap. Don't forget that whoever picks you up at the airport when you return to the states should have a car seat. But since your child has never been in one, expect some crying.

Do I send out baby announcements?

When you return from your adoption, you may want to send out an adoption announcement similar to a birth announcement. Some people buy cards from a store on which they place their child's photo. On the front you might write, "Please help us welcome (or are thrilled to announce, or placed in our loving arms) the newest addition to our family." Then her name, birth date (birth city) and adoption date. There are lots of variations, which are limited only by your imagination.

How can I change my I-600A to another country?

Try to change countries before you receive the I-171H. You can do so by simply mailing in a letter to your local BCIS amending the I-600A. If you have already received the I-171H, you must file form I-824 (Application for Action on an Approved Application or Petition) at a cost of $140.00 to have your approval sent from your old country to the U.S. Embassy issuing the child's U.S. visa. The BCIS will send a Visa 37 cable to the old and the newly designated post. In the cable to the old post it will say, "Pursuant to the petitioner's request, the Visa 37 cable previously sent to your post/office in this matter is hereby invalidated. The approval is being transferred to the other post/office addressed in this telegram. Please forward the approved advanced processing application to that destination." After a while you should email the adoption unit in the new embassy's adoption office and ask them if they have received your file. When you file your I-824 to change countries, make sure you tell them in a cover sheet that it is for an adoption. If BCIS knows it is for an adoption they will process within 30 days, otherwise it will sit for months on a desk.

Be aware that if you want approval to adopt in two countries rather than simply transferring approval, it is likely to cost you another $460 and a second I-600A, but you won't have to be fingerprinted again. Also, some people have actually received their I-171H approval even though they left line 16 blank on their I-600A. In that case all they did was to send or fax a letter to the BCIS telling them which country they wanted the approval sent to. No additional fee was required.

How do I notify the BCIS if I change agencies?

Have your new agency write a letter on their letterhead stating they are now your agency for all adoption proceedings. Then write a cover letter to the BCIS enclosing the letter from your agency and informing the BCIS to make the change in their files. Enclose a copy of your I-171H with your cover letter.

Are my children Chinese or American?

Most countries have an artificial cutoff at 18 when your child is supposed to declare her citizenship. This is usually artificial, as most countries (such as France) will allow you to submit documentation later to prove and reclaim your dual citizenship. Even the state department now recognizes dual citizenship. See more at the state department site: *http://travel.state.gov/dualnationality.html* and at *http://www.richw.org/dualcit.*

How do I adopt if I live overseas?

The BCIS regulations at 8 CFR 204.3 cover this. You can find them at *http://www.access.gpo.gov/nara/cfr/waisidx_99/8cfr204_99.html*. Your I-600A can be filed with the BCIS office in the country where you reside. You can have your home study prepared by anyone that is licensed or authorized by the foreign country's adoption authorities to conduct home studies under the laws of the foreign country. There is an indication that if you are fingerprinted at a United States Embassy or consulate then you do not need to be fingerprinted by the BCIS and are exempt from the $50 fingerprint fee. You would then file your completed fingerprint card when you file your I-600A. See the regulations for further details. If you live overseas and adopt there, if the child is with you for two years you may be able to file a Family Petition, Form I-130, rather than go the I-600 orphan route. You should check with an immigration attorney to see if this is available to you.

How long is my I-171H valid?

Just to review the time lines again, you have one year within which to file your home study after filing your I-600A. The home study or the most recent update must not be any older than six months at the time you submit it to the BCIS. Once you receive your approved advanced processing (the I-171H), the I-600 must be filed within 18 months of the date of such advanced approval. If you do adopt, it may be possible to use that very same I-171H to adopt again within that 18 months. Whether you can or not depends on your local BCIS office and your state's home study requirements. Some states will allow you to simply send in a two-page update and you are off to China again. Other states require a completely new home study. Some BCIS offices are satisfied with using your old FBI fingerprints to run a check on you, however, many offices now require a new FBI fingerprint check 15 months after the first one. The first step is to check with the U.S. Consulate by fax or email and ask them if you are approved for more children than you have already adopted and if your file is still open. If it is, find out from your home study agency what the rules are about updating the home study. Even if your file is not open, some BCIS offices will allow you to piggyback on your old I-171H, and using the home study update they will amend your I-171H. You just have to check.

Should I adopt one child or two at a time?

There are pros and cons about this. The pros are that you get all this adoption stuff over with at one time, and you don't have to go through the whole thing again. This makes sense if you are older and want to complete your family quickly. You also save money. Normally agencies only charge a third or quarter more for an additional child plus you get an additional Adoption Tax Credit and Title IV reimbursement check. The children stimulate and play with each other. They grow up as best friends. They will always be there for each other. Displacement issues may be nonexistent. Somehow, two babies together are even cuter than one, you will find yourself an instant celebrity, and everyone will want to come over and play with your babies. You've given one more child a home. They also realize that they are not the only adopted child in the family and can take comfort in the similar experience of their sibling.

Now the cons. It's hard to travel home with two children. Sometimes they both want to be fed, cuddled, and played with at the same time! It takes lots of paraphernalia (diaper bag, car seats, stroller) to go anywhere. You spend a fortune on formula and diapers. If you adopt unrelated children and one is older than the other, it could add stress in the home that could negatively affect the older child. You also are able to give only one child your full attention at a time, which he may need in order to happily integrate into your family.

If you are planning to adopt two children at once (artificial twinning), you must think through the "what-ifs." What if one or both of the children have attachment issues? What if one or both are more delayed than you anticipate? Do you have a support system and a "game plan" to deal with these types of "what-ifs?" Hopefully they won't happen, but you must think through all the "what-ifs" and decide what you would do if any of them did happen, because coming up with a game plan after the kids are home is much more difficult. The children are likely to be more developmentally delayed than you anticipate. If you adopt young toddlers you really have 2 infants on your hands and not toddlers. Infants require a lot more "hands-on" care than toddlers. Also, both kids may very well need some early intervention, speech, or OT/PT. While many families who adopt two children who are close in age say they made the right choice, they don't say it until the first year is over, as they are too tired to say anything! You really need a reality check on your support system. Still, the children will likely bond well and be the best of friends. They will spur each other on in their development.

Artificial twinning (adopting two whose ages are within 9 months of each other) does have its critics and the points raised are worthy of consideration. See *http://www.eeadopt.org/home/preparing/process/issues/twinning.htm* and *http://www.perspectivespress.com/notwinning.html.*

Is there adoption financial assistance?

The National Adoption Foundation in Danbury, Connecticut can provide such assistance. The National Adoption Foundation Loan Program offers unsecured loans and home equity line of credit loans of up to $25,000 to adopting parents. The annual percentage rate (APR) is usually very competitive compared to other unsecured loans. NAF can be contacted at (203) 791-3811 for loan applications. Also, you can call 800-448-7061 to apply for a loan over the phone. Usually you will hear something within a week. The loans are usually below credit card rates. The loans are funded by MBNA America of Wilmington, Delaware. There is some confusion as MBNA claims they really do not offer a special adoption rate. The number for MBNA is (800) 626-2760. Credit unions may also offer a special adoption loan program. NAF also offers grants that are not based on income. Call them for that information as well.

There is also a foundation called A Child Waits Foundation at *http://www.achildwaits.org*. A Child Waits is a non-profit charitable foundation that provides loans to parents needing funds to complete their adoption. There is also the DOMOI Foundation that promotes international adoptions and may provide loans. Its address is The DOMOI Foundation (Shayna Billings, Ex. Dir.), 1915 Polk Court, Mountain View, CA 94040 (650) 969-1980.Some families have also received donations from fundraisers held by their churches.

A web site with some information is at *http://adoption.about.com/cs/ financesintl.*

Other possible sources are at these web sites:
http://www.projectoz.com
http://www.hiskidstoo.org
www.jsw-adoption.org
http://www.homestead.com/brightfutures/
http://www.adoptshare.org/
www.loveknowsnoborders.com
http://www.nafadopt.org/NafGrants.htm

At what age can children not be adopted?

The current U.S. law does not permit children 16 or over from being adopted. There is an exception if you have adopted a younger sibling and the older sibling is between 16 and 18. This exception may not be available if another family has adopted other siblings. In 1999, Public Law 106-139 was signed amending the Immigration and Nationality Act to provide that an adopted alien who is less than 18 years of age may be considered a child under such act if adopted with or after a sibling who is a child under such act.

What is PAD?

PAD is post-adoption depression. It is very similar to post-pregnancy depression. It is not uncommon. Probably more than 50% of adoptive mothers get some sort of situational depression. You cry and are depressed and you don't know why because you are so happy. You cry because parenting is so hard and you want things back the way they used to be. Yet you are so in love with your new children you wouldn't change a thing. Eventually everyone gradually adjusts to the changes in the family and in time as the stress disappears the depression will too. If it becomes too serious, you may want to get help from a professional.

Physicians and the mental health community expect new birth mothers to go through a transition period after the birth of a child. Many articles about the birth mother's experience attribute the depression to hormonal changes. Others relate it to the stress of being a new parent (which probably triggers hormonal changes). Just know that post-adoption stress is real—and it can lead to post-adoption depression. Factors that can affect the depression are your support system and your goal of trying to be "Super Mom" or the "Perfect Parent." If you have a good support system of family and friends so you can catch a break every now and then and go off by yourself or with your spouse that will help you. Do not feel guilty for doing something for you for a change. If you pressure yourself so you feel you must be the perfect mom (just like a biological mom), this can trigger the depression. Also, it can be very difficult at first transitioning from working full-time to suddenly being at home full-time and away from daily contact with adults. You have to make plans to get a required dose of "adult reality" on a regular basis.

Even fathers can feel depression. The nighttime feedings, loss of independence to come and go as you please, and the demands on personal time all have an impact all your emotional well-being. This depression is not the same as unhappiness. You can feel overwhelmed with your new child, but that does not mean that you do not love your child or believe that this child is not right for your family. Just accept that it is normal to feel down after the trip to China and permit yourself to have these feelings and to recognize that they are perfectly all right.

Many parents, usually at 1 A.M. when they've been awakened for the fourth time or the baby has been crying nonstop for 2 hours, crawl into the bathroom and say, "What have I done?" This is a normal reaction. Your sweet little baby in your dreams is now a real life, screaming, smelly person all his own—and you're totally responsible! This is a frightening, paralyzing realization for *all* parents, so remember that you're not alone.

Here are a few suggestions: Sleep when the baby sleeps (or at least lie down and rest). Forget the sticky floors and dishes in the sink. They'll be there tomorrow and for 18 years after that. Take advantage of every offer of help from friends—keep saying yes whenever asked. Don't be shy about admitting that you need a hand. Give yourself and your baby time to get to know each other. Bonding happens over time. Find some books about postpartum depression. Talk to other adoptive parents. You'll find a lot of good advice. Finally, there's nothing wrong with getting a little counseling either. Talk with a therapist experienced with infertility and adoption issues. The help is out there, all you have to do is ask.

Is there a problem if I have a hyphenated name?

The only problem is if your passport is in your maiden name. It is recommended in general, not just in adoption, to change your passport if your name changes. The name on your passport is the name you travel under. You really do not want to have inconsistent documents. Simplify your life and your adoption. You can find information on passports at *http://travel.state.gov/passport_services.html*. For expedited service, check *http://travel.state.gov/passport _expedite.html*.

What happens if my child fails her visa medical exam?

This is very rare and usually involves TB. The law is that any person applying for a permanent residency visa must undergo a physical examination by a medical officer approved by the U.S. The absurdity is that IR-3 children are citizens immediately upon entering the United States and the law does not apply to them. Yet because there is a brief period between when they leave China and land on U.S. soil and are residing at 35,000 feet, you must go through this bureaucratic hoop.

The examination must look for these excludable conditions: Sexually transmitted diseases including chancroid, gonorrhea, granuloma inguinale, lymphogranuloma venereum, syphilis, active leprosy, HIV infection, active tuberculosis, mental retardation, insanity, narcotic or alcohol addiction, sexual deviation, and serious or permanent physical defects, diseases or disabilities. In addition, persons 15 years and older must have blood tests for syphilis and HIV infection and a chest X-ray checking for signs of tuberculosis. Children under 15 are not required to have these tests unless the examining physician feels the history or physical examination indicates a possibility of exposure. Notice that many contagious diseases such as hepatitis B, chicken pox, measles, intestinal parasites, and malaria are not on this list. They are missing because the conditions are already very common in the U.S., they are not spread by casual physical contact, or the conditions needed to spread the diseases are not found or are rare in the U.S.

You might think based on this list that special needs children cannot immigrate. The real answer is that it is not strictly applied, and except for children with active TB there are not usually any problems.

Most children just have a brief physical examination including a medical history (if there is any information). If the child does not have any obvious abnormalities and there is no particular reason to suspect one of the listed infectious diseases, no other tests or examinations are required. The officer will fill out the medical form that is then sealed in an envelope to be delivered to the U.S. Consulate. There, after all other documents have been approved, the medical examination is reviewed and the visa usually granted. The actual medical report goes into a sealed packet that is left with the Immigration Officer at the point of entry into the U.S.

If the examining officer were to issue an unfavorable report because he found a condition on the excludable list, you would have the right to appeal. If the child has active tuberculosis or another untreated infectious disease, the condition can be reclassified after the child has begun treatment. If the condition is a mental or physical disability, the orphan visa officer may interview the parents, if they are present, to assure himself that they realize the extent of the condition and that they are capable of caring for the child. However, for most severe disabling conditions and for HIV infection the parents will have to undertake a "waiver process." To obtain a waiver, the embassy or consulate forwards the visa medical report and any supporting evaluations or tests to the Centers for Disease Control (CDC) in Atlanta. There, the Office of Quarantine contacts the family who must then provide:

- an affidavit explaining that they understand the extent and severity of the condition and giving a compelling reason to allow the child to enter the U.S. (Adoption is considered compelling for most children!)
- proof that they have adequate financial resources to care for the child. This may include proof of health insurance and sometimes even an advance approval from the insurance company guaranteeing that the child's condition will be covered.
- n affidavit from a physician stating that she will provide care to the child after arrival in the U.S.

This information is forwarded to the CDC where a panel of physicians reviews the material and makes a determination that the child will not likely not be a threat to the health of others or become a public charge. This determination is then sent back to the embassy or consulate. The material is again reviewed and if all appears appropriate, an orphan visa granted. The waiver process typically takes 3 to 6 months to complete; however, it can be accomplished in as short a time as a week if the medical condition is life-threatening or there is some other compelling reason to move quickly. Most waivers applied for by adoptive parents are approved, probably because the parents have already had plenty of opportunity to review the child's condition and their own financial resources.

Should I take my U.S. child along on the adoption trip?

The answer varies by family. Is there a reliable caregiver at home? Sometimes grandparents are not physically up to the task of taking care of children for a whole week or so. Does your U.S. child travel well or does he have problems with food, different situations, timetables etc.? You cannot give your new child the love and attention she needs if you have to expend energy on your other child. Would it make bonding as a family easier? Will there be a lot of waiting and downtime, or will you always be on the go? Will there be room in the car? Some schools consider trips to different countries great educational experiences and are willing to work out some kind of arrangement about their schoolwork. It is a once-in-a-lifetime opportunity for them to see other cultures at a young age. It will stay with them forever. You can always ask your agency to get a van rather than a car. Remember, though, that this trip is 99% business—sleep doesn't always come when expected and there is a lot of running around.

Are adoptive children at a higher risk for ADD?

I have not seen any statistical study supporting this idea. However, once you have given a child enough time to learn English so that language acquisition is not the source of any frustration, had her eyes and ears checked, and reviewed any allergies in her diet, if she is still having problems you may need to look into that subject, just as you would with any child.

One theory about domestic adoptions is that if you assume the children come from young mothers who were involved in risky behavior and perhaps lacked appreciation of cause and effect, you would expect a higher incidence of such behavior in these children. To my knowledge, however, there has been no study to validate that theory.

Can I breastfeed my adoptive child?

If you're a guy, this could be difficult. Otherwise, the best overall source of information about adoptive breastfeeding is the book *Breastfeeding the Adopted Baby* by Debra Stewart Peterson. The La Leche League sells this book in its catalogue, but it is also available through other sources. The book is fairly short (140 pages), but it is packed with information. You probably should contact your local La Leche League for additional information and check out their web site. You need not have ever been pregnant in order to breastfeed.

Is there an adoptive single parent organization?

According to the Census Bureau, 82 million people over the age of 18 are single. Thus, it comes as no surprise that a sizeable number of adoptive parents are single as well. There are several organizations for adopting singles. There is the Association of Single Adoptive Parents (ASAP) based in the metropolitan D.C. area. It can be contacted by phone at 703-521-0632 and its email address is *ASAP-metroDC@yahoogroups.com*. There is also SPACE (Single Parents for Adoption of Children Everywhere). Its web site is *http://www.geocities.com/odsspace*.

A great resource for adoptive singles is at *http://www.calib.com/naic/parents/single.cfm*.

Where can I buy the *Big Bird in China* video?

The video *Big Bird In China* is available from several sources. To order the video or get a catalog of multicultural and adoption books, call 608-833-5238. The video also is available from the Metropolitan Museum of Art in New York City—212-879-5500, ext. 4098. The Metropolitan Museum of Art catalog also includes such things as an Ancient China Treasure Chest and a CD-ROM of the Splendors of Imperial China exhibit. Call 800-468-7386.

How is the bathroom situation in China?

The toilets at the expensive Chinese hotels frequented by foreign tourists are just like any toilets you would see at home. Otherwise, it is better to wear skirts than pants. At the Beijing Airport in the domestic terminal, the women's rest room has a couple of stalls in the Chinese style. These are basically ceramic troughs that flush. (You may want to take advantage of the restrooms on the plane while you can.) In other Chinese restrooms there may be a fee of 3 jiao (about 2 cents), which will allow you to use a stall with a hole in the floor to squat over. Some have a gutter in the floor that you straddle and no stalls. Just say to yourself that it is part of the adventure, like going to Florida with Aunt Myrtle.

In the Hong Kong Airport's international terminal, the toilets are western-style. In Japanese airports and department stores (for those of you going through Japan), there's usually a row of stalls with the first several toilets Japanese-style (the same as Chinese), and the last one or two stalls at the far end are usually western-style. Jeans present a problem for using Asian toilets, as does any other type of clothing that can't be hitched up out of the "damp" that's usually all over the floor. A full skirt is much more practical. In the new international airport in Osaka, Japan, the last stall at the far end of the women's rest room has a western toilet with a high-walled changing table right beside it.

Now a word about changing diapers: Asian children have flat behinds that are a little smaller than those of the Caucasian child. Most parents find Huggies #1 to be the right size. However, changing the diaper is not all that easy. A lot of washrooms have pedestal sinks with no place to change. Some parents end up changing their child on top of the garbage receptacle outside of the washroom, which unfortunately has a tendency to swivel. Others have simply balanced their child in mid-air like some circus act on an old Ed Sullivan Show. Always carry some collapsed toilet paper and hand wipes.

What is the Intercountry Adoption Act of 2000?

In 2000, Public Law 106-279 was signed providing for implementation by the United States of the Hague Convention on Protection of Children and Cooperation in Respect of Intercountry Adoption. The Hague Convention will impose intercountry adoptions rules on countries that have ratified and implemented the Hague Convention. In 2003 China began the process of implementing the convention. Korea has not.

The U.S. has designated the state department as our central authority and drafted regulations. These should be approved and go into effect in 2004, and at that time three things will happen: 1) A few agencies will go through the expensive process of being accredited by the state department (this accreditation will have no impact on the actual quality of adopting); 2) most agencies will either joint venture with one that is accredited or else avoid adopting in those countries that adhere to the Hague; and 3) parents will pursue more independent adoptions as these are not covered by the Hague.

The reason that accreditation will not solve the problems is that many international agencies (which do not have to be licensed in most states) are licensed to place domestic adoptions. In other words, some of the same agencies that have had problems with international adoptions have already gone through a licensing process and we still have problems.

Support for the Hague Convention as a cure for the problems of foreign adoption has diminished, however, it is all we have. The proposed regulations do have a component regarding handling complaints by parents against an agency. This was proposed and vocally supported by parents. This is the only thing in the regulations that provides any protection to parents.

The goal of the Intercountry Adoption Act of 2000 (IAA) and of the regulations and procedures promulgated thereunder is two-fold: first, to provide some accountability in an industry that has none, and second, *to do no harm* to Americans who are seeking to create a family. The state department must recognize that there is tension between these two goals. Indeed, it is my opinion that the time delay caused by the additional paperwork required by the Hague Convention, particularly Articles 16 and 17, will result in Americans greatly reducing adoptions from those countries who are full parties to the convention.

The state department needs to recognize that the goal of the IAA was not to slavishly follow the 1993 Hague Convention, but rather to remedy some problems in the following 3 ways:

(1)   Give parent(s) better education and preparation;

(2)   Give parents a more complete medical and social history on a child; and

(3)   Give parents a forum to voice complaints.

The state department should try to streamline the adoption process and make it more efficient. If the procedures promulgated under the IAA do not actually solve these issues, but simply add to the adopting parents' bureaucratic burden, nothing has been accomplished. My reservations can best be described by quoting Senator Brownback when he said "…: [w]*hile the treaty will provide significant benefits, I had serious concerns that the proposed method of implementation would have caused more harm than good.*"

One suggestion that was made at the public forum on the regulations was that the state department should get involved diplomatically in resolving the problems of inadequate medical information. While Korean adoptions generally come with a lot of information, the same cannot be said of Chinese adoptions. When this suggestion was made to the panel, which included a State Department representative, it elicited no response. More on the Hague Project can be found here: *http://www.hagueregs.org/.*

How can the BCIS process be improved?

1.   Currently the BCIS and state department share responsibility for foreign adoptions. Everyone agrees that foreign adoptions should fall under one authority. If they did, then you would not have the BCIS declaring that it makes no sense to enforce the I-864/212(a)(4) requirement on IR-3 children while the state department continues to do so.

2.   BCIS offices are currently inconsistent as to how they process I-600A Orphan Petitions. It makes little sense to have each field office handle these petitions. Instead:

   a)   Either 1 or no more than 3 offices should handle all of the petitions in the country. There is no reason for numerous locations when FedEx, UPS, and the U.S. Mail can get to the same place, regardless of location, within a day or two. It's not like a parent needs or wants to visit the local field office.

b) This office should issue a tracking number and parents should be able to check the status on a web site like a UPS, FedEx, or U.S. mail package.

c) There should be an ombudsman in the office that actually answers the phone, is trained and knowledgeable, can answer questions, and can find out status, etc. There is no ombudsman that handles adoption questions.

d) Because of country delays, the I-171H should be valid for 24 months, not 18 months. Fingerprint checks should be as valid as the I-171H or else the FBI should just run checks using the fingerprints on file and not have parents re-fingerprinted. Parents are running out of time and having to redo all their I-600A paperwork simply because of delays by the sending country.

e) Parents should have the option of letting the FBI keep their fingerprints on file for up to 5 years. BCIS fingerprinting causes the biggest delay on the petitions. Many parents adopt another child within a year or two after the first. Why should they have to redo their prints when they can just authorize the BCIS to run the check on the prints already on file?

f) The BCIS should automatically send an IR-3 Visa child a Certificate of Citizenship and not an unnecessary Green Card. This would save the BCIS and the parents a lot of time and money.

g) The BCIS should view adoptive parents with a rebuttable presumption that they will be approved. Too many BCIS offices treat adopting U.S. citizens as the enemy. This should stop.

h) Many parents adopt several times. The BCIS should keep their records on file so parents do not have to repeatedly submit the same supporting documents time after time. Having a previously approved I-171H should mean that you only have to submit documents created after the first I-600A was submitted, i.e. a new divorce or marriage.

i) The BCIS should only consider felonies and misdemeanors that occurred in the previous 10 years unless related to child or spousal abuse. The BCIS seems preoccupied with misdemeanors that occurred 20 years before when the parent was a teenager or college kid.

j)   The BCIS should work with states to standardize their procedures relating to international adoption. For example, in North Carolina a parent can use an old I-171H by filing an amended home study, but in Georgia a parent cannot use their old I-171H until they submit a brand new home study by which time the old I-171H has expired. Since the I-171H is the BCIS' approval, the BCIS should be the one to make the rules regarding how it can be used or extended.

How can I have something translated into Chinese or Korean?

There are many services in the United States that will do so. If you live near a university, it will have a language department with this service. Also, with the large numbers of Chinese immigrants in the United States there are Chinese speakers everywhere. One service is the Hudson-Neva Translation Service in the U.S at *http://www.hudson-neva.com/translation/index.html*. Also, University Language Services, Inc. 15 Maiden Lane, Suite 300, New York NY 10038; (212) 766-4111.

If you want to take some phrases with you to help get around, see those at *http://members.tripod.com/gtkelle/cards.pdf*.

What is Failure to Thrive (FTT)?

This is a nonsense label that American doctors sometimes give to a child. It is not a diagnosis. All it means is that your child is significantly below the average in height or weight, or both. The real diagnosis could be a parasite problem, a gastrointestinal problem, thyroid or human growth hormone problem, prematurity, or genetics, i.e., the biological parents were on the small side. It could even be that the child was in the institution for so long that the psychosocial dwarfism condition that is usually cured through catch-up growth cannot be completely overcome. Since the FTT label doesn't actually help parents or doctors analyze the issue, it is useless.

Are there special adoption programs for military couples?

The military will reimburse active-duty personnel for most one-time adoption costs up to $2,000 per child. Travel costs, foreign or domestic, are not covered. There is a maximum of $5,000 in a given year, even if both parents are in the military. Reimbursement is made only after the adoption is finalized and only if the adoption was completed through a state adoption agency or a non-profit private agency. Fees that can be reimbursed include adoption fees; placement fees, legal fees, court costs, and medical expenses. The DoD Instruction reference number is DODI-1341.9, dated 29 July 93, and can be found at *http://www.dtic.mil/whs/directives/corres/pdf/i13419wch1_072993/i13419p.pdf.* The reimbursement form is DD 2675.

Go to *http://web1.whs.osd.mil/icdhome/DD2500-.htm* and scroll down looking for "DD2675." An article on the obstacles military couples face is at *http://www.adopting.org/military.html.*

Other articles are at:
http://www.nmfa.org/adoption.html
http://www.calib.com/naic/pubs/militarybulletin.cfm
http://www.calib.com/naic/pubs/f_milita.cfm
http://www.anewarrival.com/military.html.

Will my infant have to relearn the sucking instinct?

It is most likely that your infant will have to relearn the sucking instinct. Sucking is very important for the development of facial muscles used for speech. Speech therapists recommend heavy sucking. You can obtain medium flow nipples and make your child really work for those calories. Frozen popsicles and a candy called "war heads" are also good tools for older toddlers. There will be a tremendous difference in your child's face and speech after she starts pursing those lips and begins sucking again. Her earlobes might even begin to grow!

The reason children in these homes lose that instinct is that the bottles are often propped up on the pillow and things are so old and worn out that the holes in the nipples are big and the formula or milk just runs down their throats—assuming the bottle didn't slip off the pillow. Going back to a bottle, even for a toddler, can be a great tool to facilitate bonding and attachment. When she asks for "baby time," remember that she missed her baby years and so did you and it really is all right to give you both a cuddle and a bottle.

0-595-29784-6

Printed in the United States
15823LVS00004B/28-45